Persian (Farsi)-
English Transliterated
Dictionary

فرهنگ لغات فارسی انگلیسی

Yavar Dehghani

Introduction

This dictionary uses transliteration as the basis for the word entries and makes it easier for the language learners who are not familiar with the Persian script or are not skilled enough in using it. In those few dictionaries which use transliterations, since the alphabetical order is based on Persian script, it is very difficult and in some cases impossible for a non-native speaker to find the word, especially for those who are at the first stages of learning the language. However, in this method, they would be able to find the transliteration as quick as the English word and they can match it with the equivalent word in the script. So, this dictionary is the first one which can be used by those who even do not know writing and reading in Persian script.

There are some words in Persian that have Arabic plural structure and to make it easier to understand them, their singular form is included in the bracket beside them. For example, a'däd is the plural for numbers. The singular is adad 'number' that is provided in brackets.

a³däd (adad)   اعداد (عدد)   numbers, digits

The verb entries are introduced in the infinitive form but since the verb is conjugated out of the present tense form, the present tense form is also added in brackets beside the infinitive formes.

jušidan (juš)   جوشیدن(جوش)   to boil

The characters which are used for the transliteration of Persian script in this dictionary, are adapted from IPA fonts. These characters are as follow:

VOWELS   väkehä
                          واکه ها
The vowel system in Persian is simple and just consists of six vowels. These vowels are:

a   as the 'a' in 'ask'
and 'fast'
e   as the 'e' in 'get'
and 'fell'

| i | as the 'i' in 'fit' |

and 'pitch'

| o | as the 'a' in 'ball' |

or the 'o' in 'mole'

| u | as the 'u' in |

'rule' and 'push'

| ä | as the 'o' in 'top' |

or 'a' in 'father'

CONSONANTS
hamxänhä   همخوان
ها

Most Persian consonants are pronounced like their English counterparts. The consonants, which are pronounced similar to the English ones, are listed here:

b	as the 'b' in 'boy'
č	as the 'ch' in 'cheese'
d	as the 'd' in 'door'
f	as the 'f' in 'feet'
j	as the 'j' in 'jar'
m	as the 'm' in 'me'
n	as the 'n' in 'net'
s	as the 's' in 'sin'
š	as the 'sh' in 'she'
t	as the 't' in 'toy'
v	as the 'v' in 'vest'
y	as the 'y' in 'yes'
z	as the 'z' in 'zip'

There are three consonants in Persian, which do not exist in English. These consonants are:

x   as the 'ch' in the scottish 'loch'. it is pronounced at the back of the mouth, when the root of tongue makes a smooth contact with the end of the palate.

q   a guttural sound like a heavy french 'r', which is also pronounced at the back of the mouth, when the root of tongue makes a sudden contact with the end of the palate ž   as the 'zh' in 'Zhivago' or the 'g' in 'mirage'

³   a glottal stop which is pronounced in the throat and marks a break in the flow of speech.

The following consonants are slightly different from their English counterparts:

l   Persian l is pronounced in the front of the mouth, so it is similar to the 'l' in 'life', but not the 'l' in 'role'

k   It is similar to the English 'k' before and after 'ä, u, o' but it is palatalised with 'i, e, a' which is similar to the 'ck' in 'backyard'

r   similar to a trilled 'r' in English but never silent or diphtongised.

h   as in the 'h' in 'hit'. It is never silent.
g   like 'k' has two forms: it is like the 'g' in 'got' before or after 'ä, o, u', and similar to the 'g' in 'get' before or after 'a, e, i'

A		
a³däd (adad)	اعداد (عدد)	numbers, digits
a³šär	اعشار	decimal
a³yän	اعیان	nobles
a³zä (ozv)	اعضا (عضو)	members, organs
äb	آب	water
äb darmäni	آب درمانی	hydrotherapy
äb kardan	آب کردن	to melt something
äb raftan	آب رفتن	to shrink
äb šodan	آب شدن	to melt
ab³äd (bo'd)	ابعاد (بعد)	dimensions
abä	ع با	clergy's cloak
abad	ابد	forever, eternity
abadi	ابدی	eternal
äbäd	آباد	habitable
äbäd kardan	آباد کردن	to make it habitable
abadan	ابدا	never, not at all
äbädi	آبادی	habituation, village
äbän	آبان	eight's Persian month
abar godrat	ابرقدرت	super power
abas	ع بس	vain, useless
äbdär	آبدار	juicy
äbdide	آبدیده	tempered
äbe garm	آب گرم	hot water
äbe ma³dani	آب معدنی	mineral water
äbe mive	آب میوه	juice
äbele	آبله	smallpox
abele morgän	آبله مرغان	chickenpox
äber	عاب ر	pedestrian
äberu	آبرو	respect, honour
äberu rizi	آبروریزی	disgrace, discredit
äberu rizi kardan	آبروریزی کردن	to make a disgrace

äbestan	آبستن	pregnant
äbestan šodan	آبستن شدن	to get pregnant
äbgarmkon	آب گرمکن	water heater
äbgušt	آبگوشت	broth, soup
šorbä	شوربا	broth, soup
äbi	آبی	blue
äbjo	آبجو	beer
äbkeš	آبکش	strainer
äbkeš kardan	آبکش کردن	to strain
ablah	ابله	stupid, silly
äbnabät	آب نبات	lollipop, candy
äbnumän	آبونمان	subscription
äbnumän šodan	آبونمان شدن	to subscribe
äbohavä	آب و هوا	weather, climate
äbpäš	آب پاش	water sprinkler
äbpäši karan	آب پاشی کردن	to sprinkle water
äbpaz	آب پز	boiled in water
abr	ابر	cloud
äbrang	آب رنگ	water colour
abri	ابری	cloudy
abrišam	ابریشم	silk
abru	ابرو	eyebrow
äbšar	آبشار	waterfall
äbtani	آبتنی	bathing, swimming
äb bäzi	آب بازی	bathing, swimming
äb bäzi kardan	آب بازی کردن	to bath, to swim
abus	ع بوس	frowning, cross, stern
äbyär	آبیار	irrigator
äbyäri	آبیاری	irrigation
äbyäri kardan	آبیاری کردن	to irrigate
abzär	ابزار	tool, device
äbzi	آبزی	aqueous, marine
äčär	آچار	screw driver

adab	ادب	politeness, civility
ädäb	آداب	ceremonies, formalities
adab kardan	ادب کردن	to discipline
adabiyyät	ادبیات	literature
adad	عدد	number, figure, digit
adälat	عدالت	justice, fairness
adam	عدم	absence, lack
ädam	آدم	human, mankind, person
ädam koš	آدمکش	assassin, killer
ädam koši	آدم کشی	homicide, murder
ädäms	آدامس	chewing gum
adas	عدس	lentil
adasi	عدسی	lens, lenticular
ädat	عادت	habit, menstruation
ädat kardan	عادت کردن	to get used to, to habituate
ädel	عادل	fair, just
adeläne	عادلانه	justly
ädi	عادی	ordinary, usual, typical
adl	عدل	justice, fairness
ädres	آدرس	address
adviye	ادویه	spices, condiments
afᵌi	افعی	viper
äfaridan(äfarin)	آفریدن	to create
äfarin	آفرین	well done!
äfat	آفت	pest, plague
äfiyat	عافیت	health, welfare, happiness
äfiyat baše!	عافیت باشه	bless you!
afräd	افراد	individuals
afräštan(afräz)	افراشتن (افراز)	to raise, to elevate
afruxtan(afruz)	افروختن (افروز)	to light, to provoke
afsäne	افسانه	fiction, myth
afsar	افسر	officer
afsär	افسار	leash, bridle, head-stall

afsär zadan	افسار زدن	to leash
afsorde	افسرده	depressed
afsordegi	افسردگی	depression
afsun	افسون	charm, spell
afsus	افسوس	regret, alas
afsus xordan	افسوس خوردن	to regret
äftab	آفتاب	sun
äftab zade	آفتاب زده	sunburnt, sunstruck
äftäbe	آفتابه	ewer
äftäbgardän	آفتاب گردان	sunflower
äftabi	آفتابی	sunny
äftabi šodan	آفتابی شدن	to show up, to appear
afv	ع فو	forgiveness, amnesty
afv kardan	عفو کردن	to forgive
afzäyeš	افزایش	increase, growth
afzäyeš yaftan	افزایش یافتن	to increase
ägäh	آگاه	aware, conscious
ägäh kardan	آگاه کردن	to warn, to inform
ägähi	آگاهی	awareness
ägahi	آگهی	ad, announcement
ägahi kardan	آگهی کردن	to advertise, to announce
agar	اگر	if, in case
äh	آه	sigh, alas
äh kešidan	آه کشیدن	to sigh
ähak	آهک	lime
ahäli	اهالی	inhabitants, citizens
ahamiyat	اهمیت	importance, significance
ähan	آهن	iron
ähan robä	آهن ربا	magnet
ähang	آهنگ	tune, music
ähangar	آهنگر	blacksmith
ähangsäz	آهنگ ساز	composer
ahd	عهد	agreement, era, oath

ahd kardan	عهد كردن	to promise
ahdäf (hadaf)	اهداف (هدف)	goals, aims
ahdnäme	عهدنامه	treaty, pact
äheste	آهسته	slow, soft
ahkäm (hokm)	احكام (حكم)	orders, sentences
ahl	اهل	native, inhabitant, citizen
ahli	اهلى	domestic, pet
ahli kardan	اهلى كردن	to domesticate
ahmaq	احمق	fool, stupid
ahriman	اهریمن	devil, satan
ahrom	اهرم	lever
ähu	آهو	deer
ahväl (häl)	احوال (حال)	conditions
äj	عاج	ivory
ajab	عجب	surprising, wonderful
ajal	اجل	death, the hour of death
ajale	عجله	hurry, rush
ajale kardan	عجله كردن	to hurry
ajdäd (jad)	اجداد (جد)	ancestors
äjez	عاجز	unable, disabled, unfit
ajib	عجيب	strange, bizarre
äjil	آجيل	dried nuts and fruits
ajir	اجير	hired worker, mercenary
ajir kardan	اجير كردن	to hire
ajnabi	اجنبى	foreigner, alien, outsider
ajnäs (jens)	اجناس (جنس)	goods, commodities
äjor	آجر	brick
ajr	اجر	reward, compensation
ajsäm (jesm)	اجسام (جسم)	substances, materials
ajul	عجول	hasty, impatient
ajzä³ (joz')	اجزا (جزء)	parts, components
akidan	اكيدا	strictly, emphatically
akkäs	عكاس	photographer

akkäsi	عکاسی	photography
akkäsi kardan	عکاسی کردن	to take photo
aknun	اکنون	now, at present
aks	عکس	photo, picture, image
aks gereftan	عکس گرفتن	to take photo
aksaran	اکثرا	mostly, generally
aksariyyat	اکثریت	majority
aksbardäri	عکس برداری	taking an x ray
aksbargardän	عکس برگردان	sticker
aksolamal	عکس العمل	reaction, reflex
alaf	علف	grass, herb
aläj	علاج	cure, remedy
alaki	الکی	groundless, phoney
alam	علم	banner, flag
älam	عالم	world, universe
alämat	علامت	sign, mark, proof
alämat gozäri	علامت‌گذاری	marking
alämate extesäri	علامت اختصاری	abbreviation
alamšange	الم شنگه	commotion, nuisance
alamšange	الم شنگه	chaos, commotion
alän	الان	now, just now
alangu	النگو	bracelet
alani	علنی	open, public, overt
alani kardan	علنی کردن	to make public, to reveal
aläqe	علاقه	interest, concern, affection
aläqe däštan	علاقه داشتن	to be interested
aläqemand	علاقه مند	interested, concerned
älat	آلت	tool, penis
älate tanäsoli	آلت تناسلی	genital organ
älät (älat)	آلات (آلت)	instruments, tools
aläve bar	علاوه بر	in addition to
älbälu	آلبالو	black cherry
albatte	البته	of course, sure

älbom	آلبوم	collection, album
aldang	الدنگ	clown, lout
alefbä	الفبا	alphabet
älem	عالم	scientist, scholar
aleyh	عـلـيه	against, opposed
äli	عالى	sublime, grand, superb
alil	عليل	invalid, disabled
alkan	الكن	stutterer
alkol	الكل	alcohol
alkoli	الكلى	alcohol drinker
alläh	الله	god
alläkolang	آلاكلنگ	see-saw
älmän	آلمان	Germany
älmäni	آلمانى	German
almäs	الماس	diamond
almosannä	المثنى	duplicate copy
alo	الـو	hello! (answering)
älu	آلو	plum
äluče	آلوچه	prunes
älude	آلوده	contaminated, polluted
älude kardan	آلوده كردن	to contaminate, to pollute
äludegi	آلودگى	pollution
älunak	آلونک	hut, shanty house
alvär	الوار	timber
alvät	الواط	rascal, wanton
älyäž	آلياژ	alloy
ämadan(äy)	آمدن (آى)	to come
ämäde	آماده	ready, prepared
ämäde kardan	آماده كردن	to prepare
ämädegi	آمادگى	readiness, fitness
amäken (makän)	اماكن (مكان)	places, locations
amal	عمل	act, action, operation
ämäl	آمال	desires, hopes

amal kardan	عمل کردن	to act, to operate
amalan	عملا	practically
amale	عمله	labourer
amali	عملی	practical, addict
amaliyyät	عملیات	operations, procedures
amalkard	عملکرد	function, revenue
amän	امان	safety, security, amnesty
amänat	امانت	honesty, deposit
amänat gereftan	امانت گرفتن	to borrow (i.e. a book)
ämär	آمار	statistics, census
ämäs	آماس	swelling, edema
ämbuläns	آمبولانس	ambulance
amdi	عمدی	deliberate, intentional
ämel	عامل	agent, factor
amin	امین	trustworthy, honest
ämin	آمین	amen!
amiq	عمیق	deep, profound
amir	امیر	prince, chief
ämixtan(ämiz)	آمیختن (آمیز)	to mix, to blend
ämixte	آمیخته	mixed
ämiyäne	عامیانه	slang, vulgar, folk
ämizeš	آمیزش	intercourse
ämizeš kardan	آمیزش کردن	to make an intercourse
ämizeši	آمیزشی	venereal
amläk (melk)	املاک (ملک)	estates, properties
ammä	اما	but
ammäme	عمامه	turban
amme	عمه	paternal aunt
ämme	عامه	common people, the public
amn	امن	peaceful, safe
amniyat	امنیت	security, peace
ämorzeš	آمرزش	forgiveness
ämpul	آمپول	shot, injection

ämpul zandan	آمپول زدن	to give a shot, to inject
amräz (maraz)	امراض (مرض)	diseases
amr	امر	order, command
amr kardan	امر کردن	to order
amri	امری	imperative
amu	عمو	paternal uncle
amudi	عمودی	vertical
ämuxtan(ämuz)	آموختن (آموز)	to learn
ämuzande	آموزنده	instructive
ämuzeš	آموزش	instruction, education
ämuzeš dädan	آموزش دادن	to instruct, to teach
ämuzeš didan	آموزش دیدن	to learn , to take lessons
ämuzešgäh	آموزشگاه	academy
ämuzgär	آموزگار	teacher
amväj (moj)	امواج (موج)	waves, tides
amvät (mot)	اموات (موت)	the dead
än	آن	that, he, she, it
an³äm	انعام	tip
an³äm dädan	انعام دادن	to give a tip
änänäs	آناناس	pineapple
anär	انار	pomegranate
anbär	انبار	warehouse, store
anbär kardan	انبار کردن	to store
anbe	انبه	mango
anbiyä	انبیا	prophets
anbor	انبر	tongs, nippers
anbuh	انبوه	thick, crowded
andak	اندک	little, few
andäm	اندام	body, limb, organ
andäze	اندازه	size, measure
andäze gereftan	اندازه گرفتن	to measure
andiše	اندیشه	thought, contemplation
anduh	اندوه	grief, sorrow

anduhgin	اندوهگین	sad, upset
änfulänzä	آنفولانزا	flue, influenza
angal	انگل	parasite
angixtan (angiz)	انگیختن (انگیز)	to motivate, to stimulate
angize	انگیزه	motivation, stimulant
angošt	انگشت	finger
angošt kardan	انگشت کردن	to tamper, to molest
angoštar	انگشتر	ring (on finger)
angur	انگور	grapes
äni	آنی	instantly, immediately
anjäm	انجام	fulfilment, ending
anjäm dädan	انجام دادن	to do, to fulfil
anjir	انجیر	fig
anjoman	انجمن	association, assembly
ankabut	عنکبوت	spider
änten	آنتن	antenna, aerial
äntibiyutik	آنتی بیوتیک	antibiotics
anvä³ (no')	انواع (نوع)	kinds, sorts
äpändis	آپاندیس	appendix (body part)
äqä	آقا	mr, sir, gentleman
aqab	ع قب	back, behind, rear
aqab nešini	ع قب ن ش ی نی	retreat, withdrawal
aqab nešini kardan	ن ش ی نی ع قب ک ردن	to retreat, to withdraw

aqab oftäde	عقب افتاده	retarded, remaining behind
aqab mände	عقب مانده	retarded, backward
aqallan	اقلا	at least
aqalliyat	اقلیت	minority
äqäz	آغاز	start, beginning
äqäz kardan	آغاز کردن	to start, to begin
aqd	ع قد	marriage contract
aqd karadn	ع قد کردن	to wed
äqebat	عاق بت	at last, end, conclusion

äqed	عاقد	a notary marrying a couple
äqel	عاقل	wise, sane
äqeläne	عاقلانه	wisely, wise
aqide	عقیده	belief, faith, opinion
aqide däštan	عقیده داشتن	to believe
aqim	عقیم	barren, sterile
aqiq	عقیق	agate
aql	عقل	wisdom, intellect
aqlab	اغلب	often
aqläni	عقلانی	intellectual, rational
aqrab	عقرب	scorpion
aqrabe	عقربه	hand (of watch)
aqsäm (qesm)	اقسام (قسم)	kinds, varieties
aqsät (qest)	اقساط (قسط)	instalment, portions
äquš	آغوش	hug
äquš gereftan	آغوش گرفتن	to hug
aqväm (qom)	اقوام (قوم)	tribes, ethnic groups
är	عار	shame, disgrace
arabestän	عربستان	Saudi Arabia
äräm	آرام	quiet, pacific
äräm baxš	آرام بخش	sedative, tranquilliser
äräm kardan	آرام کردن	to soothe, to calm down
ärämeš	آرامش	rest, peace, relaxation
ärämqäh	آرامگاه	tomb, grave
araq	عرق	sweating, perspiration
aräq	عراق	Iraq
araq kardan	عرق کردن	to sweat, to perspire
araq xor	عرق خور	habitual drinker
araqgir	عرق گیر	singlet, underwear
äräye umumi	آرای عمومی	polls
äräyeš	آرایش	make-up
äräyeš kardan	آرایش کردن	to do make-up
äräyešgäh	آرایشگاه	barber shop, hair dressing

äräyešgar	آرایشگر	hairdresser, barber
aräzel	اراذل	hoodlums, rascals
arbäb	ارباب	boss, masters
arbäb ruju	ارباب رجوع	client
arbade	عربده	drunken brawl
arbade kešidan	عربده کشیدن	to scream
ärd	آرد	flour
ärd kardan	آرد کردن	to grind
äre	آره	yes (info)
ärenj	آرنج	elbow
äreze	عارضه	complication, happening
ärezu	آرزو	wish, desire
ärezu kardan	آرزو کردن	to wish
ärezumand	آرزومند	hopeful, eager
äriyä	آریا	aryan race
arj	ارج	value, esteem
arj gozäštan	ارج گذاشتن	to value, to appreciate
arjomand	ارجمند	valuable, respected
ärmän	آرمان	ideal, aim
armani	ارمنی	armanian
armaqän	ارمغان	present, souvenir
äroq	آروغ	burp
äroq däštan	آروغ زدن	to burp
arqäm (raqam)	ارقام (رقم)	figures, numbers
arqaväni	ارغوانی	purple
arrazi	اراضی	lands, territories
arre	اره	saw
arre kardan	اره کردن	to saw
aršad	ارشد	elder, senior
arse	عرصه	field, arena
arše	عرشه	deck
äršiv	آرشیو	archives
arteš	ارتش	army, military

arus	عروس	bride, daughter-in-law
arusak	عروسک	doll
arusi	عروسی	wedding, marriage
arusi kardan	عروسی کردن	to marry
arväh (ruh)	ارواح (روح)	spirits, ghosts
ärväre	آرواره	jaw
arz	ارز	foreign currency
arz	عرض	width, breadth, remark
arz kardan	عرض کردن	to state (polite)
arzän	ارزان	cheap, inexpensive
äržäntin	آرژانتين	Argentina
arzeš	ارزش	value, worth
äs	آس	ace
äš	آش	soap, porridge
aš³är (še'r)	اشعار (شعر)	poems
asä	عصا	cane, stick
asab	عصب	nerve
asabäni	عصبانی	angry, furious, nervous
asabäniyat	عصبانيت	anger, wrath
asabi	عصبی	nervous, touchy
asal	عسل	honey
äšämidan (äšäm)	آشاميدن (آشام)	to drink (formal)
äšämidani	آشاميدنی	beverage
äsän	آسان	easy
äsänsor	آسانسور	elevator
asar	اثر	effect, result, impression
asar gozäštan	اثر گذاشتن	to affect, to impress
asäs	اساس	basis, foundation
asäs	اثاث	furniture
asäsi	اساسی	principle, basic
asäsnäme	اساسنامه	constitution, fundamental
ašäyer	عشاير	tribes, nomads
äsäyeš	آسايش	relaxation, convenience

äsäyešgäh	آسایشگاه	sanatorium
asb	اسب	horse
asb saväri	اسب سواری	horse riding
asb saväri kardan	اسب سواری کردن	to ride a horse
asbäb	اسباب	means, tools, instruments
aše³e	اشعه	rays
äsemän	آسمان	sky
äsemän qorre	آسمان غره	thunder
äsemän xaräš	آسمان خراش	sky scraper
äšenä	آشنا شدن	to be familiar
äšenä šodan	آ ش نا	acquaintance, friend
äšenäyi	آشنایی	friendship, familiarity
äšeq	عا شق	lover, in love
äšeq šodan	عاشق شدن	to fall in love
ašeqäne	عا ش قانه	loving, romantic
äsib	آسیب	harm, damage
äsib dide	آسیب دیده	damaged, victim, injured
äsib didan	آسیب دیدن	to be damaged
asir	اسیر	captive, prisoner
asir kardan	اسیرک ردن	to capture
äsiyä	آسیا	asia
äšiyäne	آشیانه	nest, den
ašk	اشک	tear (cry)
ašk rixtan	اشک ریختن	to cry
aškäl (šekl)	اشکال (شکل)	pictures, forms
äškär	آشکار	evident, obvious
äškär kardan	آشکار کردن	to reveal, to disclose
asl	اصل	basis, genuine, origin
aslahe	اسلحه	weapons, armaments
asli	اصلی	original
äsm	آسم	asthma
äšofte	آشفته	disturbed, agitated
äšofte kardan	آشفته ک ردن	to disturb

äšpaz	آشپز	cook
äšpazi	آشپزی	cooking
äšpazi kardan	آشپزی کردن	to cook
äšpazxäne	آشپزخانه	kitchen
äsperin	آسپرین	aspirin
äšqäl	آشغال	rubbish, garbage
ašqbäzi	عشق بازی	lovemaking, love affair
ašqbäzi kardan	عشق بازی کردن	to make love
asr	عصر	afternoon, age, era
ašräf	اشراف	aristocrats, nobles
asräne	عصرانه	afternoon tea
asrär (serr)	اسرار (سر)	secrets, mysteries
ašrär (šarr)	اشرار (شر)	hoodlums, hooligans
ast	است	is
ästar	آستر	lining, first coat
äšti	آشتی	peace, reconciliation
äšti kardan	آشتی کردن	to reconcile
ästin	آستین	sleeve
äšub	آشوب	riot, disturbance
äšub kardan	آشوب کردن	to disturb, to create riot
äšubgar	آشوبگر	riotous, agitator
äsude	آسوده	relieved, comfortable
äsudegi	آسودگی	tranquillity, comfort
äsuri	آسوری	Assyrian
ašxäs (šaxs)	اشخاص (شخص)	persons, people
ataš	عطش	thirst, craving
ätaš	آتش	fire
ätaš gereftan	آتش گرفتن	to set fire, to lit
ätaš zadan	آتش زدن	to catch fire
ätaš bär	آتشبار	machine gun
ätaš bas	آتش بس	cease-fire
ätaš bäzi	آتشبازی	fireworks
ätaš fešän	آتشفشان	volcano

ätaš kade	آتشکده	(zoroastrian) fire temple
ätaš nešän	آتش نشان	fire fighter
ätaš nešäni	آتش نشانی	fire station
ätaš parast	آتش پرست	fire worshiper
ätaš suzi	آتش سوزی	a fire
atbä³ (taba'e)	اتباع (تبعه)	citizens, nationals
ätefe	عاطفه	emotion, affection
atiqe	عتیقه	antique, relic
atr	عطر	perfume, fragrance, aroma
aträf (taraf)	اطراف (طرف)	sides, surroundings
atse	عطسه	sneeze
atse kardan	عطسه کردن	to sneeze
avämer (amr)	اوامر (امر)	commands
ävär	آوار	debris
ävardan(ävar)	آوردن (آور)	to bring
äväre	آواره	homeless, refugee
avärez	عوارض	taxes, charges, toll
aväset (vasat)	اواسط (وسط)	middle parts
aväxer (äxar)	اواخر (آخر)	near the end, latter parts
aväyel (avval)	اوایل (اول)	beginnings, early parts
avaz	عوض	exchange, change, return
äväz	آواز	song
avaz kardan	عوض کردن	to exchange, to change
äväz xändan (xän)	آواز خواندن (خوان)	to sing
avazi	عوضی	wrong, mistaken
ävixtan (äviz)	آویختن (آویز)	to hang
ävizän	آویزان	suspended, pending
ävizän kardan	آویزان کردن	to hang
ävril	آوریل	april
avval	اول	first, initial, first-rate
avvalan	اولا	firstly
avvalin	اولین	the first
avvaliye	اولیه	primary

äx	آخ	ouch! oh!
äxar	آخر	last, end, finish
axbär	اخبار	news information
äxerat	آخرت	futurity, afterlife
äxerin	آخرین	final, latest, the last one
äxerozzamän	آخر الزمان	end of the world
axir	اخیر	recent, late, last
axiran	اخیرا	recently
axläq	اخلاق	morals, ethics, habits
axläqi	اخلاقی	moral, ethical
axm	اخم	frown, disapproving look
axmu	اخمو	fretful, moody
äxor	آخور	manger
äxund	آخوند	clergy, theologian
äyä	آیا	whether (a question word)
ayäl	ع یال	wife
äyande	آینده	future
äyandegän	آیندگان	future generations
ayär	ع یار	standard (of gold), carat
äyät	آیات	verses (of koran)
äye	آیه	verse (of koran)
äyele	عای له	family, wife and children
äyeq	عای ق	non-conductor, insulator
äyin	آیین	custom, ceremony
äyne	آینه	mirror
ayyäm (yom)	ایام (یوم)	days, times
ayyäš	ع یاش	pleasure seeking, epicure
az	از	since, from
az beyn bordan	از بین بردن	to destroy, to ruin
az beyn raftan	از بین رفتن	to be destroyed
azä	عزا	mourning
azab	عذب	bachelor, single
azäb	عذاب	torment, pain, agony

äzäd	آزاد	free (not bound)
äzäd kardan	آزاد کردن	to free, to release
äzädäne	آزادانه	freely
azädär	عزادار	mourner
azädäri kardan	عزاداری کردن	to mourn
äzädi	آزادی	freedom, liberation
äzädi xäh	آزادی خواه	freedom seeker
azamat	عظمت	grandeur, eminence
azän	اذان	call to prayer
äžäns	آژانس	agency
äzar	آذر	ninth Persian month
äzär	آزار	harassment
äzär dädan	آزار دادن	to harass
azbar	ازبر	by memory, by heart
azbar kardan	ازبر کردن	to memorize
äzemäyeš	آزمایش	test, examination
äzemäyeš kardan	آزمایش کردن	to test, to examine
äzemäyešgäh	آزمایشگاه	laboratory
äzemäyeši	آزمایشی	experimental
äzemudan	آزمودن	to test, to examine
äzemude	آزموده	experienced
äzemun	آزمون	test, exam
azim	عظیم	grand, huge, magnificent
azimat	عزیمت	departure, leaving
azimat kardan	عزیمت کردن	departure, leaving
aziyyat	اذیت	nuisance, teasing
aziyyat kardan	اذیت کردن	nuisance, teasing
aziz	عزیز	dear, esteemed, darling
azl	عزل	dismissal, sacking
azl kardan	عزل کردن	to dismiss, to sack
azm	عزم	intention, determination
azolät	عضلات	muscles
azoläni	عضلانی	muscular

azole	عضله	muscle
äzuqe	آذوقه	supplies, provisions

B		
bä	با	with
ba³ba³	بع بع	bleating
ba³d	بعد	next, later, then
ba³dan	بعدا	afterwards, later on
ba³di	بـ عدی	next
bä³es	باعث	cause, motive
bä³es šodan	باعث شدن	to cause
ba³id	بعید	far, distant, unlikely
ba³idan(bal³)	بلعیدن	to swallow
ba³zi	بعضی	some, a few
bäbä	بابا	father, dad
bačče	بچه	child
baččegi	بچگی	childhood
bačče bäz	بچه باز	paedophile
bačče bäzi	بچه بازی	paedophilia, childish act
baččegäne	بچگانه	childish, child size
bad	بد	bad, evil, ill
bäd	باد	wind, swelling
bad dahan	بد دهن	foul mouth
bad jens	بد جنس	malicious, wicked
bäd kardan	باد کردن	to blow
bad zät	بد ذات	mischievous, mean
bädäm	بادام	almond
bädäm zamini	بادام زمینی	peanut
badan	بدن	body
badani	بدنی	bodily, physical
badane	بدنه	frame, trunk
bädbädak	بادبادک	kite
bädbän	بادبان	jib, sail
badbaxt	بدبخت	miserable, unfortunate
badbaxti	بدبختی	misfortune, bad luck

badbin	بدبین	pessimistic
badbiyäri	بد بیاری	bad luck
bädemjän	بادمجان	eggplant
badi	بدی	badness, fault
bädi	بادی	windy, pneumatic
badihi	بدیهی	obvious
bädkeš	بادکش	cupping, louver
badkonak	بادکنک	balloon
bädnamä	بادنما	weather cock
bädpiči	باند پیچی	bandage
badr	بدر	full moon
bädsanj	باد سنج	anemometer
bädzan	باد زن	fan, blower
bädzadan	باد زدن	to blow
bäft	بافت	tissue, texture
bäftan(bä)	بافتن (باف)	to weave
bäftani	بافتنی	textile
bahä	بها	price, value, cost
bahä dädan	بها دادن	to value
bäham	با هم	together
bahäne	بهانه	excuse, pretext
bahäne juyi	بهانه جویی	seeking excuses
bahär	بهار	spring
bahäri	بهاری	vernal
bahäyi	بهایی	Baha'i
bahäyiyat	بهائیت	Baha'ism
bahbah	به به	excellent, well done
bahman	بهمن	11th Persian month
bahr	بحر	sea
bahräm	بهرام	Mars
bahre	بهره	quotient, interest
bahrebardäri	بهره برداری	exploitation, operation
bahrekeši	بهره کشی	exploitation

bahrekeši kardan	بهره کشی کردن	to exploit, to abuse
bahs	بحث	discussion, argument
bahs kardan	بحث ک ردن	to discuss, to argue
bähuš	با هوش	intelligent, smart
bäje ye telefon	باجه تلفن	phone box
bakärat	بکارت	virginity
bäl	بال	wing
bal³	بلع	swallowing
bal³idan	بلعیدن	to swallow
balä	بلا	disaster, misfortune
bälä	بالا	up, top, upper part
bälä raftan	بالا رفتن	to climb
balad	بلد	familiar, guide
balad budan	بلد بودن	to know
baläl	بلال	corn, pop corn
balam	بلم	small boat
bäläye	بالای	above
bale	بله	yes
bäleq	بالغ	mature, adult
bäleq šodan	بالغ شدن	to mature
bäleš	بالش	pillow, cushion
bälini	بالینی	clinical
balke	بلکه	maybe, perhaps
balqur	بلغور	grouts, frumenty
balut	بلوط	oak
balvä	بلوا	riot, disturbance
bam	بم	bass, low voice
bäm	بام	roof
bämaze	با مزه	tasty
bämbul	بامبول	trick
bämedäd	بامداد	morning
banä	بنا	building, construction
banäder	بنادر	ports, harbours

banafš	بنفش	violet
banafše	بنفشه	violet, pansy
banäguš	بناگوش	cavity behind the ear
band	بند	band, rope, joint, string
band bäzi	بند بازی	acrobatics, rope-walking
band e kafš	بند کفش	lace
bandar	بندر	port, harbour
bande	بنده	slave, servant
bandegi	بندگی	slavery
bang	بنگ	hashish
bangi	بنگی	addicted to hashish
bäni	بانی	founder, builder
bänk	بانک	bank
bannä	بنا	builder, mason
bannäyi	بنایی	building, masonry
bänovän	بانوان	ladies, women
bänu	بانو	lady
bäq	باغ	garden
bäq vahš	باغ وحش	zoo
baqä	بـقا	survival, permanence
baqal	بغل	a cuddle, hug
baqal kardan	بغل کردن	to cuddle, to hug
baqali	بغلی	pocket-size
baqäyä (bäqi)	بقایا (باقی)	remains, remnants
bäqbäni	باغبانی	gardening
bäqelä	باقلا	broad bean
bäqi	باقی	rest, residue, left
bäqimände	باقیمانده	remaining, rest
baqiyye	بقیه	rest, remaining
bäqlavä	باقلوا	a kind of pastry
baqqäl	بقال	grocer
baqqäli	بقالی	grocery
bär	بار	load, time

bar aleyh	بر علیه	against
bar angixtan	بر انگیختن (برانگیز)	to motivate, to encourage
bar hasb e	بر حسب	in terms of, for
bär zadan	بار زدن	to load
baräbar	برابر	equal, same
baräbari	برابری	equality
barädar	برادر	brother
barädar šohar	برادر شوهر	husband's brother
baradar xände	برادر خوانده	step brother
barädar zäde	برادر زاده	niece or nephew
barädar zan	برادرزن	wife's brother
barädari	برادری	brotherhood
barädarxände	برادر خوانده	half brother
bärakalläh	بارک الله	well down
barakat	برکت	blessing
baraks	برعکس	vice versa, contrary
barämadan	برآمدن	to appear, to rise
barämadegi	برآمدگی	projection, outgrowth
bärän	باران	rain
barande	برنده	winner
barande šodan	برنده شدن	to win
bärandegi	بارندگی	rainfall
bäräni	بارانی	raincoat
barävard	برآورد	estimate, evaluation
baräye	برای	for, in order to
bärbar	باربر	porter
barčasb	برچسب	label, tag
barčasb zadan	برچسب زدن	to label
barčidan(bar čin)	برچیدن (برچین)	to remove, to put an end
bärdär	باردار	pregnant
bärdäri	بارداری	pregnancy
bardäštan	برداشتن (بردار)	to pick up, to take
barde	برده	slave

barde däri	برده داری	slavery
barf	برف	snow
barf bäzi	برف بازی	playing with snow
barf pakkon	برف پاکن	wipers
barfak	برفک	thrush, tv flakes
barg	برگ	leaf, sheet, page
barge	برگه	sheet, page
bargaštan	برگشتن (برگرد)	to return, to go back
bargozär kardan	برگذار کردن	to celebrate, to held
bargozidan	برگزیدن	to choose, to select
bärik	باریک	narrow, thin
barjaste	برجسته	projecting, prominent
barjastegi	برجستگی	projection, prominence
barkanär	برکنار	discharged, dismissed
barkanär kardan	برکنار کردن	to discharge, to dismiss
bärkeš	بارکش	lorry, truck
barmalä kardan	برملا کردن	to reveal
barnäme	برنامه	program
barnäme rizi	برنامه ریزی	planning
barnäme rixtan	برنامه ریختن	to plan
barq	برق	electricity
barqkär	برقکار	electrician
barqi	برقی	electrical
barq gereftan	برق گرفتن	to electrocute
barqarär	برقرار	established, continuing
barqarär kardan	برقرار کردن	to establish
barraq	براق	shiny, bright
barrasi	بررسی	inspection, review
barrasi kardan	بررسی کردن	to inspect, to review
barre	بره	lamb
bartar	برتر	higher, superior
bartari	برتری	superiority
bärut	باروت	gunpowder

bärvar	بارور	fertile
bärvari	باروری	fertility
bärvar kardan	بارورکردن	to fertilise
barxästan	برخاستن (برخیز)	to rise, to get up
barxeläf	برخلاف	against, contrary
barxi	برخی	some
barxordan	برخوردن (برخور)	to clash, to bump into
barzax	برزخ	limbo, uncertainty
barzegar	برزگر	farmer
bas	بس	enough
bäš!	باش	be
basämad	بسامد	frequency
bašar	بشر	human, mankind
bašariyat	بشریت	humanity
bašardust	بشردوست	philanthropist
bašardustäne	بشردوستانه	humanitarian
basäväyi	بساوایی	sense of touch, tactile
bäše	باشه	ok (for accepting, confirming)
bäšgäh	باشگاه	club
basij	بسیج	mobilization force
basiji	بسیجی	A Basij militia
basirat	بصیرت	insight
basketbäl	بسکتبال	basketball
basketbälist	بسکتبالیست	basketball player
baššäš	بشاش	cheerful, smiling
bastan (band)	بستن (بند)	to close, to tie, to fasten
bastani	بستنی	ice cream
bästänišenäsi	باستان شناسی	archaeology
bästänšenass	باستان شناس	archaeologist
bastari	بستری	hospitalised
bastari kardan	بستری کردن	to hospitalise
baste	بسته	package, parcel, closed
bastebandi	بسته بندی	packing, wrapping

bastegän	بستگان	relatives
batälat	بطالت	idleness, laziness
bätel	باطل	void, useless
bätel kardan	باطل کردن	to cancel
bäten	باطن	conscious, inner part
bäteni	باطنی	internal, hidden, spiritual
bätläq	باتلاق	swamp
bätri	باطری	battery
bävar	باور	belief, trust
bävar kardan	باور کردن	to believe
baväsir	بواسیر	haemorrhoids
baxil	بخیل	jealous, miserly
baxiye	بخیه	suture, stitch
baxiye zadan	بخیه زدن	to stitch
baxš	بخش	part, portion, section
baxšande	بخشنده	generous, merciful
baxšandegi	بخشندگی	generosity
baxšidan(baxš)	بخشیدن (بخش)	to forgive
baxšnäme	بخشنامه	circular, directive
baxt	بخت	chance, luck
bäxt	باخت	loss
bäxtan	باختن	to loss
bayän	بیان	expression, explanation
bayän kardan	بیان کردن	to express, to explain
bayäniye	بیانیه	declaration, manifesto
bayät	بیات	stale
bäyegäni	بایگانی	archives
bäyegäni kardan	بایگانی کردن	to archive, to store
bäyer	بایر	idle land, barren
bäyesti	بایستی	must
bäz	باز	open, wide, hawk
bäz kardan	باز کردن	to open
bazak	بزک	make up, grooming

bäzande	بازنده	loser
bäzär	بازار	market
bazarak	بزرک	linseed, flax
bäzargän	بازرگان	merchant, trader
bäzargäni	بازرگانی	commerce, business
bäzäri	بازاری	businessman, commercial
bazäz	بزاز	cloth-dealer
bäzdäšt	بازداشت	detention, arrest
bäzdäšt kardan	بازداشت ک ردن	to arrest
bäzdäštgäh	بازداشتگاه	detention center, prison
bäzdeh	بازده	output, efficiency
bäzdid	بازدید	inspection, audit
bäzdid kardan	بازدید کردن	to inspect, to audit
bäzgašt	بازگشت	return, homecoming
bäzgaštan	بازگشتن	to return
bäzi	بازی	game, sport, play
bäzi kardan	بازی کردن	to play
bäzigar	بازیگر	actor
bäziguš	بازیگوش	playful, careless
bäzikon	بازیکن	player
bäzju	بازجو	investigator, interrogator
bäzjuyi	بازجویی	interrogation
bäzjuyi kardan	بازجویی کردن	to interrogate
bazm	بزم	party, feast
bäzmände	بازمانده	survivor
bäznešaste	بازنشسته	retired
bäznešaste šodan	بازنشسته شدن	to retire
bäznešastegi	بازنشستگی	retirement
bäzpors	بازپرس	inspector
bäzporsi	بازپرسی	investigation
bazr	بذر	seed, grain
bäzras	بازرس	inspector
bäzrasi	بازرسی	inspection

bäzsäzi	بازسازی	restoration, renovation
bäzsäzi kardan	بازسازی کردن	to restore, to renovate
bäztäb	بازتاب	reflex, reaction
bäzu	بازو	arm
bäzuband	بازوبند	bracelet, armlet
bäzxäst	بازخواست	interrogation
be	به	to, at, by, in
be dar bordan	(بدر بر) بدر بردن	to save, to escape
be salamati	بسلامتی	cheers!
be taraf e	بطرف	towards
be³sat	بعثت	becoming a prophet
bedehi	بدهی	debt, liability
bedehkär	بدهکار	in debt, indebted
bedune	بدون	without
beh	به	quince
behbud	بهبود	recovery, improvement
behdäšt	به هدا شت	health care, health
behdäšti	بهداشتی	hygienic
behešt	بهشت	paradise, heaven
behešti	بهشتی	heavenly
behtar	بهتر	better
behtarin	بهترین	the best
behyär	بهیار	nurse aid
bejoz	بجز	except
bekr	بکر	virgin, intact
belderčin	بلدرچین	quail
belit	بلیت	ticket
belqovve	بالقوه	potential
bemoqe³	به موقع	on time, timely
benzin	بنزین	petrol, gasoline
berahne	برهنه	naked, nude
berahnegi	برهنه گی	nudity
berenj	برنج	rice, brass

berešte	برشته	toasted, browned
berešte kardan	برشته ک ردن	to toast
berjis	برجیس	jupiter
beryän	بریان	roasted, grilled
beškan	بشکن	finger snap for joy
beškan zadan	بشکن زدن	to snap fingers for joy
besmelläah	بسم الله	in the name of god
bestänkär	بستانکار	creditor
besyär	بسیار	many, a lot,
bey³äne	بیعانه	deposit
bey³at	بیعت	loyalty, homage
beyn	بین	middle, between, among
beynolmelali	بین المللی	international
beyraq	بیرق	flag
beytolmäl	بیت المال	public budget
beyze	بیضه	testicle
bezä³at	بضاعت	financial ability, means
bezehkär	بزهکار	delinquent, criminal
bezehkäri	بزهکاری	delinquency
bezudi	بزودی	soon
bi	بی	without
bi³är	بی عار	shameless, lazy
bi³äri	بی عاری	shamelessness, laziness
bi³orze	بی عرضه	incapable, incompetent
bi³orzegi	بی عرضه گی	incapability
bibi	بی بی	mistress of the house
bičäre	بیچاره	helpless, poor
bičäregi	بیچاره گی	helplessness
bičiz	بیچیز	poor
bidäne	بی دانه	seedless
bidär	بیدار	awake, alert
bidäri	بیداری	awakening, alertness
bidär šodan	بیدار شدن	to wake up

bidasto pä	بی دست و پا	clumsy, resource less
biderang	بیدرنگ	immediately, quickly
bidin	بیدین	atheist, secular
bidini	بیدینی	atheism
bigäne	بیگانه	foreign, alien, stranger
bigänegi	بیگانگی	alienation
bigonäh	بیگناه	innocent, sinless
bigonähi	بیگناهی	innocence
bihäl	بی حال	ill, weak, exhausted
bihäli	بی حالی	weakness, exhaustion
bihayä	بی حیا	immodest, rude
bihayäyi	بی حیایی	immodesty, rudeness
bihejäb	بی حجاب	unveiled, uncovered
bihejäbi	بی حجابی	without Islamic cover
bihess	بی حس	numb, anaesthetised
bihessi	بی حسی	numbness
bihosele	بی حوصله	impatient, irritable
bihoselegi	بی حوصله گی	impatience, irritability
bijä	بی جا	inappropriate
bikär	بیکار	unemployed
bikäri	بیکاری	unemployment
bil	بیل	shovel
bim	بیم	fear, panic
bimär	بیمار	ill, sick
bimärestän	بیمارستان	hospital
bimäri	بیماری	illness, disease
bime	بیمه	insurance, guarantee
bime kardan	بیمه کردن	to insure
bimnäk	بیمناک	fearful, afraid
bimohregän	بی مهرگان	invertebrates
binamak	بی نمک	tasteless
binande	بیننده	viewer, watcher
bINäyi	بینایی	visual, vision

binäyi sanj	بینائی سنج	optometrist
binäyi sanji	بینائی سنجی	optometry
bini	بینی	nose
bipanäh	بی پناه	homeless, shelter less
biparde	بی پرده	frank, open
bipedaro mädar	بی پدر و مادر	orphan
birabt	بی ربط	irrelevant
birähe	بیراهه	by-way
birahm	بیرحم	cruel, ruthless
birahmi	بیرحمی	cruelty, ruthlessness
biriyä	بی ریا	sincere, frank
birun	بیرون	outside, outdoor
birun kardan	بیرون کردن	to expel
bisaro pä	بی سروپا	rascal
bisaro tah	بی سروته	incoherent, empty
bisarosedä	بی سروصدا	quiet, hush-hush
bisaväd	ب ی سواد	illiterate
bisavädi	بی سوادی	illiteracy
bisedä	بی صدا	quiet, mute
bisim	بی سیم	wireless
bist	بیست	twenty
bištar	بیشتر	more, most
bistom	بیستم	twentieth
bitafävot	بی تفاوت	indifferent
bitafävoti	بی تفاوتی	indifference
bitaraf	بی طرف	neutral
bitarafi	بی طرفی	neutrality, impartiality
biväk	بی واک	voiceless
biväsete	بی واسطه	direct
bive	بیوه	widow
bix	بیخ	root, bottom
bixabar	بی خبر	unaware, ignorant
bixabari	بی خبری	unawareness, ignorance

bixäbi	بی خوابی	insomnia
bixänemän	بی خانمان	homeless
bixänemäni	بی خانمانی	homelessness
bixäsiyat	بی خاصیت	ineffective, useless
bixiyäl	بی خیال	absent minded
bixiyäli	بی خیالی	absent mindedness
biyäbän	بیابان	desert, wilderness
bizär	بیزار	weary, disgusted
bizäri	بیزاری	disgust
bo³d	بعد	dimension, distance
bohrän	بحران	crisis
bohräni	بحرانی	critical
boht	بهت	stunning, amazement
bohtän	بهتان	false accusation
bohtän zadan	بهتان زدن	to falsely accuse
boks	بوکس	boxing
boksel kardan	بوکسل کردن	to tow a vehicle
boland	بلند	loud, tall, long
boland kardan	بلند ک ردن	to lift, to raise
boland parväz	بلند پرواز	ambitious
boland šodan	بلند شدن	to get up, to stand up
bolandgu	بلند گو	loudspeaker
bolbol	بلبل	nightingale
boloq	بلوغ	maturity, puberty
bolqärestän	بلغارستان	Bulgaria
boluz	بلوز	shirt, blouse
bomb	بمب	bomb
bombafkan	بمب افکن	bomber
bombärän	بمباران	bombardment
bombärän kardan	بمباران کردن	to bombard
bon	بن	base, root
bonbast	بن بست	dead end, no through road
bongäh	بنگاه	agency, institution

bonyäd	بنیاد	base, foundation
bonyän	بنیان	foundation, structure
bonye	بنیه	health, physical condition
boq³e	بقعه	tomb
boqalamun	بوقلمون	turkey
boqče	بقچه	bundle, cloth wrapper
boqranj	بغرنج	complicated, intricate
boqz	بغض	spite, hatred
boräde	براده	filings, shavings
bordan(bar)	بردن (بر)	to take, to win
bores	برس	brush
bores zadan	برس زدن	to brush
boridan(bor)	بریدن (بر)	to cut
borj	برج	tower, month
boške	بشکه	barrel
bošqäb	بشقاب	plate, dish
bostän	بستان	garden
bot	بت	idol
botri	بطری	bottle
boxär	بخار	steam, vapour
boxäri	بخاری	heater, fireplace
boz	بز	goat
bozäq	بزاق	saliva
bozorg	بزرگ	large, big, grown up
bozorg kardan	بزرگ کردن	to foster, to grow
bozorg šodan	بزرگ شدن	to grow up, to mature
bozorgräh	بزرگراه	freeway, highway
bozorgsäl	بزرگسال	adult, grown up
bozorgsäli	بزرگسالی	adulthood
bu	بو	smell, odour
bu kardan	بو کردن	to smell
budan(bast)	بودن (هست)	to be
budäyi	بودائی	Buddhist

budje	بودجه	budget
bufe	بوفه	buffet
buluk	بلوک	block, civil parish
bulur	بلور	crystal
bumi	بومی	native, local, indigenous
buq	بوق	horn
bur	بور	blond, light-coloured
burän	بوران	snow-storm blizzard
buse	بوسه	kiss
busidan(bus)	بوسیدن (بوس)	to kiss
bute	بوته	bush, shrub
buyäyi	بویایی	olfaction
buyidan(buy)	بوییدن (بوی)	to smell

C		
čäbok	چابک	agile, quick
čädor	چادر	veil, tent
čädori	چادری	a woman who wears veil
čädor zadan	چادر زدن	to camp
čädornešini	چادر نشینی	nomadic, tent dwelling
čägu	چاقو	knife
čägukeš	چاقو کش	hoodlum, knife stabber
čäh	چاه	well, hole
čäh kan	چاه کن	well digger
čähär	چهار	four
čähär räh	چهار راه	intersection
čähärdah	چهارده	fourteen
čähärpä	چهارپا	quadruped, animal
čähäršanbe	چهارشنبه	wednesday
čähäršanbe suri	چهارشنبه سوری	new year celebration
čahčahe	چهچهه	twittering
čak	چک	slap
čak zadan	چک زدن	to slap
čäk	چاک	cleft, crack
čäkar	چاکر	servant
čakävak	چکاوک	lark
čakidan(čak)	چکیدن (چک)	to drip, to trickle
čakide	چکیده	summary
čakkoš	چکش	hammer
čakme	چکمه	boot, high boot
čäknäy	چاکنای	glottis
čäle	چاله	pit, trench, hole
čamadän	چمدان	suitcase
čaman	چمن	grass, lawn
čaman zadan	چمن زدن	to mow lawn
čaman zan	چمن زن	lawn mower

čamanzär	چمنزار	meadow
čanbare	چنبره	hoop, circle, curl
čand	چند	some, few, how, how
čand zel³i	چند ضلعی	polygon
čandän	چندان	so, as much as
čandin	چندین	several, many
čäne	چانه	chin
čäne zadan	چانه زدن	to bargain
čang	چنگ	harp, claw
čang zadan	چنگ زدن	to grasp
čangak	چنگک	hook
čangäl	چنگال	fork, claws
čap	چپ	left
čap gara	چپ گرا	leftist
čapi	چپی	leftist
čäp	چاپ	print, edition, press
čap dast	چپ دست	left handed
čäp kardan	چاپ کردن	to print
čapändan	چپاندن (چپان)	to stuff, to push into
čapar	چپر	wattle, fence
čapävol	چپاول	looting, fleecing
čapävol kardan	چپاول کردن	to loot
cape šodan	چپه شدن	to capsize
čäpi	چاپی	printed, typographical
čapidan(čap)	چپیدن (چپ)	to packed into a place
čäplus	چاپلوس	flatterer, toady sit
čäpxäne	چاپ خانه	press, print house
čäp kardan	چاپ کردن	to print, to publish
čäq	چاق	fat, obese
čäqi	چاقی	obesity
čäqu	چاقو	knife
čäqu zadan	چاقوزدن	to stab
čarä	چرا	grazing, pasturing

čarägäh	چراگاه	pasture, meadow
čarak	چارک	quarter
čarande	چرنده	grazer
čarb	چرب	fatty, oily, greasy
čarb jabän	چرب زبان	glib tongued
čarbi	چربی	fat, oil
čarbidan(čarb)	چربیدن (چرب)	to exceed
čärčub	چارچوب	frame, skeleton
čärdiväri	چاردیواری	house, premises
čäre	چاره	remedy, cure
čärguš	چارگوش	quadrangle, square
čaridan(čar)	چریدن	to graze
čarm	چرم	leather
čarm säzi	چرم سازی	tannery
čäroq	چاروق	rural shoe
čärpä	چارپا	quadruped
čärpäye	چارپایه	stool
čäršäne	چارشانه	broad-shouldered
čarx	چرخ	wheel, bicycle
čarx dande	چرخ دنده	gear
čarx kardan	چرخ کردن	to mince
čarx karde	چرخ کرده	minced
čarx saväri	چرخ سواری	cycling
čarxeš	چرخش	spinning, rotation
čarxidan(čarx)	چرخیدن (چرخ)	to turn, to roll
čašäyi	چشایی	gustatory
časb	چسب	glue, paste
časbän	چسبان	sticky, tight
časbidan(časb)	چسبیدن (چسب)	to glue, to paste
časbnäk	چسبناک	sticky, adhesive
čašidan(čaš)	چشیدن (چش)	to taste
čäšni	چاشنی	seasoning, dressing
čatr	چتر	umbrella, parachute

čatr bäz	چتر باز	parachutist, paratrooper
čatr bäzi	چتربازی	parachuting
čävoš	چاوش	herald
čäxän	چاخان	exaggeration, charlatan
čäxän	چاخان کردن	exaggeration, charlatan
čaxmäq	چخماق	flint
čäy	چای	tea
čäyiydan(čäy)	چاییدن (چای)	to chill, to catch cold
če	چه	what, whether
čeft	چفت	latch, hasp
čegune	چگونه	how
čegunegi	چگونگی	condition, circumstance
čehel	چهل	forty
čehre	چهره	face
ček	چک	checking, bank check
ček ček	چک چک	dropping, dripping
ček kardan	چک کردن	to check
čekke	چکه	drop, leaking
čekke kardan	چکه کردن	to leak
čeländan(čelän)	چلاندن	to squeeze, to wrench
čelčele	چلچله	swallow
čelčeräq	چلچراغ	chandelier
čelle	چله	a period of forty days
čenänče	چنانچه	if, in case
čenänke	چنانکه	as
čenär	چنار	plane tree
čenin	چنین	such, such as
čeqadr	چقدر	how much, how many
čerä	چرا	why
čeräq	چراغ	light, lamp, lantern
čeräq qovve	چراغ قوه	torch (flashlight)
čerik	چریک	guerilla, partisan
čerk	چرک	pus, filth

4

čerk kardan	چرک کردن	to fester
čerknevis	چرکنویس	draft, rough copy
čert or pert	چرت و پرت	irrelevant, nonsense
češm	چشم	eye, ok (polite)
češm bandi	چشم بندی	juggling
češm baste	چشم بسته	blindfold
česm dāšt	چشمداشت	expectation hope
česm zadan	چشم زدن	to jinx
češm pezešk	چشم پزشک	ophthalmologist
češm pezeški	چشم پزشکی	ophthalmology
češm puši	چشم پوشی	forbearance, tolerance
češm puši kardan	چشم پوشی کردن	to ignore, to forgive
česm rošani	چشم روشنی	gift, present
češm zaxm	چشم زخم	harm by evil's eye
češmak	چشمک	wink, blink, twinkle
češmak zadan	چشمک زدن	to wink, to blink
češmandāz	چشم انداز	view, outlook
češmčarāni	چشم چرانی	voyeurism, ogling
česme	چشمه	spring, source
četor	چطور	how
či	چی	what
čidan(čin)	چیدن (چین)	to pick, to pluck, to clip
čin	چین	china, wrinkle, crease
čin xordan	چین خوردن	to wrinkle
čin xorde	چین خورده	wrinkled, crumpled
čini	چ ي نی	chinese, chinaware
čire šodan	چیره شدن	to conquer, to overcome
čiregi	چیرگی	victory, dominance
čistān	چیستان	riddle, puzzle
čit	چیت	printed cotton, fabric
čit sāzi	چیت سازی	fabric factory
čiz	چیز	thing, object
čizi	چیزی	something

čo	چو	rumor
čo andäxtan	چو انداختن	to spread a rumor
čodan	چدن	cast iron
čogän	چوگان	polo-stick, bat
čollaq	چلاق	crippled, paralyzed
čomäq	چماق	club
čombätme	چمباتمه	squat
čombätme zadan	چمباتمه زدن	to squat
čomče	چمچه	ladle, scoop
čon	چون	because, for
čopoq	چپق	calumet, pipe
čopoq kešidan	چپق کشیدن	to smoke a pipe
čoqolli kardan	چوقلی کردن	To telltale, to complain
čoqondar	چغندر	beet
čort	چرت	nap
čort zadan	چرت زدن	to take a nap
čortke	چرتکه	abacus
čoruk	چروک	wrinkle, crease
čub	چوب	wood, timber, log
čub bast	چوب بست	scaffold
čub panbe	چوب پنبه	cork
čubdasti	چوبدستی	walking stick, cane
čupän	چوپان	shepherd

D		
dä³emi	دائمی	permanent, constant
da³vä	دعوا	fight, quarrel, argument
da³vä kardan	دعوا کردن	to argue, to fight
da³vat	دعوت	invitation
da³vat kardan	دعوت کردن	to invite
dabbäq	دباغ	tanner
dabbe	دبه	flask
dabestän	دبستان	primary school
dabir	دبیر	secretary, teacher
dabirestän	دبیرستان	high school, secondary school
dabirxäne	دبیرخانه	secretariat office
dad	دد	wild, beast
däd	داد	scream, justice
däd zadan	داد زدن	to scream
dädan(dah)	دادن (ده)	to give
dädäš	داداش	brother
dädgäh	دادگاه	court (legal)
dädgostari	دادگستری	office of justice
dädo bidäd	دادوبیداد	brawl, turmoil
dädo setad	دادوستد	deal, business, trade
dädras	دادرس	judge
dädsetän	دادستان	public prosecutor
dädxäst	دادخواست	petition, complaint
daf	دف	tambourine
daf³	دفع	repelling, discharge
daf³ kardan	دفع کردن	to repel, to discharge
daf³e	دفعه	time, instance
dafn	دفن	burial
dafn kardan	دفن کردن	to bury
daftar	دفتر	notebook, office, register
daftarče	دفترچه	notebook

daftardär	دفتردار	bookkeeper
daftarxäne	دفترخانه	notary public
dah	ده	ten
dahän	دهان	mouth
dahan kaji	دهن کجی	making face at
dahanbin	دهن بین	whimsical
dahandarre	دهن دره	yawning
dahane	دهانه	bridle, opening, entrance
dahe	دهه	decade
dakke	دکه	stand, booth, stall, kiosk
dälän	دالان	hall, corridor
dalil	دلیل	reason, cause
dalil ä	دلیل آوردن	to reason, to argue
dalläk	دلاک	masseur, barber
dalläl	دلال	broker, dealer
dalqak	دلقک	clown
däm	دام	trap, domestic animal
däm pezeški	دامپزشکی	veterinary
damä	دما	temperature
dämäd	داماد	groom, son-in-law
däman	دامن	lap, skirt
dämane	دامنه	foothill, extent
dämäqe	دماغه	cape, prow
damar	دمر	prone, lying on face
damäsanj	دماسنج	thermometer
damidam(dam)	دمیدن (دم)	to blow, to puff
dampäyi	دمپایی	slippers
dänä	دانا	wise, savant
dänäyi	دانایی	wisdom
dandän	دندان	tooth
dandän dard	دندان درد	toothache
dandän quruče	دندان قروچه	grating the teeth
dandäne širi	دندان شیری	milk tooth

dandänpezešk	دندانپزشک	dentist
dandänpezeški	دندانپزشکی	dentistry
dandänsäz	دندانساز	dentist, denture maker
dande	دنده	rib, gear (of a vehicle)
däne	دانه	seed, grain, piece
däneš	دانش	knowledge
däneš ämuz	دانش آموز	student (school)
däneš ju	دانـ شجو	student (university)
dänešgäh	دانشگاه	university
däneškade	دانشکده	faculty, college
dänešmand	دانشمند	scientist, scholar
dänestan(dän)	دانستن (دان)	to know (something)
däng	دانگ	share, sixth part
däq	داغ	hot, scar, bereavement
daqal	دغل	fraud, deceitful
daqdaqe	دغدغه	apprehension, worry
däqdär	داغدار	bereaved
daqiq	دقیق	subtle, careful, precise
dar	در	door, lid, cap, in, at, by
där	دار	gallows
dar ämadan	در آمدن (در آی)	to come out
dar ävardan	در آوردن (در آور)	to bring out, to earn
dar bäz kon	در باز کن	can opener
dar kardan	در کردن (در کن)	to let off, to fire off
dar raftan	در رفتن (در رو)	to escape, to dislocate
dar raftegi	در رفتگی	dislocation
dar sad	درصد	percent
därä	دارا	rich, possessor
däräyi	دارایی	property, equity, asset
däräbi	داراب ی	grapefruit
darajät	درجات	degrees, ranks
daraje	درجه	degree, rank
darajebandi	درجه بندی	graduation , rating

darajebandi kardan	درجه بندی کردن	to grade, to rate
darak	درک	hell
darämad	درآمد	income
darande	درنده	beast, predatory, fierce animal
darbän	دربان	door keeper, porter
darband	دربند	narrow pass or alley
darbär	دربار	court(royal)
darbast	دربست	exclusive, whole
darbedar	دربدر	homeless, vagabond
därčin	دارچین	cinnamon
dard	درد	pain, ache, agony
dard kardan	درد کردن	to ache
dardnäk	دردناک	painful, sore
dargir šodan	درگیر شدن	to get involved, to fight
dargozašt	درگذشت	passing away, demise
darham	درهم	chaotic, mixed
dari	دری	Dari, an Afghan language
dariče	دریچه	hatch, shatter, valve
daride	دریده	torn, ripped, impudent
dariq	دریغ	alas, denial, refusal
darj	درج	insertion, publishing
dark	درک	perception, comprehension
dark kardan	درک کردن	to understand, to realise
därkub	دارکوب	woodpecker
darmän	درمان	cure, healing, therapy
darmände	درمانده	hopeless, desperate
darmängäh	درمانگاه	clinic
därottarjome	دارالترجمه	translation office
darre	دره	valley, gorge
dars	درس	lesson, lecture
dars dädan	درس دادن	to teach, to give lessons
dars xändan	درس خواندن	to study, to learn, to take lessons

darsad	درصد	precent
däru	دارو	medicine, drug
darun	درون	in, inside, interior
daruni	درونی	internal, inner
därusäz	داروساز	pharmacist, chemist
däruxäne	داروخانه	pharmacy, chemist
darväze	دروازه	gate, goal
darväzebän	دروازه بان	gateman, goalkeeper
darviš	درویش	dervish, mystic, poor
darxäst	درخواست	request, petition
darxäst kardan	درخواست کردن	to request, to apply
daryä	دریا	sea
daryä kanär	دریا کنار	seacoast, beach
daryäče	دریاچه	lake
daryädär	دریا دار	rear admiral
daryäft	دریافت	receipt, perception
daryäft kardan	دریافت کردن	to receive
daryänavard	دریانورد	seaman, sailor
daryäsälär	دریاسالار	admiral
daryäyi	دریایی	marine, naval, maritime
darz	درز	suture, crack
däs	داس	flax, sickle
dasise	دسیسه	plot, conspiracy
dast	دست	hand, side, deck, set
dašt	دشت	plain, field
dast ämuz	دست آموز	pet
dast andäz	دست انداز	bump, puddle
dast andäzi	دست اندازی	aggression, invasion
dast äviz	دست آویز	excuse, pretext
dast däštan	دست داشتن	to be involved
dast deräzi	دست درازی	aggression, violence
dast duz	دست دوز	hand sewn
dast päče	دستپاچه	hasty, excited

dast poxt	دست پخت	hand-cooked
dast säz	دست ساز	handmade
dast šuyi	دستشویی	washstand, toilet
dast xat	دست خط	hand writing
dast xorde	دست خورده	touched, used
dast zadan	دست زدن	to touch
dästän	داستان	story, tale
däštan(där)	داشتن (دار)	to have
dastband	دستبند	bracelet, handcuff
dastband zadan	دستبند زدن	to handcuff
dastbord	دستبرد	theft, robbing
dastbord zadan	د س ت برد زدن	to rob, to steal
dastbus	دستبوس	kissing superior's hand
daste	دسته	handle, bunch, group
daste gol	دسته گل	bouquet, flower bunch
dastebandi	دسته بندی	sorting, grouping, classification
dastebandi kardan	دسته بندی کردن	to sort, to classify
dastforuš	دست فروش	peddler, hawker
dastgäh	دستگاه	system, set, apparatus
dastgire	دستگیره	handle, knob
dasti	دستی	handmade, manual
dastkeš	دستکش	gloves
dastmäl	دستمال	handkerchief
dastmäli	دستمالی	touching, fingering
dastmozd	دستمزد	wage, earning
dastnamäz	دستنماز	ablution before praying
dastnešände	دست نشانده	protégé, stooge
dastranj	دسترنج	wage
dastšuyi	دستشویی	bathroom
dastur	د س تور	order, direction, grammar
dastur dädan	دستور دادن	to order
dastur olamal	دستورالعمل	manual, guide
dastyär	دستیار	assistant, aid

davä	دوا	medicine, potion
davām	دوام	durability, stability
dävar	داور	judge, referee, umpire
dävari	داوری	judgment, being referee
davazdah	دوازده	twelve
davidan(dav)	دویدن (دو)	to run
dävtalab	داوطلب	volunteer, candidate
dävtalabäne	داوطلبانه	voluntarily
däxel	داخل	inside, in, interior
däxeli	داخلی	internal, local
daxl	دخل	income, profit, cash register
daxme	دخمه	tomb, crypt
däye	دایه	nanny
däyer	دایر	established, opened
däyere	دایره	circle, round, tambourine
däyi	دایی	maternal uncle
dayyus	دیوث	cuckold
defä³	دفاع	defense, resistance
defä³ kardan	دفاع کردن	to defend
degarguni	دگرگونی	change, transformation
deh	ده	village
dehät	دهات	villages
dehäti	دهاتی	villager
dehkade	دهکده	small village
dehliz	دهلیز	hallway, vestibule
dehqän	دهقان	farmer
del	دل	heart, guts, belly
del bastan	دل بستن	to be attached emotionally
del kandan	دل کندن	to give up
del tang šodan	دلتنگ شدن	to miss (feel absence)
delävar	دلاور	brave, courageous
delbar	دلبر	charming, sweetheart
delbari	دلبری	charm

delbastegi	دلبستگی	attachment, affection
delčasb	دلچسب	pleasing, enjoyable
deldäri	دلداری	consolation
deldäri dädan	دلداری دادن	to sympathise
delgarm	دلگرم	confident, assured
delgir	دلگیر	offended, heart rendered
delir	دلیر	brave, bold
deljuyi	دلجویی	appeasement, affability
deljuyi kardan	دلجویی کردن	to appease
delsard	دلسرد	disappointed, discouraged
delsardi	دلسردی	disappointment
delsuz	دلسوز	compassionate, sympathetic
delsuzi	دلسوزی	compassion, sympathy
deltang	دلتنگ	gloomy, nostalgic
deltangi	دلتنگی	nostalgia
delxäh	دلخواه	desirable, ideal
delxaräš	دلخراش	heart-breaking, harrowing
delxor	دلخور	annoyed, offended
delxori	دلخوری	annoyance
delxoši	دلخوشی	delight, happiness
demokrasi	دمکراسی	democracy
denj	دنج	cozy, snug
deq	دق	fatal grief
deq kardan	دق کردن	to die out of sorrow
deqqat	دقت	attention, precision
deqqat kardan	دقت کردن	to pay attention, to be careful
derang	درنگ	pause, delay
derang kardan	درنگ کردن	to pause, to delay
deraxšän	درخشان	shiny, bright
deraxšidan(deraxš)	درخشیدن (درخش)	to shine, to glow
deraxt	درخت	tree
deräz	دراز	long, prolonged, tall
deräz kešidan	دراز کشیدن	to lay down

deräzä	درازا	length
dero	درو	harvest
dero kardan	درو کردن	to harvest
desämr	د سام بر	December
deser	دسر	dessert
dešne	دشنه	dagger
dexälat	دخالت	interference, intrusion
dexälat kardan	دخالت ک ردن	to interfere, to intervene
dey	دی	tenth Persian month
deym	دی م	dry farming
deyn	دین	debt
deyr	دیر	monastery, convent
dež	دژ	castle, fort
dežbän	دژبان	military policeman
dežxim	دژخیم	executioner
did	دید	view, vision, sight
didan(bin)	دیدن (بین)	to see, to visit
didani	دیدنی	worthy of seeing
didär	دیدار	visit, meeting
didär kardan	دیدار کردن	to visit, to meet
didebän	دی ده ب ان	watchman, signalman
didgäh	دیدگاه	viewpoint
dido bäzdid	دید و باز دید	visiting each other
dig	دیگ	boiler, pot
digar	دیگر	other, another, next, more
digarän	دیگران	others, other people
digari	دیگری	another, the other one
dikšeneri	دیکشنری	dictionary
diktätor	دیکتاتور	dictator
dikte	دیکته	spelling, dictation
din	دین	religion, faith
dindär	دیندار	religious
dini	دینی	religious

diplom	ديپلم	diploma holder
dir	دير	late, delayed
dir kardan	دير ک ردن	to be late, to delay
dirine šenäsi	ديرينه شناسی	paleontology
diruz	ديروز	yesterday
dirvaqt	دير وقت	late
dis	ديس	big plate
dišab	ديشب	last night
div	ديو	demon, devil
diväne	ديوانه	mad, crazy, insane
divär	ديوار	wall, partition
divist	دويست	two thundered
diyabet	ديابت	diabetes
diyär	ديار	region, country
diye	ديه	fine, blood money
dizi	ديزی	small cooking pot
do	دو	two
do³ä	دعا	prayer, blessing
do³ä kardan	دعا کردن	to pray, to give blessing
dobär	دوبار	twice
dobäre	دوباره	again
dobb	دب	bear
dobeyti	دوبيتی	quatrain
dobini	دوبينی	diplopia
dočär	دچار	afflicted with, involved in
dočarxe	دوچرخه	bicycle
dočarxesavar	دوچرخه سوار	cyclist
dockarxe saväri	دوچرخه سواری	cycling
dodel	دودل	double minded, hesitant
dogäne	دوگانه	double
dogme	دگمه	button
dohol	دهل	kettledrum
dojänebe	دوجانبه	bilateral

dojin	دوجين	a dozen
dokän	دكان	shop, store
doktor	دكتر	doctor, physician
dolat	دولت	government, state, wealth
dolati	دولتی	related to government
dolul	دولول	double barreled
dom	دم	tail
domal	دمل	abscess
donbäl	دنبال	rear, behind, following
donbäl kardan	دنبال ک ردن	to follow
donbalän	دنبلان	sheep's testicle
donbäledär	دنباله دار	continuous
dong	دنگ	share
donyä	دنیا	world, universe
doqulu	دوقلو	twins
dor	دور	turn, rotation
dor zadan	دور زدن	to turn, to rotate
dorage	دورگه	hybrid, half blooded
dorähi	دوراهی	junction
dorän	دوران	era, period, age
dore	دوره	period, term, course
dore didan	دوره دیدن	to be trained, to take a course
doregard	دوره گرد	hawker, peddler
dornä	درنا	crane
dorobar	دوروبر	around, surrounding
doroške	درشکه	carriage, pram
dorost	درست	right, true, exact
dorošt	درشت	large, coarse, big
dorost kardan	درست کردن	to make, to build, to correct
dorr	در	pearl
doru	دورو	double faced
dorud	دورود	greeting, praise
došanbe	دوشنبه	monday

dosare	دوسره	return trip
došaxe	دو شاخه	plug (electricity)
došman	دشمن	enemy
došmani	دشمنی	hostility, animosity
došnäm	دشنام	curse, swearing
dost doxtar	دوست دختر	girlfriend
dost pesar	دوست پسر	boyfriend
došvär	د شوار	difficult, hard
dotarafe	دوسره	two way, return, bilateral
dovvom	دوم	second
doxäniyät	دخانیات	tobacco products
doxtar	دختر	girl, daughter, virgin
doxtar xände	دخترخوانده	adopted daughter
doxtaräne	دخترانه	girlish, for girls
dozabäne	دوزبانه	bilingual
dozd	دزد	thief, robber, snitcher
dozdaki	دزدکی	secret, covert
dozdi	دزدی	theft, robbery, stealing
dozdidan(dozd)	دزدیدن (دزد)	to steal, to rob, to kidnap
dozgir	دزدگ یر	security alarm, thief-catcher
dozist	دوزیست	amphibious
duble	دوبله	dubbing
dud	دود	smoke, smog
dude	دوده	smut, lampblack
dudi	دودی	smoked, dark
dudkeš	دودکش	chimney
dudmän	دودمان	dynasty, lineage
duq	دوغ	yogurt and water
dur	دور	far, remote
duri	دوری	being far, missing (someone)
durandiš	دوراندیش	farsighted, wise
durbin	دوربین	binoculars, camera
durbin furuši	دوربین فروشی	camera shop

durbini	دوربینی	farsightedness
durnamä	دورنما	landscape, view
duruq	دروغ	lie, false
duruq goftan	دروغ گفتن	to lie
duruq qu	دروغ گو	liar
duš fang	دوش فنگ	shoulder arms
dušidan(duš)	دوشیدن (دوش)	to milk
dušize	دوشیزه	girl, miss
dust	دوست	friend, mate, pal
dust däštan	دوست داشتن	to like
dustäne	دوستانه	friendly, hospitable
dusti	دوستی	friendship
duxtan(duz)	دوختن (دوز)	to sew, to tailor
duzande	دوزنده	tailor
duzax	دوزخ	hell

E		
e³däm	اعدام	execution
e³däm kardan	اعدام کردن	to execute
e³tebär	اعتبار	credit, importance
e³teläf	اعتلاف	coalition, alliance
e³temäd	اعتماد	trust, reliance
e³temäd kardan	اعتماد کردن	to trust
e³tenä	اعتنا	care, attention
e³tenä kardan	اعتنا کردن	to care, to pay attention
e³teqäd	اعتقاد	belief, faith
e³teqäd däštan	اعتقاد داشتن	to believe
e³teräf	اعتراف	confession
e³teräf kardan	اعتراف کردن	to confess
e³teräz	اعتراض	protest, objection
e³teräz kardan	اعتراض کردن	to protest
e³tesäb	اعتصاب	strike
e³tesäb kardan	اعتصاب کردن	to go on a strike
e³tiyäd	اعتیاد	addiction
e³zäm	اعزام	dispatch, sending off
e³zäm kardan	اعزام کردن	to dispatch, to send
ebädat	عبادت	worship
ebädat kardan	عبادت کردن	to worship
ebädatgäh	ع بادت گ اه	a place for worship
ebärat	ع بارت	phrase, expression
ebhäm	ابهام	ambiguity, uncertainty
eblis	ابلیس	devil, satan
ebrat	ع برت	lesson, warning
ebri	ع بری	hebrew
ebtedä	ابتدا	beginning, first
ebtedäyi	ابتدایی	elementary, primary
ebtekär	ابتکار	innovation, initiative
edälat	عدالت	justice

edäme	ادامه	continuation, prolongation
edäme däštan	ادامه داشتن	to continue
edäre	اداره	office, administration
edäre kardan	اداره کردن	to manage, to administer
edqäm	ادغام	combination, integration
edqäm kardan	ادغام ک ردن	to combine, to integrate
edräk	ادراک	perception
edrär	ادرار	urine
edrär kardan	ادرار کردن	to urinate
efäde	افاده	show off, boasting
effat	ع فت	purity, modesty
efrät	افراط	immoderation, exaggeration
efräti	افراطی	immodest, radical, extremist
efrite	ع فری ته	female demon, astringent
efšä³	افشا	revealing, disclosing
efšä³ kardan	افشا کردن	to reveal, to disclose
eftär	افطار	breaking a fast
eftetäh	افتتاح	opening, commencement
eftetäh kardan	افتتاح کردن	to open, to commence
eftexär	افتخار	honour, dignity
eftexär kardan	افتخار کردن	to be proud of
eftezäh	افتضاح	scandal, disgrace
ehänat	اهانت	insult, offence
ehänat kardan	اهانت کردن	to insult, to offend
ehäte	احاطه	surrounding, siege
ehäte kardan	احاطه کردن	to surround
ehdä	اهدا	dedication, present
ehdä kardan	اهدا کردن	to dedicate, to present
ehsän	احسان	charity, favour
ehsäs	احساس	feeling, sentiment
ehsäs kardan	احساس کردن	to feel
ehtekär	احتکار	hoarding, forestalling
ehtekär kardan	احتکار کردن	to hoard, to forestall

ehtemäl	احتمال	probability, likelihood
ehteräm	احترام	respect, regard
ehteräm kardan	احترام کردن	to respect
ehtiyäj	احتیاج	necessity, requirement, need
ehtiyäj däštan	احتیاج داشتن	to need
ehtiyät	احتیاط	caution
ehtiyät kardan	احتیاط کردن	to be careful, to watch out
ehzär	احضار	calling, summoning
ehzär kardan	احضارکردن	to call, to summon
ejäre	اجاره	rent, hire, lease
ejäre kardan	اجاره کردن	to rent, to hire
ejäze	اجازه	permission
ejäze dädan	اجازه دادن	to permit
ejbäri	اجباری	compulsory, forceful
ejläs	اجلاس	meeting, session
ejrä³	اجرا	execution, enforcement
ejrä³ kardan	اجرا کردن	to execute, to enforce
ejtemä³	اجتماع	meeting, society, gathering
ejtenäb	اجتناب	avoidance, abstinence
ejtenäb kardan	اجتناب کردن	to avoid
ekbiri	اکبیری	nasty, mangy
ekräh	اکراه	reluctance, dislike·
elähe	الهه	goddess
elähi	الهی	divine, o god
elähiyät	الهیات	theology
elhäm	الهام	inspiration
elhäm kardan	الهام کردن	to inspire
ellat	علت	reason, cause
elm	علم	science, knowledge
elqä³	الغاء	abolition, elimination
elqä³ kardan	الغاء کردن	to abolish
eltehäb	التهاب	inflammation, excitement
eltemäs	التماس	begging, requesting

eltemäs kardan	التماس ك ردن	to beg
emäm	امام	religious leader
emämat	امامت	leadership
emämzäde	امامزاده	religious shrine
emärat	عمارت	building, construction
emddad	امداد	help, assistance
emkän	امکان	possibility, feasibility
emlä³	املا	spelling, dictation
emperätor	امپراتور	emperor
emperätori	امپراتوری	empire
emruz	امروز	today
emšab	امشب	tonight
emsal	امسال	this year
emtahän	امتحان	exam, trial, test
emtahän dädan	امتحان دادن	to sit for test, to take an exam
emtahän kardan	امتحان کردن	to try on
emtedäd	امتداد	extension, length
emtenä³	امتناع	refusal, abstention
emtenä³ kardan	امتناع کردن	to refuse
emtiyäz	امتیاز	privilege, advantage, point
emzä³	امضا	signature
emzä³ kardan	امضا کردن	to sign
en³ekäs	انعکاس	reflection, reaction
enabiye	عذبیه	iris
enäyat	عنایت	favour, kindness
enbessat	انبساط	expansion
enereži	انرژی	energy
enfejär	انفجار	explosion, eruption
engär	انگار	think thou, as if
engelis	انگلیس	England
engelisi	انگلیسی	English
enheläl	انحلال	termination, dissolution
enheräf	انحراف	deviation, diversion

enhesär	انحصار	monopoly
enhesäri	انحصاری	monopolistic, exclusive
enjemäd	انجماد	freezing, solidification
enjil	انجیل	Bible
enkär	انکار	denial
enkär kardan	انکار ک ردن	to deny
enqebäz	انقباض	contraction
enqeläb	انقلاب	revolution, upheaval
enqeräz	انقراض	downfall, decline
enšä³	انشا	composition, writing
enšä³alläh	انشا الله	god willing
ensäf	انصاف	equity, justice
ensän	انسان	mankind, human
ensäni	انسانی	humane
ensäniyat	انسانیت	humanity, courtesy
enše³äb	انشعاب	branching, separation
enseräf	انصراف	giving up, changing mind
enseräf dädan	انصراف دادن	to give up
entefäyi	انتفائی	profit producing
entehä	انتها	end, limit
entehär	انتحار	suicide
enteqäd	انتقاد	criticism
enteqäd kardan	انتقاد کردن	to criticize
enteqäl	انتقال	transition, transfer
enteqäli	انتقالی	transient, interim
enteqäl dädan	انتقال دادن	to transfer
enteqäm	انتقام	revenge, vengeance
enteqäm gereftan	انتقام گرفتن	to take revenge
entesäb	انتصاب	appointment
entesäb kardan	انتصاب کردن	to appoint
entešär	انتشار	publishing, broadcasting
entešär dädan	انتشار دادن	to publish
entexäb	انتخاب	election, selection

entexäb kardan	انتخاب کردن	to select, to elect
entezämi	انتظامی	disciplinary
entezär	انتظار	waiting, expectation
entezär däštan	انتظار داشتن	to expect
enzebät	انضباط	discipline, order
eqämat	اقامت	residence, staying
eqdäm	اقدام	action, performance
eqdäm kardan	اقدام کردن	action, performance
eqmä³	اغما	faint, coma
eqräq	اغراق	exaggeration, overstatement
eqräq kardan	اغراق کردن	to exaggerate
eqrär	اقرار	confession
eqrär kardan	اقرار کردن	to confess
eqtebäs	اقتباس	adaptation, citation
eqtebäs kardan	اقتباس کردن	to adapt
eqtesäd	اقتصاد	economy
eqtesädi	اقتصادی	economical, cost effective
eqtešäš	اغتشاش	riot, revolt
eqtešäš kardan	اغتشاش کردن	to revolt
erädat	ارادت	inclination, devotion
erädatmand	ارادتمند	sincere, sincerely
eräde	اراده	will, intention
erädi	ارادی	voluntary, intentionally
erfän	عرفان	mysticism
erfäni	عرفانی	mystic
ers	ارث	inheritance, legacy
ersi	ارثی	hereditary, congenital
ers bordan	ارث بردن	to inherit
eršäd	ارشاد	guiding, leading
eršäd kardan	ارشاد کردن	to guide
ersäl	ارسال	remittance, dispatch
ersäl kardan	ارسال کردن	to dispatch, to send
erte³äš	ارتعاش	vibration, trembling

ertebät	ارتباط	connection, relation
ertefä³	ارتفاع	height, altitude
erzä³	ارضا	satisfaction
erzä³ kardan	ارضا كردن	to satisfy
esärat	اسارت	captivity, capture
ešäre	اشاره	pointing, hint, gesture
ešäre kardan	اشاره كردن	to point out
esbät	اثبات	proof, verification
esbät kardan	اثبات كردن	to prove
esfanj	اسفنج	sponge
esfenäj	اسفناج	spinach
eshäl	اسهال	dysentery, diarrhoea
eškäl	اشكال	difficulty, hardness
eskele	اسكله	dock
eskenäs	اسكناس	note (money)
eski	اسكى	skiing
esläh	اصلاح	correction, reform, haircut
eslähät	اصلاحات	corrections, reforms
esläh kardan	اصلاح كردن	to correct, to cut one's hair
esläm	اسلام	Islam
eslämi	اسلامى	Islamic
esläm garä	اسلام گرا	Islamist
esm	اسم	name, noun
esmi	اسمى	nominal
esme kučik	اسم كوچک	christian name
esme fämil	اسم فاميل	family name
espäniyä	اسپانيا	Spain
espäniyäyi	اسپانيايى	Spanish
ešq	عشق	love, passion
ešqi	عشقى	romantic
ešqäl	اشغال	occupation, invasion
ešqäl kardan	اشغال كردن	to occupy
esräf	اصراف	extravagance, wasting

esräf kardan	اسراف ک ردن	to waste, to use extravagantly
esrär	اصرار	insistence, persistence
esrär kardan	اصرار ک ردن	to insist
establ	اصطبل	stable, mews
estädiyom	استادیوم	stadium
estaxr	استخر	pool (swimming)
este³äre	استعاره	metaphor, simile
este³äri	استعاری	metaphoric, ironic
este³däd	استعداد	talent, gift
este³fa	استعفا	resignation
este³fa kardan	استعفا ک ردن	to resign
este³mäl	استعمال	usage, application
este³mäl kardan	استعمال ک ردن	to use
este³mär	استعمار	colonization
este³märi	استعماری	colonizer
este³mär kardan	استعمار ک ردن	to colonize
eštebäh	اشتباه	mistake, error
eštebäh kardan	اشتباه ک ردن	to make a mistake
estebdäd	استبداد	dictatorship
estebdädi	استبدادی	dictator, totalitarian
estedläl	استدلال	argument, reasoning
estedläl kardan	استدلال ک ردن	to argue
estefäde	استفاده	use, benefit
estefäde kardan	استفاده ک ردن	to use
estefräq	استفراغ	vomiting, puke
estefräq kardan	استفراغ کردن	to vomit
eštehä	اشتها	appetite
estehläk	استهلاک	spending away, consuming
estehqäq	استحقاق	merit, right
estehzär	استحضار	notice, information
estekäk	اصطکاک	friction, contact
estekän	استکان	tumbler-shaped, tea cup
esteläh	اصطلاح	term, idiom

estemnä	استمناع	masturbation
estemnä kardan	استمناع کردن	to masturbate
esteqämat	استقامت	resistance, endurance
esteqämat kardan	استقامت کردن	to resist
esteqbäl	استقبال	welcome, reception
esteqbäl kardan	استقبال کردن	to welcome
esteqläl	استقلال	independence, liberty
esteqrä	استقرا	induction
esteqräyi	استقرایی	inductive
esteqrär	استقرار	settlement
esterähat	استراحت	resting, relaxation
esterähat kardan	استراحت کردن	to rest, to relax
ešteräk	اشتراک	partnership, subscription
ešteräki	اشتراکی	shared
ešteräk däštan	اشتراک داشتن	to participate
estesmär	استمرار	continuation
estesmäri	استمراری	continuous
estesnä	استثنا	exception, exclusivity
estesnäyi	استثنایی	exceptional, special
estetär	استتار	camouflage, under cover
estevä	استوا	equator
esteväyi	استوایی	equatorial
estexdäm	استخدام	employment, recruitment
estexdäm kardan	استخدام کردن	to employ
estexräj	استخراج	extraction, drawing out
estexräj kardan	استخراج کردن	to extract
eštiyäq	اشتیاق	eagerness, enthusiasm
estizäh	استیضاح	impeachment
estizäh kardan	استیضاح کردن	to impeach
ešve	ع شوه	coyness, playfulness
etä³at	اطاعت	obedience, following
etä³at kardan	اطاعت کردن	to obey, to follow
etläf	اتلاف	wasting, losing

etminän	اطمینان	confidence, trust
etminän kardan	اطمینان ك ردن	to trust
ettefäq	اتفاق	event, incident
ettefäqi	اتفاقى	accidental
ettehäd	اتحاد	alliance, union
ettehadiye	اتحادیه	unions
ettehäm	اتهام	accusation, charge
ettelä	اطلاع	information, notice
ettelä³ät	اطلاعات	information, news
ettelä³iyye	اطلاعیه	announcement
ettesäl	اتصال	link, junction
exläl	اخلال	trouble, sabotage
exräj	اخراج	dismissal
exräj kardan	اخراج كردن	to dismiss, to fire
extär	اخطار	notification, warning
extär kardan	اخطار كردن	to warn, to notify
exteläl	اختلال	disorder, disturbance
exteläs	اختلاس	embezzlement
exterä³	اختراع	invention, innovation
exterä³ kardan	اختراع كردن	to invent
extiyär	اختیار	authority, power, option
extiyäri	اختیارى	optional
eyädat	ع یادت	visiting the sick
eyb	ع یب	fault, shortcoming
eybjuyi	ع ی بجوی ى	criticism
eyd	ع ید	festival, feast, celebration
eydi	ع یدى	new year's gift
eynak	ع ی نک	glasses, spectacles
eynaki	عینکى	one who wears glasses,
eynak äftäbi	عینک آفتابى	sun glasses
eynak tebbi	عینک طبى	prescription glasses
eynan	عینا	exactly similar
eyni	ع ی نى	objective

eyšo nuš	عیش و نوش	life in extreme pleasure
eyvän	ایوان	balcony
ezäfe	اضافه	excess, extra
ezäfe kardan	اضافه کردن	to add, to increase
ezdehäm	ازدحام	crowd, gathering
ezdehäm kardan	ازدحام کردن	to gather
ezdeväj	ازدواج	marriage, wedding
ezdeväj kardan	ازدواج کردن	to marry
ezdiyäd	ازدیاد	increasing, increase
ezhär	اظهار	expression, statement
ezhär kardan	اظهار کردن	to express, to state
ezhäriyye	اظهاریه	declaration
ezn	اذن	permission
ezteräb	اضطراب	anxiety, worry
ezteräri	اضطراری	urgent

F		
fa³äl	ف عال	active, energetic, activist
fa³äliyat	ف عال یت	action, activity, effort
fä³el	ف اعل	subject, actor, factor, agent
fa³le	ف عله	labourer
fadä	ف دا	sacrifice, devotion
fadä kardan	ف دا كردن	to sacrifice, to devote
fadäkär	ف داكار	devoted, self-sacrificing
fadäkäri	ف داكارى	devotion, self-sacrifice
fäheše	ف احشه	prostitute, whore
fäheše gari	ف احشه گرى	prostitution
fäheše xäne	ف احشه خانه	brothel, whorehouse
fahm	ف هم	comprehension
fahmidam(fahm)	فهميدن (فهم)	to understand
fahmide	ف هم یده	wise, intelligent
fahšä³	ف حشا	prostitution
fäje³e	ف اجعه	disaster, tragedy, catastrophe
faji³	ف ج یع	tragic, horrible, brutal
fajr	ف جر	dawn
fakk	ف ک	jaw
fäktor	ف اک تور	invoice, list, bill
fäl	ف ال	omen, fortune
fäl gereftan	ف ال گرفتن	to tell fortune, to read tarot
falaj	ف لج	paralysed, paralysis
falaj šodan	فلج شدن	to paralyse
falak	ف لک	destiny, fortune, bastinado
faläkat	ف لاک ت	poverty, misery
falake	ف ل که	roundabout, belt pulley
falakzade	ف لک زده	unfortunate, miserable
falät	ف لات	plateau
fälbin	فال بين	fortune teller
fälgiri	ف ال گ یرى	fortune telling

falsafe	ف ل س فه	philosophy, reason
falsafi	ف ل س فى	philosophical
fämil	ف ام يل	family
fämily	ف ام ي لى	familial, surname
fan	ف ن	technique, skill
fanä	ف نا	destruction, annihilation
fanar	ف نر	spring, coil
fandak	ف ندك	lighter
fandoq	ف ندق	hazelnut
fäni	ف ان ى	mortal, transitory, finite
fanländ	ف نلاند د	Finland
fanländi	ف نلاند دى	Finnish
fann	فن	technique
fanni	ف نى	technical
fäntezi	ف از تزى	fancy goods
fänus	ف از وس	lantern, bellows
faqän	ف غان	wailing, groaning
faqat	ف قط	only, just
fäqed	ف اق د	missing, lacking
faqid	ف ق يد	the late, deceased
faqih	ف ق يه	clergy
faqir	ف ق ير	poor, needy, beggar
faqr	ف قر	poverty, impoverishment
far³	ف رع	secondary, subsidiary
far³i	ف رعى	secondary, subordinate
farägereftan	فرا گرفتن (فراگير)	to learn, to embrace
faräham	ف راهم	available, ready
faräham kardan	فراهم كردن	to prepare
farahbaxš	ف رح بخش	pleasant, refreshing
farämuš	ف راموش	forgetting, disregarding
farämuš kardan	فراموش كردن	to forget
farämuši	ف رامو شى	amnesia, forgetfulness
faränesavi	ف راز سوى	French

faränese	فرانسه	France
farang	فرنگ	overseas, abroad, west
farangi	فرنگی	westerner
farangi maᵌäb	فرنگی ماب	westernised
faräq	فراق	separation, departure
faräqat	فراغت	leisure, rest
farär	فرار	escape, running away
farärasidan	فرا رسیدن (فرا رس)	to arrive, to come
faräri	فراری	escapee, fugitive
farävän	فراوان	many, a lot, plenty, numerous
faräväni	فراوانی	abundance, plenty
farävorde	فرآورده	product
faräxäni	فراخوانی	recall, summon
faräyand	فرآیند	process
fard	فرد	person, individual, single, odd
fardä	فردا	tomorrow
fardi	فردی	personal, individual
färeq	فارغ	free, disengaged, released
färeqottahsil	فارغ التحصیل	graduate
färeqottahsil šodan	فارغ التحصیل شدن	to graduate
färeqottahsili	فارغ التحصیلی	graduation
farhang	فرهنگ	culture, dictionary
farhangestän	فرهنگستان	academy
farhangi	فرهنگی	cultural
farib	فریب	deceit, deception, cheating
farib xordan	فریب خوردن	to be deceit, to be cheated
farib dädan	فریب دادن	to deceit, to cheat
faribande	فریبنده	deceitful, charming, enticing
farize	فریضه	religious duty
farjäm	فرجام	end, termination, appeal
farjäm xästan	فرجام خواستن	to appeal (to court)
farmän	فرمان	command, steering-wheel
farmän dädan	فرمان دادن	to order

farmändär	فرماندار	governor general
farmändäri	فرمانداری	governor's office
farmändeh	فرمانده	commander
farmändehi	فرماندهی	command office, headquarter
farmänravä	فرمانروا	ruler
farmäyeš	فرمایش	order, remarks, words
farmudan(farmä)	فرمودن (فرما)	to order, to say, to do(pol)
farq	فرق	difference, discrimination
farq däštan	فرق داشتن	to differ
farrär	فرار	vaporizable, volatile
farräš	فراش	servant, waiter, janitor
farš	فرش	rug, carpet
farsang	فرسنگ	length unit, 6 kilometre
farsäyeš	فرسایش	erosion, wearing out
färsi	فارسی	Persian, Farsi
färsi zabän	فارسی زبان	Persian speaker
farsudan(farsä)	فرسودن (فرسا)	to wear out, to erode
farsude	فرسوده	worn out, eroded
fart	فرط	excess
fartut	فرتوت	old, senile
farvardin	فروردین	first Persian month
faryäd	فریاد	scream, shouting, yell
faryäd zadan	فریاد زدن	to scream, to shout, to yell
farz	فرض	supposition, assumption
farzi	فرضی	hypothetical
farz kardan	فرض کردن	to suppose, to assume
farzand	فرزند	child, offspring
farzand e rezä³i	فرزند رضائی	foster-child
farzand xände	فرزند خوانده	adopted child
farzäne	فرزانه	wise, sagacious
farziyye	فرضیه	hypothesis
fäš	فاش	revealed, obvious, overt
fäš kardan	فاش کردن	to reveal, to expose

fasäd	ف ساد	corruption, decay
fäsed	ف ا سد	corrupt, rotten, perverted
fäsed šodan	ف ا سد شدن	to corrupt, to rot
fäsele gereftan	ف ا صله گرفتن	to keep distance
fäsele	ف ا صله	distance, interval, extent
fasl	ف صل	season, chapter, section
fasli	فصلی	seasonal
fasx	ف سخ	dissolution, cancellation
fasx kardan	ف سخ	to cancel, to terminate
fäteh	ف اتّ ح	victor, conqueror, champion
fätehe	ف اتّ حه	a verse of koran
fätehe xändan	ف اتّ حه خواندن	to pray for the dead
fath	ف تح	victory, triumph
fath kardan	فتح كردن	to conquer, to overcome
fatq	ف تق	hernia, rupture
fatvä	ف توا	fatwa, judicial decree
fatvä dädan	ف توادادن	to give a fatwa
favarän	ف وران	eruption, outbreak, outburst
favarän kardan	ف وران	to erupt, to outburst
favväre	فواره	fountain
faxr	ف خر	pride, boasting
faxr kardan	فخر كردن	to boast
fäyede	ف اید ده	use, profit, utility
fazä	ف ضا	space, area
fazähat	ف ضاحت	disgrace, scandal, shame
fazänavard	ف ضانَورد	astronaut
fazäpeymä	ف ضاپ یما	spaceship
fazäyi	ف ضاىی	spatial
fäzel	ف ا ضل	spiritual, scholar
fäzeläb	ف ا ضلاب	drainage, sewerage
fazl	ف ضل	excellence, merit, virtue
fazle	ف ضله	bird dropping, dung
fe³l	ف عل	verb, action

fe³li	فعلی	verbal, current
fe³lan	ف علا	currently, at the moment
fehrest	ف هر ست	index, list, glossary
fekr	ف کر	thought, thinking, mind
fekri	ف کری	mental, intellectual
fekr kardan	فکر کردن	to think
felän	ف لان	such and such
felestin	ف لسط ین	Palestine
felestini	فلسطینی	Palestinian
felezz	ف لز	metal
felezzi	ف لزی	metallic
felfel	ف ل فل	pepper
fenjän	ف نجان	cup
feqdän	ف قدان	lack, absence, shortage
feqh	ف قه	religious law
fer	ف ر	curl, ringlet, oven
fer³on	ف رعون	Pharaoh
ferämäsoneri	ف راما سوذری	Freemasonry
ferdos	ف ردوس	paradise
ferekäns	ف رک ان س	frequency
ferestädan(ferest)	فرستادن (فرست)	to send, to despatch, to mail
ferestäde	ف ر سـ تاده	messenger, envoy
ferestande	ف ر سـ تـ نده	sender, broadcaster
ferešte	ف ر شـ ته	angel
ferfere	فرفره	peg-top, whirligig
ferferi	ف رف ری	curly, wavy
ferni	ف رذ ی	a type of pudding
ferqe	ف رقـه	sect, faction, denomination
ferz	ف رز	quick, agile, fast
fešang	ف شـ نگ	cartridge
fešär	ف شار	force, pressure, strain, push
fešär dädan	فشار دادن	to press, to push
fešare xun	فشار خون	blood pressure

fešärsanj	ف شار س نج	barometer
fesenjän	ف س نجان	a type of stew
fešfeše	ف ش ف شه	torpedo, rocket
fešorde	ف شرده	pressed, compressed
fešordan	فشردن	to press, to squizze
fetile	ف ت یله	wick
fetne	ف ت نه	revolt, conspiracy, trouble
fetr	ف طر	end of ramadan
fetrat	ف طرت	nature, disposition, instinct
fetri	ف طری	innate, inborn
fevriye	ف وریه	february
feys	ف یس	boasting
feyz	ف یض	blessing, profit
fil	ف یل	elephant
filipin	ف یل ی پ ین	Philippines
filipini	فیلیپینی	Pilipino
film	ف یلم	film, movie
film gereftan	ف یلم گرفتن	to take film
filmbardär	ف یلم ب ردار	cinematographer
filmbardäri	فیلم برداری	shooting a film
filmbardäri kardan	فیلم برداری کردن	to shoot a film
filmnäme	فیلم نامه	movie script
filmnäme nevis	فیلم نامه نویس	scriptwriter
filsuf	ف یل س وف	philosopher
filsufäne	فیلسوفانه	philosophical
fin	ف ین	snot
fin kardan	فین کردن	to blow nose
firuze	ف یروزه	azure, turquoise
fizik	ف یزی ک	physics
fiziki	فیزیکی	physical
fizikdän	فیزیک دان	physicist
fohš	ف حش	swear word, verbal abuse
fohš dädan	فحش دادن	to swear

fokähi	ف ﮑاهى	humorous, funny
fokol	ف ﮑل	tie, collar
foqoläde	فوق العاده	brilliant, great
foran	ف ورا	immediately, right away
fori	فورى	urgent, express
forje	فرجه	respite, delay
form	ف رم	form, figure
formul	ف رمول	formula
forsat	ف ر صت	opportunity, chance, occasion
forsattalab	ف ر صت ط لب	opportunist
forsattalabi	فرصت طلبى	opportunism
foru raftan	فرو رفتن	to sink, to go in
forud	ف رود	descending, landing
forud ämadan	فرود آمدن	to land, to descend
forudgäh	ف رودگ اه	airport
forugozäri	ف روگ ذارى	neglect, refrain
forukeš	ف روك ش	subsiding, allaying
foruraftegi	ف رورف ﺘگى	dent, depression, cavity
foruš	ف روش	sale, selling, auction
forušande	ف رو ش نده	shopkeeper, seller, salesman
forušgäh	ف رو ش ﮕاه	store, shop, market
foruši	فروشى	for sale
forutan	ف روتَ ن	humble, modest
forutani	فروتنى	humility, modesty
foruxtan(foruš)	فروختن (فروش)	to sell
foruzän	ف روزان	bright, light
fošordan(fešär)	فشردن (فشار)	to squeeze, to press
fošorde	فشرده	intensive, pressed
fot	ف وت	death, passing away
fot kardan	فوت كردن	to passing away, to die
fozul	ف ضول	intruder, nosy, meddler
fozuli	فضولى	intrusion, meddling
fozulät	ف ضولات	waste matters, excrement

fuläd	ف ولاد	steel
fulädi	ف ولادی	made of steel, strong
furušqah	فروشگاه	store, supermarket
furušqahe zanjireyi	فروشگاه زنجیره ای	department store
fut	ف وت	blow, puff
fut kardan	فوت کردن	to blow
futbäl	ف وت بال	football, soccer
futbäl dasti	فوتبال دستی	table football
futbälist	ف وت بال یست	football player

G		
gač	گ چ	chalk, plaster
gahgäh	گ ه گاه	sometimes
gähgähi	گ اهکاهی	occasionally, once in a while
gähi	گ اهی	sometimes
gahväre	گ هواره	cradle, crib, hammock
gäl	گ ال	scabies
galangedan	گ ل ن گدن	breechblock
galle	گ له	cattle, herd, flock
galu	گ لو	throat
galu dard	گ لو درد	sore throat
gäm	گام	step, pace, gait
gand	گ ند	stink, foul smell
gandidan(gand)	گندیدن (گند)	to rot, to decompose, to spoil
gandide	گ ندیده	rotten, spoiled
gandom	گ ندم	wheat
gandomi	گندمی	brunet
ganj	گ نج	treasure
ganje	گ نجه	cupboard, cabinet, wardrobe
ganjine	گ نجینه	treasure, store
gap	گ پ	chat, chattering
gap zadan	گپ زدن	to chat up
gap zani	گ پ زنی	chatting
gar	گ ر	bald, mangy, scabbed
garär	قرار	date (appointment)
garär däd	قرارداد	contract, treaty
garär gozaštan	قرار گذاشتن	to make a an appointment
gäräž	گ اراژ	garage
garče	گ رچه	although
gard	گ رد	dust, powder
gardgiri	گ رد گیری	dusting
gärd	گ ارد	guard, watchman

gardan	گردن	neck
gardan band	گردن بند	necklace
gardan koloft	گردن کلفت	bully, ruffian
gardändan(dardän)	گرداندن (گردان)	to turn, to spin, to rotate
garde	گرده	pollen, powder
garde afšäni	گرده یگ شاذ اف	pollination
gardeš	گردش	walk, circulation, excursion
gardgiri kardan	گردگیری کردن	to dust
gardidan(gard)	گردیدن (گرد)	to turn, to rotate, to revolve
gäri	گاری	cart
garm	گرم	warm, hot, passionate
garmä	گرما	heat, warmth
garmäbe	گرمابه	turkish bath
garmäzadegi	گرمازدگی	heat stroke, exhaustion
garmi	گرمی	heat, warmth, affection
garmsir	گرمسیر	tropical, warm climate
garmxäne	گرمخانه	greenhouse
gärson	گارسن	waiter
gašt	گشت	tour, walk, patrol
gaštan(gard)	گشتن (گرد)	to search, to look for, to turn
gašti	گشتی	patrol
gäv	گاو	cow, ox, bull
gäv sanduq	گاو صندوق	safe (box)
gävähan	گاو آهن	ploughshare
gavähi	گواهی	certificate, license
gavähinäme	گواهینامه	certificate, license
gavazn	گوزن	deer, reindeer
gävčarän	گاو چران	cowboy
gäyiydan(gäy)	گائیدن (گای)	to fuck, to screw
gäz	گاز	bite, nip, gas, gauze
gäzi	گازی	powered by gas
gäz anbor	گاز انبر	pliers
gäz gereftan	گاز گرفتن	to bite

gazand	گ ز ن د	damage, injury
gäzdär	گ ا زدار	gassy
gazidan(gaz)	گزیدن (گز)	to bite, to sting
gäzo³il	گ ازو ئ یل	gasoline
gedä	گ دا	beggar
gedäyi	گ دای ی	begging
gedäyi kardan	گدایی کردن	to beg
gel	گل	mud, clay
geli	گلی	muddy
gelälud	گ ل آل و د	muddy, full of mud
geläviz šodan	گ ل آو پ زشدن	to grapple, to scuffle
geläyol	گ لای ل	sword lily
gele	گ له	complaint, grievance
gele kardan	گله گردن	to complain
gelgir	گ ل گ یر	mudguard, fender
gelim	گ ل یم	coarse carpet
geram	گ رم	gram
gerämäfon	گ راماف ون	record player
gerämi	گ رامی	dear, honourable, respectful
gerän	گ ران	expensive, costly
gerän bahä	گ راذ بها	precious, valuable, priceless
gerän foruši	گ ران ف رو شی	overcharging, fleecing
geräni	گ رانی	expensiveness, high cost
geräyeš	گ رای ش	tendency, inclination
geräyidan(geräy)	گراییدن (گرای)	to intend, to believe, to tend
gerd	گ رد	round, circular
gerdäb	گ رداب	whirlpool, swirl
gerdävari	گ ردآوری	gathering, compiling
gerdbäd	گ ردب اد	cyclone, hurricane, tornado
gerdehamäyi	گرد هم آیی	rally
gerdo	گ ردو	walnut
gereftan(gir)	گرفتن (گیر)	to get, to take, to hold
gereftär	گرفتاری	involved, captured, very busy

gereftäri	گرفتاری	trouble, preoccupation
gerefte	گرفته	dull, taken, closed, overcast
gereh zadan	گره زدن	to knot, to tie
gerim	گریم	make up (for acting)
geris	گریس	grease
gero	گرو	bond, pledge, pawn
gerogän	گروگان	hostage, pledge
gerogän giri	گروگانگیری	hostage taking
gerogän gereftan	گروگان گرفتن	to take hostage
geryän	گریان	weeping, tearful
gerye	گریه	crying, weeping, tears
gerye kardan	گریه کردن	to cry, to weep
gešniz	گشنیز	coriander
gij	گیج	dizzy, giddy, confused
gij šodan	گیج شدن	to be confused, to get dizzy
giji	گیجی	dizziness, giddiness
giläs	گیلاس	cherry, glass
gir	گیر	difficulty, stoppage, clog
gir kardan	گیرکردن	to stuck, to clog
girä	گیرا	attractive, grasping
girande	گیرنده	receiver, recipient
girboks	گیربکس	gearbox
gire	گیره	clip, hairpin, clamp
girodär	گیرودار	in the heat of, conflict
gis	گیس	women's hair
giše	گیشه	ticket office, counter
gitär	گیتار	guitar
gity	گیتی	cosmos, universe
give	گیوه	cotton shoes
giyäh	گیاه	plant, herb
god	گود	deep, profound
godäl	گودال	pit, ditch, puddle
godäxte	گداخته	melted, smelted

godäze	گدازه	lava
godi	گودی	depth, groove
goftan(guy)	گفتن (گوی)	to say, to tell
goftär	گفتار	speech, discourse, statement
goftegu	گفتگو	conversation, dialogue
goftegu kardan	گفتگو کردن	to converse, to discuss
gofto šenud	گفت و شنود	conversation, dialogue
goh	گه	shit, faeces
goje	گوجه	plum
goje farangi	گوجه فرنگی	tomato
gol	گل	flower, goal
gol zadan	گل زدن	to score a goal
gol foruš	گل فروش	florist
goläb	گلاب	rose-water
goläbi	گلابی	pear
golčin	گلچین	selection, digest
goldän	گلدان	vase, flowerpot
golduzi	گلدوزی	embroidery
gole sorx	گل سرخ	rose
golestän	گلستان	rose garden
golf	گلف	golf
golule	گلوله	bullet, shot, ball
golule bärän	گلوله باران	shelling, cannonade
gom	گم	lost, missing
gom kardan	گم کردن	to lose
gomän	گمان	guess, supposition
gomäštan(gomär)	گماشتن (گمار)	to appoint, to assign
gomnäm	گمنام	anonymous, incognito
gomräh kardan	گمراه کردن	to misled, to deceive
gomrok	گمرک	customs
gomšode	گم شده	lost, missing, misplaced
gonäh	گناه	sin, guilt, fault
gonäh kardan	گناه کردن	to commit a sin

gonähkär	گ ناه ک ار	sinner, guilty, offender
gonbad	گ ن بد	dome, arch
gonde	گ نده	large, huge
gong	گ نگ	dumb, mute, silent
gonjändan(gonjän)	گنجاندن (گنجان)	to include, to insert
gonjäyeš	گ نجای ش	capacity, volume, size
gonješk	گ نج شک	sparrow
gor	گ ر	flame, blaze
goräz	گ راز	boar
gorbän	ق رب ان	sir (polite)
gorbän kardan	قربانی کردن	to sacrifice
gorbäni	قربانی	victim, sacrifice
gorbe	گ رب ه	cat
gorg	گ رگ	wolf
gorixtan(goriz)	گریختن (گریز)	to escape, to run away
goriz	گ ری ز	escape, runaway
gorosne	گ ر س نه	hungry, starved
gorosnegi	گ ر س نگی	hunger, starvation
goruh	گ روه	group, band
goruhän	گ روهن	company
goruhbän	گ روه بان	sergeant
goruhe xuni	گروه خونی	blood type
gošäd	گ شاد	wide, broad, loose
gošädi	گ شادی	width, shallowness
gošäyeš	گ شای ش	opening, improvement
gosil kardan	گ س یل کردن	to despatch, to deploy
gosixte	گ س یخ ته	broken, torn, disconnected
gošne	گ ش نه	hungry (informal)
gostareš	گ س ترش	expansion, extension
gostareš yäftan	گ س ترش یافتن	to expand, to extend
gostäx	گ س تاخ	rude, bold
gostäxi	گستاخی	rudeness, boldness
goväh	گ واه	witness, testimony

govähi	گواهی	certificate, evidence, diploma
goväreš	گ وارش	digestion
goväreši	گ وار شی	digestive
gozarä	گ ذرا	transient, temporary
gozarän	گ ذران	livelihood, subsistence
gozarändan	گذراندن (گذران)	to spend, to pass, to transmit
gozäreš	گ زارش	report, news
gozäreš dädan	گزارش دادن	to report
gozäreš gar	گزارش گر	reporter, journalist
gozargäh	گ ذرگ اه	passage, crossing
gozarnäme	گ ذر ذامه	passport
gozašt	گ ذ شت	concession, forgiveness
gozaštan(gozar)	گذشتن (گذر)	to pass, to cross, to forgive
gozäštan(gozär)	گذاشتن (گذار)	to put, to set, to deposit, to let
gozašte	گ ذ ش ته	past, bygone, last
gozaštegän	گ ذ ش ت گان	the deceased
gozide	گ ز ی ده	chosen, selected
gozine	گ ز ی نه	option, selection
gozineš	گ ز ی نش	selection, choice
gugerd	گ وگ رد	sulphur
gul	گ ول	deceit, deception
gul xordan	گول خوردن	to be cheated
gul zadan	گول زدن	to deceit, to cheat
gunägun	گ وذاگ ون	various, diverse
gune	گ وذه	kind, species, type, cheek
guni	گ وذ ی	big sack to carry fabrics
gur	گور	grave, tomb, mausoleum
gurestän	گ ور س تان	cemetery, graveyard
guri	ق وری	teapot
guril	گوریل	gorilla
gurkan	گورکن	badger
gurxar	گ ورخر	zebra
guš	گوش	ear

guš dädan	گوش دادن	to listen
guš mähi	گ وش ماهی	sea shell
gusäle	گ و ساله	calf
guše	گ و شه	corner, angle
guše gir	گ و شه گ یر	isolated, withdrawn
gusfand	گ و س فند	sheep
guši	گ و شی	receiver, earphone
gušmäli	گ و شمال ی	punishment
gušmäli dädan	گ و شمال ی دادن	to punish
gušt	گ و شت	meat
guštälu	گ و ش تالو	plump, chubby, fat
gušte xuk	گوشت خوک	ham
guštkub	گ و شتکو ب	masher
guštxär	گ و شت خوار	carnivore
gušväre	گ و شواره	earring
gušzad kardan	گوشزد کردن	to remind, to hint
guvatr	گ واتَ ر	goitre
guyä	گ و یَ ا	expressive, clear, self-evident
guyande	گ و یَ نده	broadcaster, announcer
guyeš	گ و یَ ش	dialect
guz	گ وز	fart
guzidan(guz)	گوزیدن (گوز)	to fart

H		
hab	حب	pill
habbe	حبه	grain, seed
habs	حبس	prison, jail
habs kardan	حبس کردن	to block, to jail
häd	حاد	acute
hadaf	هدف	aim, target, goal
hadafgiri	هدف گیری	aiming
hadar	هدر	waste, futile
hadar dädan	هدر دادن	to waste
hadd	حد	limit, extent
hadde aksar	حد اکثر	maximum
hädese	حادثه	accident, event
hadis	حدیث	religious narrations
hads	حدس	guess, assumption
hads zadan	حدس زدن	to guess
häfeze	حافظه	memory, recollection
haffäri	حفاری	digging, excavation
hafr	حفر	digging, excavation
hafr kardan	حفر کردن	to dig
haft	هفت	seven
haftäd	هفتاد	seventy
haftädom	هفتادم	seventieth
hafte	هفته	week
haftegi	هفتگی	weekly
haftom	هفتم	seventh
haftsad	هفتصد	seven hundred
häg	هاگ	spore
häjat	حاجت	necessity, requirement
häji	حاجی	one who pilgrims mecca
hajj	حج	pilgrimage to mecca
hajm	حجم	capacity, mass, volume

hajmi	حجمی	cubic
hajv	هجو	lampoon, satire
häkem	حاکم	governor, ruling
häki	حاکی	indicating, designating
hakk	حک	engraving, carving
hakkäki	حکاکی	engraving
häl	حال	present, condition
hälä	حالا	now, at the moment
halab	حلب	tin
haläk	هلاک	death, perished, downfall
haläkat	هلاکت	death, ruin
haläl	حلال	legitimate, permissible
haläl zäde	حلال زاده	legitimate child
hälat	حالت	state, mood, case
hälät	حالات	conditions, circumstances
halazun	حلزون	snail, cochlea
häle	هاله	halo, aura
halim	حلیم	porridge made of wheat
hall	حل	dissolving, solution
hall kardan	حل کردن	to dissolve, to solve
halläji kardan	حلاجی کردن	to analyze
halq	حلق	pharynx
halqe	حلقه	ring, loop, link
halvä	حلوا	sweet paste
ham	هم	also, too, both, either
ham hame	همهمه	noise, commotion, turmoil
ham ma³ni	هم معنی	synonymous
ham otaqi	هم اتاقی	roommate
ham qadd	همقد	of the same height or size
ham sen	همسن	of the same age
ham vatan	هم وطن	compatriot, fellow citizen
ham zisti	همزیستی	coexistence
hamähang	هماهنگ	coordinated, harmonious

hamähangi	هماهنگی	harmony, coordination
hamän	همان	the same, that very same
hamänä	همانا	indeed, certainly
hamänand	همانند	alike, identical, like, same
hamäse	حماسه	epic poem
hamäväzi	هم آوازی	chorus, concord
hambastari	هم بستری	sleeping together
hamčenän	همچنان	accordingly, in that way
hamčenin	همچنین	too, as well, also, likewise
hamčešmi	همچشمی	rivalry, competition
hamd	حمد	praise
hamdam	همدم	companion, confident
hamdardi	همدردی	sympathy
hamdast	همدست	collaborator, accomplice
hamdasti	همدستی	collaboration, conspiracy
hamdeli	همدلی	agreement, consensus
hamdigar	همدیگر	one another, each other
hame	همه	all, every, whole, everyone
hame porsi	همه پرسی	referendum
hamegi	همگی	all, whole, entire
hamegir	همه گیر	epidemic
hämel	حامل	carrier, transporters
hämele	حامله	pregnant
hämelegi	حاملگی	pregnancy
hamgen	همگن	congenial, cohort
hamgerä	همگرا	convergent
hämi	حامی	supporter, protector
hamin	همین	only this, this same
hamin alän	همین الان	right now
hamin ke	همینکه	as soon as, when, just as
hamiše	همیشه	always, forever
hamišegi	همیشگی	permanent, everlasting
hamjavär	همجوار	neighbour, adjacent

hamjens	همجنس	homogeneous
hamjes bäz	همجنس باز	homosexual
hamkär	همکار	colleague, co-worker
hamkäri	همکاری	cooperation, collaboration
hamkäri kardan	همکاری کردن	to cooperate, to collaborate
hamkeläs	همکلاس	classmate
haml	حمل	carrying, transport
haml kardan	حمل کردن	to carry
hamle	حمله	attack, rush, assault
hamle kardan	حمله کردن	to attack, to rush
hamlo naql	حمل و نقل	transportation, conveyance
hammäl	حمال	carrier, porter
hammäm	حمام	bath, turkish bath
hamnišini	هم نشینی	companionship, friendship
hamno³	هم نوع	homogenous, same species
hamotäqi	هم اطاقی	roommate
hamqatär	همقطار	colleague, co-worker
hamräh	همراه	companion, fellow, company
hamrähi	همراهی	accompanying, escorting
hamsafar	همسفر	fellow traveller
hamšahri	همشهری	fellow citizen
hamsäl	همسال	of the same age
hamsän	همسان	alike, same
hamsar	همسر	spouse, husband, wife
hamsäye	همسایه	neighbour
hamsäyegi	همسایگی	neighbourhood, vicinity
hamšekam	هم شکم	twin
hamšire	همشیره	sister
hamsohbat	هم صحبت	interlocutor
hamtä	همتا	match, peer, equal
hamvär	هموار	plane, flat, level
hamväre	همواره	always, ever, all the time
hamyäri	همیاری	cooperation

hamzabän	همزبان	speaking same language
hamzäd	همزاد	twin, born together
hamzamän	همزمان	concurrent, simultaneous
hanä	حنا	henna
hang	هنگ	regiment
hangoft	هنگفت	enormous, large, huge
hanjare	حنجره	larynx
hanuz	هنوز	yet, still
haq	حق	right, duty, privilege
haq koši	حق کشی	injustice
haq šenäs	حق شناس	grateful
haqäyeq	حقایق	facts
haqiqat	حقیقت	truth, reality, fact
haqiqi	حقیقی	real, true
haqir	حقیر	humble, small, modest
haqqäniyat	حقانیت	truth, legitimacy
har	هر	each, any, every
här	هار	rabid, mad
har čand	هر چند	although, though
har če	هر چه	whatever, what
har čeqadr	هر چه قدر	as much as, whatever
har do	هر دو	both
har kodäm	هر کدام	each
har ruz	هر روز	every day
harakat	حرکت	movement, departure
harakat kardan	حرکت کردن	to move, to depart
haram	حرم	shrine, holy tomb
haräm	حرام	prohibited, illegitimate
haräm kardan	حرام کردن	to prohibit by religious law
haramsarä	حرمسرا	harem
harämzäde	حرامزاده	bustard, illegitimate
harärat	حرارت	heat, temperature
haräs	هراس	fear, fright, dread

haräsän	هراسان	scared, fearful, frightened
haräsidan(haräs)	هراسیدن (هراس)	to scare, to be afraid
haräsnäk	هراسناک	dreadful, frightful
harbe	حربه	weapon, excuse
harf	حرف	talking, letter, speech
harf šeno	حرف شنو	obedient, heedful
harf zadan	حرف زدن	to speak, to talk
hargäh	هرگاه	whenever, in case
hargez	هرگز	never, not at all, ever
häri	هاری	rabidity
harif	حریف	rival, opponent
harim	حریم	boundary, limit
hariq	حریق	fire
harir	حریر	silk
haris	حریص	greedy
harjo marj	هرج و مرج	chaos, anarchy, confusion
harjo marj talab	هرج و مرج طلب	anarchist
harkas	هرکس	anybody, everybody
harräf	حراف	talkative, verbose
harräj	حراج	on sale, auction
harräj kardan	حراج کردن	to auction
harz	هرز	vain, worn out, waste
harze	هرزه	libertine, lewd, profligate
harzegi	هرزگی	libertinism, profligacy
häšä	حاشا	denial
hasad	حسد	jealousy
hašare	حشره	bug, insect
hašare koš	حشره کش	insecticide
hašare šenäs	حشره شناس	entomologist
hašari	حشری	lustful, horny
hasbe	حصبه	typhoid fever
häsel	حاصل	produce, crop, harvest
häsel xiz	حاصل خیز	fertile, productive

hasir	حصیر	mat
hašiš	حشیش	hashish
häšiye	حاشیه	margin, edge, border
hasrat	حسرت	regret, rue
hasrat xordan	حسرت خوردن	to regret
hassäs	حساس	sensitive, critical
hassäsiyat	حساسیت	sensitivity, allergy
hast	هست	is, there is
hašt	هشت	eight
haštäd	هشتاد	eighty
haštädom	هشتادم	eightieth
hastand	هستند	they are, are
haste	هسته	nucleus, stone of fruit
hasteyi	هسته ای	nuclear
hasti	هستی	existence, life, being
haštom	هشتم	eighth
haštpä	هشت پا	octopus
haštsad	هشتصد	eight hundred
hasud	حسود	jealous, envious
hatk	هتک	dishonouring, violating, rape
hatman	حتما	sure, certainly
hatmi	حتمی	certain, indispensable
hattä	حتی	even
hattäki	هتاکی	swearing, defamation
hattal emkän	حتی الامکان	as far as possible
havä	هوا	air, weather, atmosphere
havädär	هوادار	admirer, fan, supporter
havädes	حوادث	accidents, occurrences
haväkeš	هواکش	air vent, chimney
haväle	حواله	draft, transfer, assignment
havÄli	حوالی	vicinity, environs
havänavard	هوانورد	navigator, airman, pilot
haväpeymä	هواپیما	aeroplane

haväpeymäyi	هواپیمایی	aviation, airline
havär	هوار	loud cry, scream
havas	هوس	passion, whim, longing
havas	هوس کردن	to long for
haväs	حواس	senses, memory
havas bäz	هوسباز	whimsical, playful
havas rän	هوسران	playful, capricious
haväšenäsi	هواشناسی	meteorology
haväxori	هواخوری	catching fresh air , strolling
haväyi	هوایی	aerial, related to air
haväzi	هوازی	aerobe
hävi	حاوی	containing, comprising
havij	هویج	carrot
havu	هوو	a rival wife
havvä	حوا	eve
havväri	حواری	disciple, apostle
hayä	حیا	decency, modesty
hayähu	هیاهو	commotion, brawl, noise
hayät	حیاط	yard, courtyard
hayät	حیات	life, living
hayäti	حیاتی	vital
hayejän	هیجان	excitement, agitation
hayejän ävar	هیجان آور	exciting, moving, stimulating
häyhäy	های های	noisy crying
hayulä	هیولا	monster
häzeme	هاضمه	digestive
häzer	حاضر	ready, prepared, present
hazf	حذف	deletion, elimination
hazf kardan	حذف کردن	to delete, to eliminate
hazine	هزینه	expense, cost, charge
hazm kardan	هضم کردن	to digest
hazrat	حضرت	highness, excellency
hazyän	هذیان	delirium, hallucination

hazyän goftan	هذیان گ ف تن	to hallucinate
hazz	حظ	enjoyment, pleasure
hazz kardan	حظ کردن	to enjoy
hebbe	هبه	gift, donation, endowment
hedäyat	هدایت	guidance, conduction
hedäyat kardan	هدایت ک ردن	to guide, to lead
hedye	هدیه	gift, present
hefäzat	حفاظت	protection, shielding
hefäzat kardan	حفاظت کردن	to protect
hefdah	هفده	seventeen
hefdahom	هفدهم	seventeenth
hefz	حفظ	memorising, protecting
hejä	هجا	syllable
hejäb	حجاب	covering, wearing veil
hejämat	حجامت	venesection
hejäyi	هجایی	syllabic
hejdah	هجده	eighteen
hejdahom	هجدهم	eighteenth
hejji	هجی	spelling
hejji kardan	هجی کردن	to spell
hejle	حجله	bridal chamber
hejrän	هجران	separation, isolation
hejrat	هجرت	Hijra, Prophhet's migration
hejri	هجری	related to hejrat
hejriye qamari	هجری قمری	Islamic lunar calendar
hejriye šamsi	هجری شمسی	Iranian solar calendar
hekäyat	حکایت	story, anecdote, narrative
hekmat	حکمت	wisdom, philosophy
hektär	هکتار	hectare
hel	هل	cardamoms
heläl	هلال	crescent, new moon
helhele	هلهله	cheers, exultation
hemäqat	حماقت	stupidity, foolishness

hemäyat	حمایت	protection, support
hemäyat kardan	حمایت کردن	to protect, to support
hemmat	همت	ambition, aspiration, effort
hend	هند	india
hendi	هندی	indian
hendese	هندسه	geometry
hendesi	هندسی	geometrical
hendeväne	هندوانه	watermelon
hendočin	هندوچین	indochina
hendu	هندو	hindu
hengäm	هنگام	time, occasion
heqärat	حقارت	inferiority, scorn
heram	هرم	pyramid
heräst	حراست	guarding, guard
herfe	حرفه	job, profession, trade
herfeyi	حرفه ای	professional
heroin	هروئین	heroin
heroini	هروئینی	heroin addict
hers	حرص	greed
hesäb	حساب	account, calculation, math
hesäb där	حساب دار	accountant, bookkeeper
hesäb däri	حساب داری	accounting, bookkeeping
hesäb ras	حساب رس	auditor
hesäb rasi	حساب رسی	auditing
hesäb kardan	حساب کردن	to calculate, to pay bills
hesädat	حسادت	jealousy, envy
hesär	حصار	fence, wall
hess	حس	feeling, sense
hess kardan	حس کردن	to feel
hessabi	حسابی	reasonable, reliable
hexämaneši	هخامنشی	achaemenid
heyᵊat	هیئت	board, council
heybat	هیبت	awe, dignity, appalling

heyf	حیف	pity
heyhät	هیهات	alas
heykal	هیکل	figure, shape, body
heyn	حین	during, at the moment of
heyrän	حیران	amazed, astound
heyrat angiz	حیرت انگیز	puzzling, stunning
heys	حیث	regard, respect
heysiyat	حیثیت	prestige, reputation
heyvän	حیوان	animal, beast
heyväni	حیوانی	brutal, beastly
heyz	حیض	menstruation
hezänat	حضانت	fostering, custody
hezär	هزار	thousand
hezäre	هزاره	millennium
hezärom	هزارم	thousandth
hezärpä	هزارپا	myriapod
hezb	حزب	party
hič	هیچ	nothing, not, no, any, none
hič čiz	هیچ چیز	nothing, anything
hič gäh	هیچ گاه	never, ever
hič gune	هیچگونه	under no condition
hič jä	هیچ جا	nowhere
hič käre	هیچ کاره	good for nothing, worthless
hič kas	هیچ کس	no one, nobody
hič kodäm	هیچ کدام	neither, none of them
hič vaqt	هیچ وقت	never, ever
hič yek	هیچیک	no one, none
hičo puč	هیچ و پوچ	nothing, vain, futile
hijdah	هجده	eighteen
hile	حیله	trick, deceit
hipätit	هپاتیت	hepatitis
hipnotism	هیپنوتیزم	hypnosis
hite	حیطه	domain, enclosure

hiz	هیز	catamite, lascivious
hizom	هیزم	firewood
ho kardadan	هوک ردن	to defame
hobäb	حباب	bubble, globe
hobubät	حبوبات	grains, cereals
hoči	هوچی	rumour monger, totter
hodhod	هدهد	hoopoe
hodud	حدود	limits, boundaries
hodudan	حدودا	approximately
hohuq begir	حقوق بگیر	stipendiary, salary earner
hohuq begiri	حقوق بگیری	living on salary
hojäj (häji)	حجاج (حاجی)	hajjis
hojb	حجب	modesty, shyness
hojre	حجره	old type of business office
hojum	هجوم	attack, rush, invasion
hokm	حکم	sentence, conviction, order
hokm kardan	حکم کردن	to order
hokmrän	حکمران	ruler, governor
hokumat kardan	حکومت کردن	to govern, to rule
hol dädan	هل دادن	to push
hol kardan	هول کردن	to startle
holand	هلند	Holland, Netherlands
holandi	هلندی	Dutch
hole	حوله	towel
holnäk	هولناک	terrifying, frightening
holqum	حلقوم	throat, pharynx
home	حومه	suburbs, outskirts
honar	هنر	art, craft, skill, talent
honarestän	هنرستان	technical school
honari	هنری	artistic
honarmand	هنرمند	artist, artistic, industrious
honarpiše	هنرپیشه	actor, artist, movie star
hoqqe	حقه	trick, cheating

hoqqe bäz	حقه باز	impostor, cheat
hoquq	حقوق	rights, salary
hoquq dän	حقوق دان	lawyer
hoquqe bašar	حقوق بشر	human rights
hoquqe madani	حقوق مدنی	civil rights
hoquqi	حقوقی	civil, legal
hormat	حرمت	respect, regard
horuf (harf)	حروف (حرف)	letters
hošdär	هشدار	warning, alert, beware
hošdär dädan	هشداردادن	to warn
hosele	حوصله	patience, tolerance
hosn	حسن	beauty, virtue
hotel	هتل	hotel
hoveydä	هویدا	obvious, apparent
hoviyyat	هویت	identity, identification
hoz	حوض	pond, pool, basin
hozeye	حوضه	region, area, district
hozur	حضور	presence, attendance
hozur däštan	حضور داشتن	to be present, to attendance
hozzär	حضار	audience
hulu	هلو	peach
huri	حوری	nymph
huš	هوش	intelligence, memory, sense
hušyär	هوشیار	aware, alert, cautious
hušyäri	هوشیاری	awareness, alertness
hut	حوت	pisces

I		
ijäd	ایجاد	creation, production
ijäd kardan	ایجاد کردن	to create
il	ایل	tribe, clan
iman	ایمن	safe, secure
imän	ایمان	faith, belief
imani	ایمنی	security, safety
in	این	this
ingilis	انگلیس	England
ingilisi	انگلیسی	English
inhä	اینها	these
injä	اینجا	here
injäneb	اینجانب	i(polite)
iräd gereftan	ایراد گرفتن	to criticize, to blame
irän	ایران	Iran
iräni	ایرانی	Iranian
irland	ایرلند	Ireland
irlandi	ایرلندی	Irish
isä	عیسی	Jesus
isavi	عیسوی	christian
išän	ایشان	they (pol)
isär	ایثار	sacrifice, generosity
isär kardan	ایثار	to sacrifice
ist	ایست	stop!
istädan(ist)	(ایست) ایستادن	to stand, to stand up, to wait
istädegi	ایستادگی	resistance, insistence
istgäh	ایستگاه	station, stop
istgähe metro	ایستگاه مترو	subway station
istgähe täksi	ایستگاه تاکسی	taxi stand
iyälat	ایالت	province, state
iyäläte mottahede	ایالات متحده	USA
izad	ایزد	God

J		
jä	جا	place, seat, space
jä oftädan	جا افتادن	to settle
jä oftäde	جا افتاده	matured
ja³be	جعبه	box, case, carton
ja³fari	جعفری	parsley
ja³l	جعل	forgery, fabrication
ja³li	جعلی	forged, fake
ja³l kardan	جعل کردن	to forge
jäbejä	جابجا	displaced, dislocated
jäbejä kardan	جابجا کردن	to transfer, to move
jabin	جبین	forehead
jad	جد	grandfather
jädde	جاده	path, road, route
jädu	جادو	magic, spell, charm
jädu kardan	جادو کردن	to cast a spell, to memorise
jädugar	جادوگر	magician
jadval	جدول	table, kerb, puzzle
jafang	جفنگ	nonsense, silly
jahäd	جهاد	holy war
jahäd kardan	جهاد کردن	to fight a holy war
jahälat	جهالت	ignorance
jahän	جهان	world, universe
jahängard	جهانگرد	tourist
jahängardi	جهانگردی	tourism
jahäni	جهانی	universal, global
jahannam	جهنم	hell
jahannami	جهنمی	belonging to hell
jahat	جهت	direction, side, cause
jahät	جهات	directions, reasons
jähel	جاهل	ignorant, unlearned
jaheš	جهش	jump, mutation

jahiziye	جهیزیه	trousseau
jahl	جهل	ignorance
jähtalab	جاه طلب	ambitious
jähtalabi	جاه طلبی	ambition
jäjim	جاجیم	coarse woollen blanket
jak	جک	jack (for car)
jäkeš	جاکش	pimp
jäkeši	جاکشی	pimping
jalab	جلب	deceitful, prostitute
jaläl	جلال	glory, grandeur
jalase	جلسه	session, meeting
jalb	جلب	arrest, subpoena
jalb kardan	جلب کردن	to arrest
jäleb	جالب	attractive, interesting
jälebäsi	جالباسی	clothes hanger
jalläd	جلاد	executioner
jalq	جلق	masturbation
jalq zadan	جلق زدن	to masturbate
jäm	جام	cup, pane
jam³	جمع	sum, addition, group
jam³ ävari	جمع آوری	collection, gathering
jam³ kardan	جمع کردن	to add, to collect, to gather
jam³an	جمعا	totally, altogether
jamä³	جماع	intercourse, coitus
jamä³at	جماعت	congregation, community
jäme jahäni	جام جهانی	world cup
jäme varzeši	جام ورزشی	league
jäme³	جامع	comprehensive, universal
jäme³e	جامعه	community, society
jäme³e šenäs	جامعه شناس	sociologist
jäme³e šenäsi	جامعه شناسی	sociology
jämed	جامد	solid, firm
jämedät	جامدات	solids

jän	جان	soul, power, essence, life
jän dädan	جان دادن	to die
jän fešäni	جانفشانى	devotion, self-sacrifice
jän nesäri	جان نثارى	devotion, sacrifice
janäb	جناب	excellency, highness
janäb ³äli	جنابعالى	your excellency
jänamäz	جانماز	a cloth for praying
janäq	جناق	wishbone, sternum
jänavar	جانور	animal, beast
jänavar šenäsi	جانورشناسى	zoology
janäze	جنازه	corpse, carcass
jänbäz	جانباز	veteran of Iran Irag war
janbe	جنبه	side, beside to, adjacent
jändar	جاندار	animate
jändärän	جانداران	fauna
jäneb	جانب	side, direction
jänebdäri	جانبدارى	support
jänebdäri kardan	جانبدارى كردن	to support, to take side
jänešin	جانشين	successor, substitute
jänešini	جانشينى	replacement
jang	جنگ	war, battle
jang afzär	جنگ افزار	weapon, arms
jang kardan	جنگ كردن	to fight
jangal	جنگل	forest, wood, bush
jangal zodayi	جنگل زدایى	deforestation
jangalbän	جنگلبان	forester, ranger
jangande	جنگنده	fighter
jangi	جنگى	martial, military
jangju	جنگجو	fighter, belligerent
jäni	جانى	criminal, murderer
janin	جنين	foetus, embryo
janjäl	جنجال	commotion, brawl, scandal
janjäli	جنجالى	scandalous

jannat	جنت	paradise
janub	جنوب	south
janubi	جنوبی	southern
jarä³ed	جراید	newspapers
jarä³em (jorm)	جرائم (جرم)	crimes, fines
jarähat	جراحت	injury, wound
jaraqqe	جرقه	spark, sparkle
jaraqqe zadan	جرقه زدن	to spark
jarasaqil	جرثقیل	crane
järaxti	جارختی	clothes hanger
jarayän	جریان	flowing, circulation
jarayän däštan	جریان داشتن	to flow, to circulate
jarb	جرب	scabies
järči	جارچی	pubic crier, herald
jär zadan	جار زدن	to announce to pubic
järi	جاری	flowing, running, current
jarime	جریمه	fine, penalty
jarime kardan	جریمه	to fine, to penalise
jarräh	جراح	surgeon
jarrähi	جراحی	surgery
jarrähi kardan	جراحی کردن	to operate a surgery
järu	جارو	broom
järu kardan	جارو کردن	to sweep
jasad	جسد	corpse, carcass
jasärat	جسارت	courage, boldness
jašn	جشن	festival, celebration
jašn gereftan	جشن گرفتن	to celebrate
jašnvare	جشنواره	festival
jäšu	جاشو	seaman
jasur	جسور	bold, daring
jäsus	جاسوس	spy, agent
jäsusi	جاسوسی	espionage, spying
javäb	جواب	answer, reply

javäb dädan	جواب دادن	to answer, to reply
javäher	جواهر	jewellery, gems
javäher furuš	جواهر فروش	jeweller
javäher furuši	جواهر فروشی	jeweller shop
javäherät	جواهرات	jewellery
javäme³ (jäme'e)	جوامع (جامعه)	societies
javän	جوان	young
javän mard	جوانمرد	generous, brave
javän mardi	جوانمردی	generosity, braveness
javän marg	جوانمرگ	dying in youth
javandegän	جوندگان	rodents
javäne	جوانه	bud, sprout
javäne zadan	جوانه زدن	to sprout
javäni	جوانی	youth
javäz	جواز	permit, licence
jävedän	جاودان	eternal, perpetual
jävid	جاوید	eternal, immortal
javidan(jav)	جویدن (جو)	to chew
javv	جو	atmosphere, space
jäxäli	جا خالی	blank space, missing
jäyegäh	جایگاه	place, quarter
jäyez	جایز	permissible
jäyeze	جایزه	prize, award
jazä	جزا	penalty, punishment
jazäyer (jazire)	جزایر (جزیره)	islands
jazäyi	جزایی	penal
jazb	جذب	absorption
jazb kardan	جذب کردن	to absorb
jäzebe	جاذبه	gravity, attraction
jazire	جزیره	island
jazr	جذر	square root
jazro mad	جذر ومد	tide, flux and reflux
jazzäb	جذاب	attractive, charming

jazzäbiyyat	جذابیت	attraction, charm
jebhe	جبهه	frontline, weather front
jedäl	جدال	quarrel, brawl, fight
jeddan	جدا	seriously
jeddi	جدی	serious, energetic
jegar	جگر	liver, guts
jegarsuz	جگرسوز	painful, heart-rending
jeld	جلد	cover, copy, volume
jelf	جلف	indecent, immodest
jelo	جلو	front, ahead, advanced
jelogiri	جلوگیری	prevention, hindrance
jelogiri kardan	جلوگیری کردن	to prevent
jelve dädan	جلوه دادن	to pretend
jenäh	جناح	wing, side
jenahe čap	جناح چپ	left-wing
jenahe rast	جناح راست	right-wing
jenäyat	جنایت	crime, murder, offence
jenäyat kär	جنایت کار	criminal, murderer
jenäyi	جنایی	criminal
jende	جنده	prostitute, whore
jende xäne	جنده خانه	brothel
jendegi	جندگی	prostitution
jengir	جن گیر	exorcist
jenn	جن	jinni, jinn
jens	جنس	gender, goods, made (of)
jense gerayi	جنس گرایی	sexism
jensi	جنسی	sexual
jensiyyat	جنسیت	sexuality, sex
jeqjeqe	جغجغه	rattle box
jerm	جرم	body, mass
jesm	جسم	body, object, material
jeyrän	جیران	gazelle, deer
jib	جیب	pocket

jib bor	جیب بر	pickpocket
jibi	جیبی	pocket size
jin	جین	jeans
jip	جیپ	jeep
jiq	جیغ	scream, cry
jiq zadan	جیغ زدن	to scream, to cry
jire	جیره	allocation, share
jirjirak	جیرجیرک	cricket(insect)
jiš	جیش	piss, urine
jiš kardan	جیش کردن	to piss, to urinate
jive	جیوه	mercury
jo	جو	barley
jobrän	جبران	compensation, indemnity
jobrän kardan	جبران کردن	to compensate
jodä	جدا	separate, loose
jodägäne	جداگانه	separate, one by one
jodäyi	جدایی	separation
jodä kardan	جدا کردن	to separate
joft	جفت	pair, even , couple, placenta
joftak	جفتک	kicking
joftgiri	جفت گیری	mating, coitus
jogandomi	جوگندمی	grey
johar	جوهر	essence, ink
jok	جوک	joke
jolän	جولان	show off, flaunting
jolbak	جلبک	seaweed, algae
jolge	جلگه	plain
jom³e	جمعه	friday
jomhuri	جمهوری	republic
jomjome	جمجمه	skull, cranium
jomle	جمله	sentence (words) , all
jonbeš	جنبش	movement, motion
jonbidan (jonb)	جنبیدن (جنب)	to move, to shake

jong	جنگ	anthology, collection
jonob	جنب	having a wet dream
jonub	جنوب	south
jonubi	جنوبی	southern
jonun	جنون	madness, insanity
joqd	جغد	owl
jor	جور	cruelty, tyranny
jor³at	جرات	courage, daring
jor³e	جرعه	sip, draught
joräb	جوراب	socks, stockings
jorm	جرم	crime, offence
josse	جثه	built, bulk
josteju	جستجو	search, quest
josteju kardan	جستجو کردن	to search
joz	جز	except
joz³	جزء	part, section, ingredient
joz³i	جزئی	slight, trivial, partial
joz³iyät	جزئیات	details
jozäm	جذام	leprosy
jozve	جزوه	pamphlet, lecture notes
juhud	جهود	jew, jewish
juje	جوجه	chicken, chick
juje kabäb	جوجه کباب	chicken kebab
juje tiqi	جوجه تیغی	porcupine
jur	جور	sort, type, assorted
jur kardan	جور کردن	to sort, to match, to solve
juš	جوش	acne, pimple, rash
jušidan(juš)	جوشیدن (جوش)	to boil
jušide	جوشیده	boiled, stewed
juškär	جوش کار	welder
juxe	جوخه	squad, section
juyande	جوینده	seeker, finder
juybär	جویبار	brook, small river

J		
kä³uču	كائوچو	rubber
kabäb	ک باب	kebab, roasted meat
kabäbi	ک بابی	kebab seller
kabed	ک بد	liver
käbin	ک ابـ ین	marriage portion
käbine	ک ابـ ینه	cabinet (government)
kabir	ک بـ یر	mature, great
kabise	ک بـ یسه	leap year
kabk	ک بک	partridge
käbl	ک ابـ ل	cable
kabud	ک بود	dark blue, pale, bruised
kabudi	ک بودی	paleness, bruise
käbus	ک ابـ وس	nightmare
kabutar	ک بوتر	pigeon
kačal	ک چل	bald, having scalp disease
kačali	کچلی	baldness
kadbänu	ک دبـ انو	housewife
kädo	کادو	souvenir
kädr	ک ادر	personnel, staff, frame
kadu	ک دو	pumpkin
kadxodä	ک دخدا	headman, elder man
kaf	ک ف	foam, bubble, palm, floor
kafan	ک فن	shroud, grave clothes
käfar	ک افـ ر	unbeliever, secular, pagan
kafbini	ک ف بـ ینی	chiromancy, palm reading
käfe	ک افـ ه	cafeteria
kaffäre	ک فاره	ransom, redemption, alms
kaffäš	ک فاش	shoemaker
kaffäši	کفاشی	shoemaker shop
kafgir	ک فـ گ یر	skimmer
käfi	ک افـ ی	enough, sufficient

kafš	ک فش	shoe
kafš duzak	ک ف شدوزک	ladybird
kaftar	ک ف تر	pigeon
kaftär	ک ف تار	hyena
kaftar bäz	ک ف تر ب از	pigeon fancier
käfur	ک اف ور	camphor
käh	ک اه	hay, straw
kähen	ک اهن	jewish priest
käheš	ک اهش	decrease, reduction
käheš yaftan	ک اهش یافتن	to decrease, to reduce
kahkašän	ک ه ک شان	the milky way, galaxy
kähu	ک اهو	lettuce
kaj	ک ج	tilted, slanting, crooked
käj	ک اج	pine tree
kaj šodan	کج شدن	to tilt
kak	ک ک	flea
käkol	ک اک ل	topknot, forelock
kakomak	ک ک و مک	freckles
kal	ک ل	bald
käl	ک ال	unripe, premature
kälä	ک الا	goods, merchandise
kaläf	کلاف	hank
kaläfe	ک لاف ه	distressed, confused
kalak	ک لک	trick, phoney
kalak zadan	کلک زدن	to trick, to fool
kalam	ک لم	cabbage
kaläm	ک لام	word, speech
kalame	ک لمه	word
kalän	ک لان	big, large, massive
kaläntar	ک لان تر	sheriff
kaläntari	ک لان تری	police station
kaläq	ک لاغ	crow
kälbäs	ک ال باس	salami

kälbod	کالبد	body
kälbod šekäfi	کالبد شکافی	autopsy
kälej	کالج	college
käleske	کالسکه	carriage, coach, pram
kalimi	کلیمی	jew
kalläš	کلاش	sponger, charlatan
kalle	کله	head, top, mind
kalle päče	کله پاچه	sheep trotters
kalle šaq	کله شق	stubborn
kalux	کلوخ	clod
kam	کم	few, little, less
käm	کام	palate, mouth
kam šodan	کم شدن	to decrease
kam xuni	کمخونی	anaemia
kamän	کمان	bow, arc
kamänče	کمانچه	a musical instrument
kamäne	کمانه	hoop, rim
kamar	کمر	waist
kamar band	کمربند	belt, waistband, seat belt
kambud	کمبود	shortage, deficit, lack
kämel	کامل	complete, perfect, thorough
kami	کمی	a little
kamin	کمین	ambush, lying in wait
kamin kardan	کمین کردن	to ambush
kämiyäb	کامیاب	successful, prosperous
kämiyon	کامیون	lorry, truck
kamiyyat	کمیت	quantity
kamkam	کم کم	little by little
kammi	کمی	quantitative
kamrang	کم رنگ	light, faint, pale
kamru	کمرو	shy, timid
kamruyi	کمرویی	shyness, timidity
kamtar	کم تر	lesser, fewer, less often

kamtarin	کم ترین	least
kamyäb	کم یاب	rare, scarce
kamyäbi	کمیابی	rarity, scarcity
kanaf	کنف	cannabis, hemp
känäl	کانال	canal
kanär	کنار	side, edge, away, beside
kanäre giri	کناره گیری	resignation, quitting
kandan(kan)	کندن (کن)	to dig, to engrave, to pull off
kandekäri	کنده کاری	engraving, carving
kändid	کاندید	candidate, applicant
kandokäv	کند و کاو	search, investigation
kandu	کندو	hive
kane	کنه	leech
kangar	کنگر	acanthus
kanise	کنیسه	synagogue
kaniz	کنیز	female servant
kankäš	کنکاش	deliberation, research
känun	کانون	centre, focus
känuni	کانونی	central, focal
kapak	کپک	mould, must
kapak zade	کپک زده	mouldy
kapar	کپر	hut
käput	کاپوت	bonnet, condom
käqaz	کاغذ	paper, letter
kar	کر	deaf
kär	کار	work, job, profession
kär gardän	کارگردان	director, stage manager
kär kardan	کار کردن	to work
karafs	کرفس	celery
kärägäh	کارگاه	detective
karam	کرم	generosity, courtesy
kärämuz	کارآموز	trainee, apprentice
karäne	کرانه	coast, shore

käräyi	کارآیی	efficiency, merit
kärbord	کاربرد	application, use
kärd	کارد	knife
kärd	کارد	knife
kärdän	کاردان	experienced, efficient
kardan(kon)	کردن (کن)	to do, to make, to fuck
kare	کره	butter
kärfarmä	کارفرما	employer
kargadan	کرگدن	rhinoceros
kärgäh	کارگاه	workshop, studio
kärgar	کارگر	worker, labourer
kärgari	کارگری	labour work
kärgozär	کارگزار	agent, correspondent
kärgozini	کارگزینی	human resources
kari	کری	deafness
kärikätor	کاریکاتور	cartoon, caricature
kärkard	کارآمد	output, yield
karkas	کرکس	vulture
kärkonän	کارکنان	personnel, employees, crew
kärkošte	کارکشته	experienced
kärmand	کارمند	employee, office worker
kärnäme	کارنامه	test result
kärpardäz	کارپرداز	in charge of supplies
käršekani	کارشکنی	sabotage, obstruction
käršekani kardan	کارشکنی کردن	to sabotage, to obstruct
käršenäs	کارشناس	expert, specialist
käršenäsi	کارشناسی	expertise, bachelor degree
kärt	کارت	card
kärt postäl	کارت پستال	post card
kärte e³tebäri	کارت اعتباری	credit card
kärte šenäsäyi	کارت شناسایی	identification card
kärte telefon	کارت تلفن	phone card
kärton	کارتن	carton, board box

kärvän	کاروان	caravan, convoy
kärvarzi	کارورزی	internship, training
kärxäne	کارخانه	factory
kas	کس	person, kin, someone
käš	کاش	i wish
kasabe	کسبه	traders, merchants
kasäd	کساد	stagnant, stale, dull market
kasälat	کسالت	illness, being unwell
kasälat ävar	کسالت آور	boring
kasb	کسب	earning, job, trade
käse	کاسه	bowl, socket
käseb	کاسب	tradesman, merchant
käšef	کاشف	discoverer
kasel	کسل	tired, bored, sluggish
kašf	کشف	discovery, deciphering
kašf kardan	کشف کردن	to discover
kašfiyät	کشفیات	discoveries
käši	کاشی	glazed tile
kasif	کثیف	dirty, messy, untidy, filthy
käšikär	کاشی کار	tiler
kašk	کشک	dried whey
kaški	کشکی	groundless, without bases
käsni	کاسنی	chicory
kasr	کسر	decimal, deduction, fraction
kästan(käh)	کاستن (کاه)	to reduce, to decrease
käštan(kär)	کاشتن (کار)	to plant, to sow
kašti	کشتی	ship, vessel
käštiräni	کشتیرانی	sailing, shipping
katäni	کتانی	cotton, linen
katbi	کتبی	written
kate	کته	boiled rice
katibe	کتیبه	inscription
kätolik	کاتولیک	Catholic

kavir	کویر	salt desert, dry climate
kävoš	ک اوش	digging, excavation, search
käx	ک اخ	palace, mansion
kazäyi	ک ذایی	so and so
käzeb	ک اذب	fake, false, untrue
ke	ک ه	when, that
kebrit	ک بریت	matches
keder	ک در	blurred, dim, dull, opaque
kefälat	ک فالت	guardianship
kefäyat	ک فایت	adequacy, sufficiency
keläj	کلاج	clutch (car)
keläs	ک لاس	class, grade, classroom
kelid	ک ل ید	key, switch
kelisä	کلیسا	cathedral, church
keliše	ک ل یشه	cliché, stereotype
kenär	کنار	beside
kenär raftan	کنار رفتن	to withdraw, to go away
kenäre daryä	کنار دریا	seaside
kenäye	ک نایه	irony, sarcasm
kenäye ämiz	ک نایه آم یز	sarcastic
kenäye zadan	کنایه زدن	to be sarcastic
kenise	ک ن یسه	synagogue
kerävät	ک راوات	tie
keräye	ک رایه	lease, rent, hire, fare
keräye kardan	کرایه کردن	to lease, to rent, to hire
keräye nešin	ک رایه ن ش ین	tenant, renter
kerdär	ک ردار	behaviour, deed, manner
kerem	ک رم	cream
kerex	ک رخ	numb
kerkere	ک رک ره	venetian blinds
kerm	ک رم	worm
kerm xordan	ک رمخوردن	to decay, to rote
kerm xordegi	ک رم خوردگ ی	tooth decay, decay

keš	ک ش	elastic band, rubber band
keš raftan	ک شرفتن	to steal (informal)
kesäfat	ک ثاف ت	dirt, filth, mess
kesäfat käri	ک اری ک ثاف ت	dirty work, making mess
kešäle	ک شاله	groin
kešävarz	ک شاورز	farmer
kešävarzi	ک شاورزی	agriculture, farming
kešeš	ک شش	attraction, draught
kesi	کسی	somebody, someone
kešidan(keš)	کشیدن (کش)	to pull, to draw, to drag
kešide	ک ش یده	extended, pulled, long, slap
kešik	ک ش یک	guard, patrol, post
kešiš	ک ش یش	priest
kešmakeš	ک شم کش	struggle, conflict
kešmeš	ک شمش	raisins, sultanas
kešo	ک شو	drawer
kešt	ک شت	cultivation, plantation
kešti	کشتی	ship
keštzär	ک ش تزار	field, farm
kešvar	ک شور	country, homeland
keši	کشی	elastic
ketäb	ک تاب	book
ketäbi	کتابی	bookish, written form
ketäb där	ک تاب دار	librarian
ketäb foruš	ک تاب ف روش	book seller
ketäb foruši	کتاب فروشی	bookshop
ketäb xäne	ک تاب خانه	library
ketäbče	ک تاب چه	booklet
ketf	ک تف	shoulder
ketmän	ک تمان	denial, concealment
ketmän kardan	ک تمان کردن	to deny
key	ک ی	when, what time
keyf	ک یف	euphoria, joy, pleasure

keyf kardan	ک یف کردن	to enjoy
keyfar	ک ی فر	penalty, punishment
keyfari	ک ی فری	penal
keyfi	ک ی فی	qualitative
keyfiyyat	ک ی ف یت	quality
keyhän	ک یهان	cosmos, universe
keyk	کیک	cake
keyvän	ک یوان	saturn
kezb	ک ذب	lie, untrue
ki	ک ی	who, whom
kif	ک یف	purse, bag, briefcase
kilo	ک ی لو	kilo
kilometre	ک ی لو م تر	kilometre
kine	ک ی نه	animosity, hatred
kinejuyi	ک ی نه جوی ی	revengefulness
kir	ک یر	penis
kiš	ک یش	religion, check mat
kise	ک ی سه	bag, sack, flannel
kise xäb	کیسه خواب	sleeping bag
kišmät	ک یش مات	checkmate
kist	کیست	cystitis
kodäm	ک دام	which, which one
kodan	ک ودن	stupid, dumb
kodurat	ک دورت	opacity, annoyance
kofr	ک فر	profanity, blasphemy
kofr goftan	ک فرگفتن	to blaspheme
kohan	ک هن	ancient, archaic
kohne	ک ه نه	old, used, out-dated, cloth
kohulat	ک هولت	senility, old age
kojä	ک جا	where
koläh	کلاه	hat, helmet, cap
koläh gozäštan	کلاه گذاشتن	to trick, to deceive
koläh bardär	ک لاه بردار	cheat, fraudulent, conman

kolāh gis	کلاه گیس	wig
kolang	کلنگ	pick
kolangi	کلنگی	wreck house
kolbe	کلبه	cottage, hut
kolfat	کلفت	maid, housemaid
koli	کولی	gypsy
koliye	کلیه	kidney
koll	کل	all, whole, entire
kollan	کلا	entirely, totally
kolli	کلی	general, total
koloft	کلفت	thick, coarse
koluče	کلوچه	cookie
komak	کمک	help, aid, assistance
komak kardan	کمک کردن	to help
komaki	کمکی	aid, auxiliary, hand, helping
komedi	کمدی	comedy
komisiyon	کمیسیون	commission
komod	کمد	wardrobe, shelf
komonist	کمونیست	communist
komonism	کمونیسم	communism
kond	کند	slow, blunt, sluggish
konde	کنده	log
kongere	کنگره	congress
konj	کنج	corner, angle
konjkävi	کنجکاوی	curiosity
konjod	کنجد	sesame
konsert	کنسرت	a concert
konserv	کنسرو	canned food
konsul	کنسول	consul
konsulgari	کنسولگری	consulate
konterät	کنترات	contract, agreement
kontor	کنتور	counter, meter, gauge
kontorol	کنترل	control, inspection

konuni	کنونی	present, current
konyäk	کنیاک	brandy
konye	کنیه	nickname
kopon	کوپن	coupon
kord	کرد	Kurdish person
kordi	کردی	Kurdish language
koreyi	کره ای	Korean
koravi	کروی	round
kore	کره	planet, globe, sphere, Korea
koreye zamin	کره زمین	planet earth
kork	کرک	soft hair, fluff
korre	کره	colt
korset	کرست	bra, corset
korsi	کرسی	seat, traditional heater
kos	کس	vagina, vulva
košande	کشنده	fatal, lethal, deadly
koskeš	کس کش	pimp
koštan(koš)	(کشتن(کش)	to kill, to murder
koštär	کشتار	killing, slaughter, massacre
koštärgäh	کشتارگاه	slaughterhouse
košte	کشته	murdered, killed
košti	کشتی	wrestling
košti gereftan	کشتی گرفتن	to wrestle
kosuf	کسوف	eclipse of the sun
kot	کت	jacket
kotak	کتک	beating, hitting
kotak zadan	کتک زدن	to beat, to hit
kubidan(kub)	کوبیدن (کوب)	to pound, to mash, to bash
kubide	کوبیده	minced, mashed, pounded
kuč	کوچ	moving, migrating
kuč kardan	کوچ کردن	to move, to migrate
kuče	کوچه	alley, lane
kuček	کوچک	small, little, tiny

kučnešin	کوچ نشین	nomadic tribes
kučulu	کوچلو	tiny, little kid
kud	کود	fertilizer, compost
kudak	کودک	child, baby, toddler
kudakestän	کودک ستان	kindergarten
kudaki	کودکی	childhood
kudetä	کودتا	coup
kufte	کوفته	bruised, a type of meal
kuftegi	کوفتگی	bruise
kuh	کوه	mountain
kuh navardi	کوه نوردی	mountain climbing
kuh peymäyi	کوه پیمایی	mountaineering
kuhän	کوهان	hump of camel
kuhestän	کوهستان	mountain ranges
kuhestäni	کوهستانی	mountainous, hilly
kuhpäye	کوهپایه	mountain side
kuk	کوک	stitch, tune, winding
kuk zadan	کوک زدن	to stitch
kuku	کوکو	vegetable omelette
kul	کول	shoulder
kuläk	کولاک	snowy storm
kule pošti	کوله پشتی	backpack
kuli	کولی	anchovy
kun	کون	ass, anus, arse, butt
kunde	کونده	passive homo-sexual
kuni	کونی	passive homo-sexual
kur	کور	blind
kurän	کوران	draught, air current
kure	کوره	crematory, kiln, furnace
kuri	کوری	blindness
kurkuräne	کورک وراژه	blindly
kurs	کورس	race
kurtäž	کورتاژ	abortion

kuse	ک و سه	shark, thin-bearded
kušeš	کوشش	effort, struggle, attempt
kušidan(kuš)	کوشیدن (کوش)	to try, to struggle
kutäh	ک وت اه	short, low, brief
kutähi	ک وت اهی	shortcoming, negligence
kutule	ک وت وله	dwarf, midget
kuy	ک وی	alley, narrow street, quarter
kuze	ک وزه	jug, pitcher

L		
lä	لا	fold, ply, inside, among
lä aqal	لا اقل	at least
lä ebäli	لا ابالی	careless, reckless
la³in	لعین	cursed, damned
la³l	لعل	ruby
la³n	لعن	cursing, damning, swearing
la³nat	لعنت	curse, damning
la³nati	لعنتی	damned, cursed
lab	لب	lip, edge
lab šekari	لب شکری	harelip, cleft lip
labälab	لبالب	brimful
labaniyät	لبذیات	dairy products
labe	لبه	edge, rim
läbod	لابد	perhaps, certainly
labu	لبو	boiled beetroot
labxand	لبخند	smile, sneer
labxand zadan	لبخند زدن	to smile
lačak	لچک	scarf
läf	لاف	puff, boast, vaunt
läf zadan	لاف زدن	to boast
laffäfe	لفافه	cover, guise
lafz	لفظ	word
lafzi	لفظی	verbal
lagad	لگد	kick
lagad zadan	لگد زدن	to kick
lagadmäl kardan	لگد مال کردن	to trample, to defeat
lagan	لنگ	pelvis, pan, urinal
lahäf	لحاف	quilt
lahäz	لحاظ	respect, view, connection
lähe	لاهه	the hague
lahim	لحیم	solder

lahje	لهجه	dialect, accent
lahlah	لهله	panting
lahn	لحن	tune, tone, manner
lahze	لحظه	moment, instant
lahze be lahze	لحظه به لحظه	gradually, momentarily
laj	لج	spite, grudge
laj kardan	لج کردن	to grouch
lajäjat	لجاجت	grudge, stubbornness
lajan	لجن	sludge, loose mud, morass
läjavardi	لاجوردی	azure
lajbäz	لج باز	stubborn, spiteful
lajuj	لجوج	stubborn, pig-head
lak	لک	freckle, spot
läk	لاک	shell, nail polish
läken	لاکن	but, however
lakkäte	لکاته	prostitute, whore
lakke	لکه	spot, stain, stigma
laklak	لک لک	stork
läkpošt	لاک پشت	turtle, tortoise
läl	لال	mute, dumb, speechless
läläyi	لالایی	lullaby
lale	لله	nanny
läle	لاله	tulip
lam dädan	لم دادن	to lean
lämazhab	لامذهب	secular, atheist
lämese	لامسه	sense of touch
lamidan(lam)	لمیدن (لم)	to loll, to relax, to lean
lämp	لامپ	lamp, globe
lams	لمس	touching, contact
lams kardan	لمس کردن	to touch, to feel
landan	لندن	london
läne	لانه	nest, den
lanf	لنف	lymph

lang	لنگ	paralysed, crippled, stalled
langänlangän	لنگ لنگان	limping
langar	لـ ن گر	anchor, gravity
langargäh	لـ ن گرگ اه	harbour, anchorage
langidan(lang)	لنگیدن (لنگ)	to limp
lape	لـ په	split peas
laq	لـ ق	loose, shaky
laqab	لـ قب	title, cognomen, epithet
läqar	لاغر	thin, skinny
läqari	لاغری	thinness
laqv	لـ غو	cancellation, void
laqv kardan	لغو کردن	to cancel
laqzän	لـ غزان	slippery, sliding
laqzande	لـ غزدده	slippery, sliding
laqzeš	لـ غزش	slip, error, mistake
laqzidan(laqz)	لغزیدن (لغز)	to slip, to slide
lärubi	لاروبـ ی	dredging
larz	لـ رز	shivering, shaking
larzän	لرزان	shaky, vibrant, shivery
larzeš	لـ رزش	tremor, vibration, quake
larzidan(larz)	لرزیدن (لرز)	to shiver, to tremble
laš	لـ ش	lumpish, nerveless
läs	لا س	flirting
lase	لـ ثه	gum (of teeth)
läše	لا شه	corpse, carcass
laškar	لـ شـ کر	army, force
laškargäh	لـ شـ کرگ اه	camp (army)
laškarkeši	لـ شـ کرک شی	military expedition
lästik	لا سـ تـ یک	rubber, tyre
läšxor	لا شخور	vulture
lät	لات	vagabond, destitute
latäfat	لـ طافـ ت	purity, fineness, tenderness
latif	لـ ط یف	tender, pure, delicate, fine

latife	لطيفه	joke, satire, humour
latme	لطمه	damage, harm, loss
latme zadan	لطمه زدن	to harm
lavä	لوا	banner, flag
lavand	لوند	coy
laväš	لواش	a type of bread
lavät	لواط	paedophilia
laväzem	لوازم	necessities, equipment
laväzem ottahrir	لوازم التحرير	stationery
laxt	لخت	flaccid, limp, lax
laxte	لخته	clot, clog
läye	لايه	layer, stratum
läyehe	لايحه	bill(legislation)
läyeq	لايق	deserved, competent, fit
lazej	لزج	viscous, slippery, sticky
läzem	لازم	necessary, essential
läzem däštan	لازم داشتن	to need
laziz	لذيذ	delicious, tasty
lebäs	لباس	clothes, dress, costume
leh	له	crushed, mashed, squashy
lehestän	لهستان	Poland
lejäm	لجام	bridle, reins
lemm	لم	trick, know how
leng	لنگ	leg
lenge	لنگه	pair, half a load, mate
lent	لنت	(brake) shoe
leqäh	لقاح	fertilization
lezzat	لذت	pleasure, joy, satisfaction
lezzat baxš	لذت بخش	delightful, enjoyable
lezzat bordan	لذت بردن	to enjoy
libi	ليبی	Libya
libiyi	ليبيايی	Libyan
lif	ليف	bathing sponge

limu	لـيمو	lime, lemon
lis	لـيس	licking
lisäns	لـيسانس	bachelor degree
lisidan(lis)	لیسیدن (لیس)	to lick
list	لـيست	menu, table, list
livän	لـيوان	glass
liyäqat	لـياقت	merit, virtue, efficiency
liz	لـيز	slippery, viscous
liz xordan	لـيز خوردن	to slip, to skid
lo dädan	لـودادن	to disclose, to betray
lo raftan	لو رفتن	to be disclosed
lo³äb	لـعاب	glaze, coating, polish
lobb	لـب	essence, gist
lobnän	لـبنان	Lebanon
lobnäni	لـبنانی	Lebanese
loh	لـوح	board, tombstone
loknat	لـکنت	stuttering, stammering
loknati	لکنتی	stutterer, stammerer
lolä	لـولا	hinge, joint
long	لـنگ	apron, bathing cloth
lop	لـپ	cheek
loqat	لـغت	word
loqat näme	لـغتنامه	dictionary
loqme	لـقمه	morsel, mouthful
los	لوث	contaminated, soiled
lotf	لـطف	kindness, favour, courtesy
lotfan	لـطفا	please
loxm	لخم	lean (meat), boneless
loxt	لخت	naked, nude, bare
loxti	لـختی	nakedness, nudity
loze	لـوزه	tonsil
lozi	لـوزی	lozenge
lozolme³de	لـوزالمعده	pancreas

lozum	لزوم	necessity, need, essentiality
lozuman	لزوما	necessarily
lubiyä	لوبیا	bean
luč	لوچ	squint, cross-eyed
luks	لوکس	luxury, elegant
lul	لول	intoxicated
lule	لوله	pipe, tube
lulidan(lul)	لولیدن (لول)	to squirm, to wriggle
lulu	لولو	bogyman
lus	لوس	spoiled
luster	لوستر	chandelier
luti	لوطی	pederast, buffoon

M		
mä	ما	we, us, our, ours
mä ošša³ir	ما ال شعير	barely water
ma³äd	معاد	resurrection day
ma³äref	معارف	education, culture
ma³äš	معاش	living, sustenance
ma³bad	معبد	temple
ma³bar	معبر	passage, road, path
ma³dan	معدن	mine
ma³dani	معذى	mineral
ma³dud	معدود	few, limited
ma³dum	معدوم	destroyed, executed, extinct
ma³išat	معيشت	living, earning
ma³jun	معجون	mixture, electuary
ma³kus	معكوس	reversed, upside down
ma³lul	معلول	handicapped, invalid, effect
ma³luliyat	معلوليت	invalidity, handicap
ma³lum	معلوم	obvious, evident
ma³lumät	معلومات	knowledge, qualifications
ma³mul	معمول	usual, customary
ma³mulan	معمولا	usually, ordinarily
ma³muli	معمولى	usual, ordinary
ma³mur	مامور	official, appointed, agent
ma³muriyat	ماموريت	mission, duty, assignment
ma³nä	معنا	meaning
ma³navi	معنوى	spiritual
ma³naviyat	معنويت	spirituality
ma³ni	معنى	meaning, sense
ma³nidär	معنى دار	meaningful
ma³qul	معقول	reasonable, rational
ma³rake	معركه	battle field, jugglers' display
ma³raz	معرض	exposure, exposed to

ma³refat	معرف ت	knowledge, insight, wisdom
ma³ruf	معروف	popular, famous
ma³siyat	معصيت	sin, guilt
ma³sum	معصوم	innocent, chaste
ma³sumiyat	معصوميت	innocence
ma³šuqe	معشوقه	mistress, lover
ma³tuf	معطوف	inclined, focused on
ma³yub	معيوب	defective, faulty
ma³yus	مايوس	disappointed, hopeless
ma³zerat	معذرت	apology, excuse
ma³zerat xästan	معذرت خواستن	to apologise
ma³zur	معذور	excused, exempted
mab³as	مبعث	Start of the prophethood
mabädä	مبادا	never ever, let it not be
mabäni (mabnä)	مبانی (مبنا)	bases, essentials
mabda³	مبدا	foundation, beginning
mabhas	مبحث	subject, topic, part
mabhut	مبهوت	stunned, astonished
mablaq	مبلغ	amount, fee
mabnä	مبنا	bases, foundation
mäč	ماچ	kiss
mäč kardan	ماچ کردن	to kiss
mäd	ماد	medes
madad	مدد	help, aid, assistance
madadkär	مددکار	social worker
madani	مدنی	civil, civic, urban
madär	مدار	orbit, circuit, axis
mädar	مادر	mother, mum
mädar bozorg	مادر بزرگ	grandmother
mädar šohar	مادر شوهر	mother in law (for a woman)
mädar xände	مادر خوانده	stepmother
mädar zädi	مادر زاد	congenital
mädar zan	مادر زن	mother in law (for a man)

mädaräne	مادرانه	motherly
mädari	مادری	maternity
madd	مد	flow(tide)
maddähi	مداحی	eulogy, praise
mädde	ماده	substance, material, article
mäddi	مادی	material, corporal
mäde	ماده	female, feminie
madfan	مدفن	grave, resting place
madfu³	مدفوع	excrement, faeces
madfun	مدفون	buried, entombed
madh	مدح	praise, eulogy
mädiyän	مادیان	mare
madrak	مدرک	document, papers, proof
madrase	مدرسه	school, academy, institute
mädun	مادون	inferior, sub-
madyun	مدیون	in debt, owing
maf³ul	مفعول	object, passive homosexual
maf³uli	مفعولی	objective, accusative
mafäsed (fesäd)	مفاسد (فساد)	corruptions, mischief
mafhum	مفهوم	concept, sense, meaning
mafluk	مفلوک	miserable, unfortunate
mäfoq	مافوق	beyond, superior
mafqud	مفقود	missing, lost
mafsal	مفصل	joint, articulation
maftul	مفتول	twisted wire
magar	مگر	unless
magas	مگس	fly
magas koš	مگس کش	fly swat
mäh	ماه	month, moon, beautiful
mahäfel	محافل	meetings, sources
mahak	محک	touchstone, criterion
mahal	محل	place, venue, locality
mahäl	محال	impossible

mahalle	محله	parish, district
mahalli	محلی	local, native
mähäne	ماهانه	monthly
mahär	مهار	bridle, harness, leading rope
mahärat	مهارت	skill, dexterity, mastery
mahäsen	محاسن	virtues, beauties, beard
mahavvate	محوطه	surroundings, area, yard
mahbel	مهبل	vagina
mahbub	محبوب	beloved, favourite, darling
mahbubiyat	محبوبیت	popularity
mahdud	محدود	limited, confined, restricted
mahdud kardan	محدود کردن	to limit, to restrict
mahdude	محدوده	confined, area, limit
mahdudiyat	محدودیت	limitation, restriction
mäher	ماهر	skilled, expert
mahfaze	محفظه	case, container
mahfel	محفل	meeting, circle, gathering
mahfuz	محفوظ	safe, secure, guarded
mähi	ماهی	fish, monthly
mähi täbe	ماهی تابه	frying pan
mahib	مهیب	scary, terrible, frightening
mähiče	ماهیچه	muscle, fillet
mähigir	ماهیگیر	fisherman
mähigiri	ماهیگیری	fishery
mähiyäne	ماهیانه	per month
mähiyat	ماهیت	nature, essence, entity
mahkum	محکوم	convicted, condemned
mahkum kardan	محکوم کردن	to condemn, to charge
mahkumiyat	محکومیت	conviction, condemnation
mahlake	مهلکه	dangerous situation
mahlul	محلول	solution, liquid
mahr	مهر	marriage portion, dowry
mahram	محرم	close kin, confidant

mahramäne	محرمانه	confidential, classified
mahriye	مهریه	marriage portion, dowry
mahrum	محروم	deprived, denied
mahrum kardan	محروم کردن	to deprive
mahrumiyat	محرومیت	deprivation
mahšar	محشر	resurrection day
mahsub	محسوب	counted, taken into account
mahsul	محصول	product, crop, output
mahšur	محشور	associated with
mahsus	محسوس	sensible, tangible
mahtäb	مهتاب	moonlight
mahtäbi	مهتابی	florescent, terrace
mähut	ماهوت	felt
mahv	محو	faded, wiped out
mahv kardan	محو کردن	to wipe out, to erase
mähväre	ماهواره	satellite
mahz	محض	mere
mahzar	محضر	notary public, presence
majalle	مجله	magazine
mäjarä	ماجرا	adventure, event
mäjaräju	ماجراجو	adventurous
mäjaräjuyi	ماجراجویی	seeking adventure
majbur	مجبور	obliged, forced
majbur kardan	مجبورکردن	to force
majhul	مجهول	passive, unknown
majjani	مجانی	free (of charge)
majles	مجلس	parliament, gathering
majma³	مجمع	assembly, association
majmu³	مجموع	total, sum
majmu³e	مجموعه	collection, set, series
majnun	مجنون	mad, crazy
majrä	مجرا	canal, passage, duct
majruh	مجروح	wounded, injured

majruh kardan	مجروح کردن	to injure
majzub	مجذوب	attracted, fascinated
majzub kardan	مجذوب کردن	to attract
majzur	مجذور	square (root)
makän	مکان	place, location
makäni	مکانی	local
makidan(mak)	مکیدن (مک)	to suck, to suckle
makkar	مکار	deceitful, crafty
makke	مکه	mecca
makr	مکر	trick, deceit
makruh	مکروه	disapproved by religious law
maks	مکث	pause, halt
maktab	مکتب	old-fashioned school
mäl	مال	asset, possession, animal
mal³un	ملعون	damned, cursed
maläfe	ملافه	bed sheet, linen
maläj	ملاج	fontanel
malak	ملک	angel
malake	ملکه	queen
maläl angiz	ملال انگیز	boring, annoying
malämat	ملامت	blame, taunt
maläqe	ملاقه	ladle
malavän	ملوان	sailor, seaman
malaväni	ملوانی	seamanship
malax	ملخ	locust
mäle	ماله	trowel
malek	ملک	king
mälek	مالک	owner, proprietor, lord
mälekiyat	مالکیت	ownership, possession
mäleš	مالش	rubbing, scrubbing
mälidan(mäl)	مالیدن(مال)	to rub, to massage
mälixuliyä	مالیخولیا	melancholy
mäli	مالی	financial

mäliyät	مالیات	tax, duty, toll
malul	ملول	weary, sad, bored
malus	ملوس	cuddly, catamite
mämä	ماما	midwife
mämän	مامان	mum, mother
mämäyi	مامایی	midwifery
mame	مه مه	breast, dummy
mamnu³	ممنوع	forbidden, restricted
mamnu³ kardan	ممنوع کردن	to forbid
mamnun	ممنون	thankful, grateful
man	من	i, me, mine
män	مان	our, ours, us
man³	منع	prohibition, forbidding
män³	مانع	obstacle, barrier
man³ kardan	منع کردن	to prohibit, to forbid
manäl	منال	property, asset
manba³	منبع	source, reservoir, origin
manbar	منبر	pulpit, preacher's seat
mändan(män)	ماندن (مان)	to stay, to remain, to last
mändegär	ماندگار	lasing, permanent
maneš	منش	manner, nature, disposition
manfa³at	منفعت	gain, benefit, profit
manfaz	منفذ	opening, passage, hole
manfi	منفی	negative, negation
manfibäf	منفی باف	negativist, pessimist
manfibäfi	منفی بافی	pessimism
mang	منگ	dizzy, giddy
mangi	منگی	dizziness, giddiness
mangane	منگنه	punch, press
mangule	منگوله	tassel, knot
mani	منی	semen, sperm
manjaläb	منجلاب	sewer, sewage water
mänovr	مانور	war game

manqal	م ذ قل	brazier
manša³	م ذ شا	source, origin
mansab	م ذ صب	position, rank, status
mansub	م ذ صوب	appointed, selected
mansub kardan	منصوب کردن	to appoint
manšur	م ذ شور	prism, charter
mansux	م ذ سوخ	obsolete, abolished
mansux kardan	منسوخ کردن	to abolish
mantaqe	م نط قه	area, zone, region
mantaqeyi	منطقه ای	regional
manteq	م نطق	logic, rationality
manteqi	م نط قی	logical
manut	م نوط	depending, pending
manzare	م نظره	sight, view, landscape
manzel	م نزل	home, house
manzelat	منزلت	respect, status
manzume	م نظومه	poem, solar system
manzur	م نظور	purpose, aim, intention
maq³ad	م قعد	anus, butt, arse
mäqabl	م قابـ ل	preceding, before
maqäle	م قالـه	paper, article, essay
maqäm	م قام	position, rank, status
maqämät	م قامات	authorities
maqäze	مغازه	shop, store
maqäzedär	مغازه دار	shop keeper
maqbare	م ق بره	shrine, tomb
maqbul	م ق بول	accepted
maqbun	مغ بون	hoaxed, cheated
maqdam	م قدم	arrival
maqduniye	م قدونـ یه	macedonia
maqdur	م قدور	possible, feasible
maqferat	مغ فرت	forgiveness
maqlate	مغ لطه	sophistry, misleading

maqlub	مغلوب	defeated, beaten
maqlub kardan	مغلوب کردن	to defeat, to beat
maqne³e	مقنعه	veil, scarf
maqreb	مغرب	west, morocco
maqrebi	مغربی	moroccan
maqrur	مغرور	arrogant, haughty, snobbish
maqruz	مقروض	indebted
maqsad	مقصد	destination, aim, intention
maqsud	مقصود	aim, purpose, intension
maqšuš	مغشوش	disturbed, chaotic
maqta³	مقطع	section, cut
maqta³i	مقطعی	temporary, sectional
maqtul	مقتول	killed, murdered
maqule	مقوله	category, class
maqz	مغز	brain
mär	مار	snake, serpent
mar³i	مرئی	visible, evident
marä	مرا	me
maräje³at	مراجعت	returning, coming back
maräje³at kardan	مراجعت کردن	to return
maräkeš	مراکش	morocco
maräkeši	مراکشی	moroccan
maräm	مرام	aim, objective
maräm näme	مرام نامه	doctrine, articles
maräsem	مراسم	ceremonies, customs
maraz	مرض	illness, disease, sickness
marbut	مربوط	relative, connected
marbute	مربوطه	relevant, related
märčube	مارچوبه	asparagus
mard	مرد	man, male, mankind
mardak	مردک	little man, little fellow
mardäne	مردانه	masculine, brave
mardänegi	مردانگی	courage, generosity

mardi	مردی	manhood, masculinity
mardom	مردم	people, folks
mardom šenäsi	مردم شناسی	anthropology
mardomak	مردمک	pupil (of eye)
mardomi	مردمی	humanity, humanism
mardud	مردود	failed, rejected, discarded
marg	مرگ	death, demise, end
margbär	مرگ بار	deadly, mortal
märgir	مارگ یر	snake charmer
margomir	مرگ و میر	mortality, fatality
marhabä	مرح با	well done, bravo
marhale	مرحله	stage, step, phase
marham	مرحم	cure, medicine
marhamat	مرحمت	favour, mercy, kindness
marhum	مرحوم	deceased, the late
marhum šodan	مرحوم شدن	to pass away
mariz	مریض	ill, sick, unwell, patient
marizi	مریضی	illness, sickness, disease
marizxäne	مریضخانه	hospital
marja³	مرجع	source, resort, reference
marjän	مرجان	coral
markaz	مرکز	centre, head office, middle
markazi	مرکزی	central
märmähi	مارماهی	eel
marmar	مرمر	marble
märmulak	مارمولک	lizard
marmuz	مرموز	mysterious, mystical
märpič	مارپیچ	spiral, helix, coil
marqad	مرقد	shrine, tomb, grave
marqub	مرغوب	high quality, desirable
märs	مارس	march
märš	مارش	marching
marsiye	مرثیه	elegy, mourning

marsum	مرسوم	customary, habitual
marta³	مرتع	pasture, meadow
martabe	مرتبه	grade, floor, time, stage
martub	مرطوب	damp, moist, humid
maryam	مریم	mary
marz	مرز	border, frontier, boundary
marzbän	مرزبان	frontier guard, border guard
marznešin	مرزدشین	borderer, frontiersman
marzobum	مرزوبوم	country, homeland
mäš	ماش	chikling vetch
maš³al	مشعل	torch
mas³ale	مسذله	problem, affair
mas³ul	مسئول	in charge, responsible
mas³uliyat	مسئولیت	responsibility, liability, duty
masäfat	مسافت	distance
masähat	مساحت	measurement, area, survey
masäleh	مصالح	interests, materials
mäšällä	ماشاالله	well done
mašäm	مشام	smelling
mašäqel	مشاغل	jobs, occupations
mašaqqat	مشقت	hardship, difficulty
mäsäž	ماساژ	massage
mäsäž dädan	ماساژدادن	to give a massage
masdar	مصدر	infinitive, source
masdud kardan	مسدود کردن	to block
masdud	مسدود	closed, blocked
mäse	ماسه	sand
mäše	ماشه	trigger, tongs
mašgul	مشغول	busy, occupied, engaged
mašguliyat	مشغولیت	preoccupation, hobby
mašhud	مشهود	obvious, evident
mašhur	مشهور	famous, well-known
masih	مسیح	messiah, christ

masihi	مسیحی	christian
masihiyat	مسیحیت	christianity
mäšin	ماشین	car, machine
mašin älät	ماشین آلات	machinery
mašine lebasšuyi	ماشین لباس شویی	washing machine
mašini	ماشینی	mechanical, urban
masir	مسیر	pass, route, direction
masjed	مسجد	mosque
mäsk	ماسک	mask
maskan	مسکن	residence, home
maškuk	مشکوک	doubtful, suspicious
maskuni	مسکونی	residential, inhabited
maskut	مسکوت	hushed, kept quiet
maslahat	مصلحت	advisable, good intention
maslak	مسلک	religion, belief, ideology
maslub	مصلوب	crucified
mašmul	مشمول	including, subject to
masmum	مسموم	poisoned
masmumiyat	مسمومیت	poisoning
masnad	مسند	seat, position, throne
masno³i	مصنوعی	artificial, forged, synthetic
mašq	مشق	homework, drill, practice
mašqul	مشغول	busy, engaged
masraf	مصرف	consumption, usage
mašreq	مشرق	east, orient
masru³	مشروع	legitimate, legal
mašrub	مشروب	alcoholic drink
mašrub foruši	مشروب فروشی	liquor store
mašrub xär	مشروب خوار	drinker
mašruh	مشروح	detailed, comprehensive
mašrut	مشروط	conditional
mašrute	مشروطه	constitutional
mašrutiyat	مشروطیت	constitutionalism

mast	مست	drunk, intoxicated
mäst	ماست	yoghurt
mäst mäli	ماست مالی	slurring over
masti	مستی	drunkenness, intoxication
masun	مصون	secure, immune
masuniyat	مصونیت	immunity, security
mašvarat	مشورت	consultation
mašvarat kardan	مشورت کردن	to consult
masx	مسخ	metamorphosis
masxare	مسخره	mockery, ridicules
masxare kardan	مسخره کردن	to ridicule
masxarebäzi	مسخره بازی	horseplay, mockery
mašy	مشی	policy, pace
mät	مات	astound, mate, opaque
matab	مطب	surgery, clinic
mätaht	ماتحت	button, ass, anus
matalak	متلک	sarcasm, taunting
matalak goftan	متلک گفتن	to taunt, to flirt
mätam	ماتم	mourning, grieving
matänat	متانت	dignity, poise
matarsak	مترسک	scarecrow
matbu³	مطبوع	pleasant, desirable
matbu³ät	مطبوعات	press, newspapers
mate	مته	drill, auger
mätik	ماتیک	lipstick
matin	متین	self-possessed, dignified
matlab	مطلب	topic, subject, text
matlub	مطلوب	desired, pleasant
matn	متن	text, context
matrah	مطرح	under consideration
matrah kardan	مطرح کردن	to offer, to raise, to suggest
matrud	مطرود	expelled, rejected
matruk	متروک	abandoned, deserted

mavädde moxadder	مواد مخدر	drugs
maväjeb	مواجب	wage, salary
mavälid	موالید	births
mavät	موات	uncultivated land
maväzin	موازین	standards, scales
maviz	مویز	raisins
maxfi	مخفی	hidden, secret, covered
maxfi kardan	مخفی کردن	to hide, to cover
maxfiyäne	مخفیانه	in secret
maxluq	مخلوق	creature, created, people
maxlut	مخلوط	mixed, blended, mixture
maxlut kardan	مخلوط کردن	to mix
maxmal	مخمل	velvet
maxmalak	مخملک	scarlet fever
maxmase	مخمصه	trouble, difficulty
maxraj	مخرج	outlet, anus, denominator
maxrube	مخروبه	ruined
maxrut	مخروط	cone
maxsus	مخصوص	special, specific
maxsusan	مخصوصا	especially, particularly
maxuf	مخوف	scary, terrifying
maxzan	مخزن	reservoir, storage
mäye	مایه	ferment, capital, yeast
mäye³	مایع	liquid, fluid
mäyel	مایل	slant, oblique, inclined
mäyo	مایو	bathing suit, swim suit
mäz	ماز	maze, twist
mäzäd	مازاد	excess, surplus
mazanne	مظنه	price, rate
mazäq	مذاق	taste
mazär	مزار	tomb, shrine
mazbur	مذبور	mentioned, aforementioned
maze	مزه	taste, flavour

mazhab	مذهب	religion, faith
mazhabi	مذهبی	religious
mazhar	مظهر	manifestation, appearance
mäzi	ماضی	past tense
maziqe	مضیقه	difficulty, hardship, distress
mäziye ba³id	ماضی بعید	past participle
mäziye estemräri	ماضی استمراری	continuous past
mäziye naqli	ماضی نقلی	present participle
mazkur	مذکور	mentioned, said
mazlum	مظلوم	oppressed
mazlumäne	مظلومانه	submissively
mazlumiyat	مظلومیت	submissiveness, innocence
maznun	مظنون	suspect, mistrustful
mazrab	مضرب	multiple
mazre³e	مزرعه	farm, field, ranch
me³de	معده	stomach
me³mär	معمار	architect
me³märi	معماری	architecture
me³yär	معیار	criterion, standard
medäd	مداد	pencil
medäd päkkon	مداد پاككن	rubber, eraser
medäd taräš	مدادتراش	pencil sharpener
medäl	مدال	medal, badge
meh	مه	fog, mist, smog, may
mehälud	مه آلود	foggy, misty, hazy
mehmän	مهمان	guest, visitor
mehmän där	مهماندار	host(ess), stewardess
mehmän dust	مهمان دوست	hospitable
mehmän naväzi	مهمان نوازی	hospitality
mehmän xäne	مهمان خانه	guest house, inn, hostel
mehmäni	مهمانی	party, feast
mehmiz	مهمیز	spur, prick
mehr	مهر	7th Persian month

mehräb	محراب	adytum
mehrebän	مهربان	kind, affectionate, gracious
mehrebäni	مهربانی	kindness, compassion
mehvar	محور	pivot, axis
mehvari	محوری	pivotal, main
mekänik	مکانیک	mechanic
mekäniki	مکانیکی	mechanical, garage
mekänize	مکانیزه	mechanised
mekzik	مکزیک	mexico
mekziki	مکزیکی	mexican
meläk	ملاک	proof, criterion, basis
melk	ملک	property, real estate
melki	ملکی	possessive (grammar)
melkiyyat	ملکیت	possession, ownership
mellat	ملت	nation, people
melli	ملی	national
melliyat	ملیت	nationality
menär	منار	minaret, lighthouse
menhä	منها	minus, subtraction
mennat	منت	favour, indebtedness
mennmenn	من من	mumbling, muttering
menqär	منقار	beak, bill, nob
meqdär	مقدار	amount, quantity, sum
meqdäri	مقداری	some
meqnätisi	مغناطیسی	magnetic
meqyäs	مقیاس	scale, measure
mercy	مرسی	thanks, thank you
meri	مری	oesophagus
merrix	مریخ	mars
mes	مس	copper
mesäl	مثال	example, instance
meški	مشکی	black
meskin	مسکین	poor, needy

mesr	مصر	Egypt
mesri	مصری	Egyptian
mesrä³	مصرع	half verse
mesväk	مسواک	toothbrush
mesväk zadan	مسواک زدن	to brush one's teeth
metr	مﺗر	meter
metro	مﺗرو	subway
mey	می	wine, liquor
meydän	مﻳدان	square, roundabout, field
meygu	مﻳﮕو	shrimp, prawn
meyl	مﻳل	desire, will, tendency
meymun	مﻳمون	monkey, prosperous
meyxäne	مﻳخاﻧﻪ	pub, bar
meyxäre	مﻳخواره	drinker, alcohol addict
meyyet	مﻳت	dead, corpse
mezäh	مزاح	joke, jest, kidding
mezäj	مزاج	condition, temperament
mi³äd	مﻳﻌاد	promise, covenant
mihan	مﻳهن	homeland, motherland
mihan parast	مﻳهن پرست	patriot
mihani	مﻳهﻧی	patriotic
mihan parasti	مﻳهن پرسﺗی	patriotism
mikrob	مﻳکروب	germ, microbe
mil	مﻳل	bar, shaft, axle
miläd	مﻳلاد	birth, birth of christ
milädi	مﻳلادی	christian calendar
mile	مﻳلﻪ	rod, shaft, axle
milimetr	مﻳلی مﺗر	millimetre
milyärd	مﻳلﻳارد	billion
milyon	مﻳلﻳون	million
milyoner	مﻳلﻳوﻧر	millionaire
minä	مﻳﻧا	enamel
minä käri	مﻳﻧاکاری	enamelwork

miräs	مـیراث	heritage, legacy
miš	مـیش	ewe
misäq	مـیثاق	promise, pact, treaty
mive	میوه	fruit
mix	مـیخ	nail, peg
mixak	مـیخک	carnation
mixi	مـیخی	cuneiform
miyän	مـیان	middle, between, among
miyän bor	مـیان بـر	short cut
miyän säl	مـیان سال	middle age
miyäne	مـیانه	middle, median
miyäne ravi	مـیانه روی	moderation
miyäne ro	میانه رو	moderate
miyängin	مـیان گـین	average, median, mean
miyäni	مـیانی	middle, central
miyänji	مـیانجی	mediator, arbitrator
miyänji gari	مـیانجی گـری	mediation, arbitration
miyänji gari kardan	میانجیگری کردن	to mediate
miyu	مـیو	meow
miz	مـیز	table, desk
mizän	مـیزان	amount, quantity, degree
mizbän	مـیزبـان	host
mizbäni	میزبانی	hosting
mo	مو	vine
mo³addab	مودب	polite, courteous
mo³addel	مـعدل	mean, median, average
mo³ädel	مـعادل	equivalent, equal
mo³ädele	مـعادلـه	equation, parity
mo³äf	مـعاف	exempt, excused, forgiven
mo³äf kardan	معاف کردن	to excuse, to exempt
mo³äfiyat	مـعاف یت	exemption
mo³ähede	مـعاهده	pact, treaty, agreement
mo³äleje	مـعالـجه	treatment, cure, healing

mo³äleje kardan	معالجه کردن	to treat
mo³allaq kardan	معلق کردن	to suspend
mo³allef	مولف	author, writer
mo³allem	معلم	teacher, trainer, master
mo³allemi	معلمی	teaching, instruction
mo³ämele	معامله	deal, trade, bargain
mo³ämele kardan	معامله کردن	to make a deal
mo³ammä	معما	riddle, puzzle, enigma
mo³ammam	معمم	clergy
mo³annas	مونث	female
mo³arref	معرف	sponsor, referee, introducer
mo³arrefi	معرفی	introducing, presenting
mo³arrefi kardan	معرفی کردن	to introduce
mo³äšeqe	معاشقه	love-making, fondling
mo³äser	معاصر	contemporary
mo³äšerat	معاشرت	relationship, company
mo³asser	موثر	influential, effective, efficient
mo³asses	موسس	founder
mo³assese	موسسه	institute, foundation
mo³attal	معطل	waiting, detained, stood up
mo³attal kardan	معطل کردن	to delay, to procrastinate
mo³attali	معطلی	delay, suspension
mo³attar	معطر	scented, aromatic, fragrant
mo³även	معاون	assistant, deputy
mo³äveze	معاوضه	exchange, swap
mo³äxeze	مواخذه	reprimanding, rebuke
mo³äyene	معاینه	examination, check up
mo³äyene kardan	معاینه کردن	to examine (medical)
mo³ayyan	معین	specified, fixed, known
mo³ayyan kardan	معین کردن	to specify, to allocate
mo³azzab	معذب	uneasy, bothered
mo³azzab kardan	معذب کردن	to make uneasy
mo³azzaf	موظف	responsible, ordered

mo³ed	موعد	due date, time, deadline
mo³eze	موعظه	preaching, sermon
mo³eze kardan	موعظه کردن	to preach
mo³jeze	معجزه	miracle
mo³tabar	مع تَ بر	reliable, valid
mo³täd	مع تاد	addict, hooked on
mo³tadel	مع تدل	mild, moderate, gentle
mo³tamed	مع تَمد	confidant, trusty
mo³taqed	مع تَ قد	believer, faithful
mo³taqedät	مع تَ قدات	beliefs, credos
mo³tarez	مع ترض	protester, objecting
mo³tareze	مع تر ضه	parenthetical
mo³ud	موعود	promised
mo³zalät	مع ضلات	problems, complexities
mobädele	مـ بادلـه	exchange, trade
mobähät	مـ باهت	pride, boasting
mobähese	مـ باحـ ثه	dispute, discussion
mobäleqe	مـ بالـ غه	exaggeration, overstatement
mobäleqe kardan	مـ بالـ غه کردن	to exaggerate
mobäleqe ämiz	مـ بالـ غه آمـ یز	exaggerated
moballeq	مـ بـ لغ	missionary, publicist
mobärak	مبارک	blessed, happy
mobärez	مـ بارز	fighter, challenger
mobäreze	مـ بارزه	fighting, combat, battle
mobäreze kardan	مـ بارزه کردن	to fight, to combat
mobarrä	مـ برا	exempt, acquitted, cleared
mobäšer	مـ باشر	foreman, conductor
mobed	موبـ د	zoroastrian priest
mobham	مـ بهم	ambiguous, vague
mobl	مـ بل	furniture, lounge
mobser	مـ بـصر	students' representative
mobtadi	مـ بـ تدى	novice, beginner
mobtaker	مـ بـ تَ کر	resourceful, innovator

mobtalä šodan	مـ ب تلا شدن	to suffer from, to be afflicted
mobtazal	مـ ب تذل	commonplace, obscene
moč	مچ	wrist
močäle	مچاله	crumpled, rumpled
močäle kardan	مچاله‌کردن	to crumpled, to rumple
mod	مد	fashion, style
modäfe³	مداف ع	defender, defendant, guard
modäfe³e	مداف عه	defence
modäm	مدام	continually, all the time
modarraj	مدرج	graduated, scaled
modarres	مدرس	teacher, lecturer
modävä	مداوا	treatment, cure
modävä kardan	مداوا کردن	to treat
modävem	مداوم	continuous, lasting
modavvan	مدون	compiled
modavvar	مدور	round, spherics
modäxele	مداخله	interference, intervention
modäxele kardan	مداخله کردن	to interfere, to intervene
modda³i	مدعی	claimant, plaintiff
modda³i olumum	مدعی العموم	public prosecutor
moddat	مدت	period, duration
model	مدل	model, design, guide
modir	مدیر	director, manager
modiriyyat	مدیریت	management, direction
mofäd	مـ فاد	contents, context
mofassal	مـ ف صل	detailed, full, elaborate
mofasser	مـ ف سر	commentator
mofid	مـ ف ید	useful, helpful
mofles	مـ ف لس	poor, needy
mofrad	مـ فرد	singular, single
moft	مـ فت	free, complimentary
moftaxar	مـ ف تخر	proud
mofti	مـ ف تی	free of charge

moftxor	مـ فـ تخور	parasite, sponger
mohabbat	محـبت	kindness, affection
mohabbat amiz	محـبت آمـیز	affectionate, kind
mohaddab	محدب	convex
mohäfez	محاف ظـ	guard, protector
mohäfezat	محاف ظت	protection, conservation
mohäfezat kardan	محافظت کردن	to protect
mohäfezekär	محاف ظه کـ ار	conservative
mohäjer	مهاجر	immigrant, migrant
mohäjerat	مهاجرت	immigration, migration
mohäjerat kardan	مهاجرت کردن	to immigrate, to migrate
mohäkeme	محاک مه	trial, hearing
mohäkeme kardan	محاک مه کردن	to try (in court)
mohäkemeye sahräyi	محاک مه صحرایـ ی	court marshal
mohandes	مه ندس	engineer
mohandesi	مه ند سی	engineering
mohaqqar	محقر	small, humble
mohaqqeq	محقق	researcher, scholar
moharrek	محرک	motive, stimulus
mohäsebe	محا سـ به	calculation, computation
mohäsere	محا صره	siege, surrounding
mohäsere kardan	محا صره کردن	to surround
mohassel	محصل	student, learner
mohävere	محاوره	conversation, dialogue
mohayyä kardan	مه یا کردن	to prepare
mohayyej	مه یج	exciting, provocative
mohebat	موهبت	gift, blessing
mohemm	مهم	important, serious
mohemmät	مهمات	ammunitions
mohen	موهن	insulting, offensive
mohit	محـیط	environment, circumference
mohite zist	محـیط زیـ ست	ecology
mohiti	محـیطی	environmental

mohkam	محکم	firm, strong, tight
mohlat	مهلت	deadline, respite, time
mohlek	مهلک	fatal, lethal, dangerous
mohmal	مهمل	nonsense, absurd, silly
mohr	مهر	seal, stamp, seal ring
mohr zadan	مهر زدن	to seal, to stamp
mohre	مهره	bead, marble, vertebra
mohre därän	مهره داران	vertebrate
mohtäj	محتاج	needy, poor
mohtaker	محتکر	hoarders
mohtaram	محترم	respected, honourable
mohtaramäne	محترمانه	respectfully
mohtät	محتاط	cautious, careful
mohtavi	محتوی	containing, consisting
mohum	موهم	imaginary, fanciful
mohumät	موهومات	superstitions, imaginations
moj	موج	wave, surge, surf
mojdär	موج دار	wavy, curly
mojaddad	مجدد	again, once more
mojähed	مجاهد	fighter of holy war
mojahhaz	مجهز	equipped, prepared
mojallal	مجلل	glorious, grand
mojarrad	مجرد	single, bachelor
mojarradi	مجردی	bachelorhood
mojassame	مجسمه	statue, sculpture
mojavvez	مجوز	warrant, licence
mojazzä	مجزا	isolated, analysed
mojeb	موجب	cause, causing
mojer	موجر	landlord, owner, lender
mojrem	مجرم	guilty, criminal
mojri	مجری	director, executive
mojtahed	مجتهد	high ranking clergyman
mojtame[3]	مجتمع	complex, gathering

mojud	موجود	existing, creature, present
mojud budan	موجود بودن	to exist
mojudät	موجودات	creatures, species
mojudi	موجودی	asset, stock
moka³ab	مكعب	cube, cubic
mokäfät	مكافات	retribution, retaliation
mokallaf	مكلف	bound, mature to practice
mokammel	مكمل	complementary
mokarrar	مكرر	repeated, recurrent
mokassar	مكسر	irregular
mokätebe	مكاتبه	correspondence
mokul	موكول	dependent, pending
moläheze	ملاحظه	consideration, notice
moläqät	ملاقات	meeting, visit
moläqät kardan	ملاقات كردن	to meet, to visit
moläqäti	ملاقاتی	visitor
molavvan	ملون	coloured
moläyem	ملايم	mild, gentle, quiet
molayyen	ملين	laxative
molhaq šodan	ملحق شدن	to join
molhed	ملهد	atheist, apostate
mollä	ملا	clergy, theologian
molokol	ملكول	molecule
moltafet	ملتفت	aware, attentive
moltaheb	ملتهب	inflamed, burning
molud	مولود	born, generated, birthday
momäne³at	ممانعت	prevention, prohibition
momäs	مماس	touching, tangent
momayyez	مميز	decimal, point, auditor
momen	مومن	believer, faithful
momken	ممكن	possible, feasible
momtad	ممتد	continuous, extended
momtane³	ممتنع	abstention, blank vote

mon³akes kardan	منعکس کردن	To reflect, to echo
mon³aqed kardan	منعقد کردن	To hold, to tie
monabbat	منبت	inlaid, embossed
monabbat käri	منبت کاری	inlaid work, embossment
monäfät	منافات	incompatibility, contradiction
monäfeq	منافق	hypocrite, double-crosser
monäjät	مناجات	prayer, chanting
monajjem	منجم	astronomer, astrologer
monäqese	مناقصه	tender
monäqeše	مناقشه	dispute, controversy
monäseb	مناسب	proper, suitable, fit
monäsebat	مناسبت	connection, pertinence
monavvar	منور	bright, lighted
monäzere	مناظره	debate, dispute
monazzam	منظم	disciplined, regular, orderly
mondares	مندرس	worn out
monfa³el	منفعل	passive, inactive
monfajer	منفجر	blown up, exploded
monfajer šodan	منفجرشدن	to blow up, to explode
monfajere	منفجره	explosive
monfared	منفرد	single, isolated
monhadem kardan	منهدم کردن	to destroy, to demolish
monhal kardan	منحل کردن	to dissolved, to close
monhani	منحنی	curve, bend
monharef	منحرف	deviated, pervert
monharef šodan	منحرف شدن	to deviate
monhaser	منحصر	confined, exclusive
monjamed šodan	منجمد شدن	to freeze
monjar šodan	منجرشدن	to result in, to lead to
monji	منجی	saviour
monker šodan	منکر شدن	to deny
monqabez šodan	منقبض شدن	to contract
monqaleb šodan	منقلب شدن	to changed

monqarez šodan	مـ ذ قرض شدن	to extinct, to overthrow
monqate³ šodan	مـ ذ قطع شدن	to cut off, to be truncated
monqazi šodan	مـ ذ قـ ضـی شدن	to expire, to end
monša³eb šodan	منشعب شدن	to branch, to be subdivided
monsaref šodan	مـ ذ صـرف شدن	to change mind, to give up
monsef	منصف	just, fair
monsefäne	مـ ذ صـ فـاذه	fair, impartially
monši	مـ ذ شـی	secretary
monšigari	مـ ذ شـ يـگری	secretarial job
montabeq	مـ نط بق	conforming, coinciding
montahä	مـ ذ تها	end, extreme, by and large
montaqed	مـ ذ تـقد	critic
montaqel kardan	مـ ذ تـقل كردن	to move, to transfer
montašer kardan	مـ ذ شركردن	to publish, to print
montaxab	مـ ذ تخب	selected, chosen, elected
montazer	مـ ذ تظر	waiting, expectant
moqa³arr	مـ قـعر	concave
moqäbel	مـ قاب ل	front, opposite, against
moqäbele kardan	مـ قاب له كردن	to confront
moqaddam	مـ قدم	preferred, foremost
moqaddamät	مـ قدمات	rudiments, first steps
moqaddamäti	مـ قدماتـ ى	preliminary, primary
moqaddame	مـ قدمه	preface, introduction
moqaddarät	مـ قدرات	destiny, decrees
moqaddas	مـ قدس	holy, scared, saint
moqalled	مـ قـلد	follower in faith
moqanni	مـ قـ نـى	well digger
moqärebat	مـ قارب ت	intercourse, coition, mating
moqärebati	مـ قارب تـى	venereal, sexual
moqären	مـ قارن	coinciding with, synchronic
moqarrar	مـ قرر	decided, arranged
moqarrari	مـ قررى	income, salary, wage
moqarrarät	مـ قررات	rules, regulations

moqasser	مـقـصر	guilty, offender, responsible
moqäte³e	مـقاطـعه	contract
moqäte³e kär	مـقاطـعه کـار	contractor
moqatta³	مـقطع	interrupted, cut into pieces
moqattar	مـقطر	distilled
moqävem	مـقاوم	resistant, enduring
moqävemat	مـقاومت	resistance, perseverance
moqävemat kardan	مـقاومت کردن	to resist
moqavvä	مـقوا	cardboard
moqavvi	مـقوی	tonic, nourishing
moqäyer	مغايـر	contradictory, incompatible
moqäyerat	مغايـرت	contradiction, disagreement
moqäyese	مـقايـسه	comparison
moqäyese kardan	مـقايـسه کردن	to compare
moqayyad	مـقـيد	bound, conservative
moqazzi	مغذی	nutritional, rich
moqe³	موقع	time, occasion, moment
moqe³iyyat	موقـعـيت	position, circumstance
moqim	مـقـيم	resident
moqolestän	مغول سـتان	Mongolia
moqol	مغول	Mongolian
moqrez	مغرض	biased, spiteful
moqtader	مـقـتدر	powerful, strong, potent
moqtanam	مغـتنم	valued, useful
moqtazi	مـقـتضی	appropriate, advisable
moqtaziyät	مـقـتضـيات	circumstances, exigencies
moquf	موقـوف	suspended, abolished
moqufät	موقـوفـات	endowment, charity
morä³ät	مراعات	observance, consideration
morabbä	مربـا	jam, preserve
morabba³	مربـع	square, quadrangle
morabbi	مربـی	trainer, coach, mentor
moräd	مراد	wish, desire, intension

moraddad	مردد	uncertain, hesitant
moräje³e	مراجعه	reference, referral
morakkab	مركب	ink, compound, consist of
morakkabät	مركبات	citrus fruits
moräqeb	مراقب	observant, alert, vigilant
moräqebat	مراقبت	attention, supervision, watch
moräqebat kardan	مراقبت كردن	to watch, to guard, to care
morattab	مرتب	tidy, orderly, punctual
morattab kardan	مرتب كردن	to tidy up, to arrange
moraxxas	مرخص	released, dismissed
moraxxasi	مرخصى	leave of absence, release
mordäb	مرداب	lagoon, marsh
mordäd	مرداد	fifth Persian month
mordan (mir)	مردن (مير)	to die, to pass away
mordani	مردنى	dying, doomed to death
mordär	مردار	corpse
morde	مرده	dead, deceased, obsolete
mordešur	مرده شور	washer of the dead
mored	مورد	case, instance, application
morid	مريد	disciple, follower
morovvat	مروت	compassion, generosity
morq	مرغ	hen, chicken
morqäbi	مرغابى	duck
moršed	مرشد	spiritual guide, instructor
morta³eš šodan	مرتعش شدن	to tremble, to vibrate
mortad	مرتد	apostate
mortafe³	مرتفع	high, elevated, raised
mortaje³	مرتجع	conservative, fanatic
mortakeb šodan	مرتكب شدن	to commit an action
mortäz	مرتاض	yogi
morur	مرور	review, passing
morur kardan	مرور كردن	to review, to rehearse
morvärid	مرواريد	pearl

mosä³ed	مساعد	in accord, favourable
mosä³edat	مساعدت	assistance, aid
mosä³ede	مساعده	advance payment
mošäbeh	مشابه	identical, similar, alike
mošäbehat	مشابهت	similarity, resemblance
mosäbeqe	مسابقه	competition, race, match
mosäbeqe dädan	مسابقه دادن	to compete, to race
mosädef	مصادف	coincident, concurrent
mosäfer	مسافر	passenger, traveller
mosäferat	مسافرت	travel, journey, trip
mosäferat kardan	مسافرت کردن	to travel
mosäferxäne	مسافرخانه	inn, motel, lodge
mosähebe	مصاحبه	interview
mosähebe kardan	مصاحبه کردن	to interview
mošähede	مشاهده	observation, noticing
mošähede kardan	مشاهده کردن	to observe, to notice
mošäjere	مشاجره	quarrel, dispute, debate
mošäjere kardan	مشاجره کردن	to quarrel, to dispute
mosakken	مسکن	sedative, pain killer
mosälehe	مصالحه	compromise, settlement
mosälehe kardan	مصالحه کردن	to compromise, to settle
mosallä	مصلا	place for public prayer
mosallah	مسلح	armed, equipped
mosallahäne	مسلحانه	armed
mosallam	مسلم	certain, definite, proved
mosallaman	مسلما	certainly, definitely
mosallat	مسلط	dominant, predominant
mosalmän	مسلمان	moslem
mosalmäni	مسلمانى	being moslem
mosalsal	مسلسل	machine gun, serial
mosammam	مصمم	determined
mošärekat	مشارکت	partnership, participation
mošärekat kardan	مشارکت کردن	to attend, to participate

mosattah	مسطح	flat, plane
mosävät	مساوات	equality
mošäver	مشاور	counsellor, advisor
mošävere	مشاوره	consultation, advice
mosävi	مساوى	equal, alike, even, the same
mosavvabe	مصوبه	approved, passed
mosavvat	مصوت	vowel, voiced
mošavveq	مشوق	motive, patron
mošaxxas	مشخص	distinct, specific
mošaxxas kardan	مشخص کردن	to specify, to clarify
mošaxxasät	مشخصات	features, particulars
mošäye³at kardan	مشایعت کردن	to see off, to escort
mosen	مسن	old, aged, senile
moshel	مسهل	laxative
mosibat	مصیبت	disaster, catastrophe
moškel	مشکل	difficult, hard, problem
moškel pasand	مشکل پسند	fussy, fastidious
mosko	مسکو	moscow
mosleh	مصلح	reformist, peace maker
moslem	مسلم	moslem
moslemin	مسلمین	moslems
mosnad	مسند	predicate
mošref	مشرف	close to, adjacent, near
mošrek	مشرک	dualist, polytheist
mošt	مشت	fist, punch, handful
mosta³är	مستعار	pen name
mosta³ed	مستعد	talented, fit, ready
mosta³jer	مستاجر	tenant
mosta³mal	مستعمل	second hand, used
mosta³mere	مستعمره	colony
mostabed	مستبد	autocrat, dictator
mostahab	مستحب	religious precepts
mostahjan	مستهجن	obscene, pornographic

mostahlak	مـسـتهـلك	worn out, absorbed
mostakber	مـسـتـكـبر	arrogant
mostalzem	مـسـتـلزم	requiring
mostamar	مـسـتمر	continuous, constant
mostame³	مـسـتمع	listener, audience
mostamerri	مـسـتمرى	pension
mostanad	مـسـتـند	documentary, supported
moštäq	مـشـتاق	eager, keen
mostaqarr šodan	مـسـتـقرشدن	to settle
mostaqell	مـسـتـقل	independent, autonomous
mostaqim	مـسـتـقـيم	straight, direct
mostaqiman	مـسـتـقـيما	directly
mostaräh	مستراح	toilet, lavatory
moštarak	مـشـترك	shared, joint, common
moštarek olmanäfe³	مـشـترك الـمـنافـع	commonwealth
moštari	مـشـترى	customer, client, jupiter
mostatil	مـسـتطـيل	rectangle
mostaxdem	مـسـتخدم	employee, servant, janitor
moštbäzi	مـشتـبـازى	boxing
mostmand	مـسـتهـند	poor, needy
moštzan	مـشتزن	boxer
mosuf	موصوف	characterised by
mosum	موسوم	called, named, labelled
mot	موت	death, demise
mota³added	مـتعددد	numerous, several
mota³ädel	متعادل	balanced, stable
mota³ahhed	مـتعهد	committed, bound, obliged
mota³ahhel	مـتاهل	married
mota³ajjeb	مـتعجب	surprised, amazed
mota³äl	مـتعال	exalted, sublime
mota³alleq	مـتعـلق	belonging, pertaining
mota³asseb	مـتعـصب	fanatical, zealous
mota³assef	مـتاسف	sorry, sad

mota³assefäne	مـ تا س فانـه	unfortunately
mota³asser	مـ تاثّ ر	sorry, sad, touched
motäbeq	مطابـ ق	according to, corresponding
motäbeqat	مطابـ قت	conformity, contrast
motadävel	مـ تداول	common, usual
motadayyen	مـ تديـ ن	religious
motafakker	مـ تـ فـکر	thoughtful, contemplating
motafarreqe	متفرقه	miscellaneous, different
motafävet	مـ تـ فاوت	different, varied
motahammel šodan	مـ تحمل شدن	to suffer, to bear, to sustain
motaharrek	مـ تحرک	mobile, moving
motahavvel šodan	مـ تحول شدن	to change, to evolve
motahayyer šodan	مـ تحـ یر شدن	to be astonished
motahhar	مطهر	pure, holy, scared
motajadded	مـ تجدد	modernised, modern
motajävez	مـ تجاوز	aggressive, offensive
motakabber	مـ تـ کـ بر	arrogant, snob
motakkä	مـ تـ کا	pillow
motäle³e	مطالعه	study, survey, consideration
motäle³e kardan	مطالـ عه کردن	to study, to consider
motälebe kardan	مطالـ به کردن	to demand
motallaqe	مطل ا قه	divorced
motamadden	متمدن	civilised, cultured
motamalleq	مـ تمـ لق	flattering, toady
motamarkez	مـ تمرکـ ز	concentrated, centralised
motammem	مـ تمم	supplement
motanaffer	مـ تـ نـ فر	hating, disgusted
motanäseb	مـ تـ نا سب	proportionate, symmetrical
motanavve³	مـ تـ نوع	various, diverse
motaqalleb	مـ تـ قـ لب	cheater, dishonest
motaqayyer	مـ تـ غـ یر	changing, variable, unstable
motaqäzi	مـ تـ قا ضی	applicant
motarädef	مـ ترادف	synonym

motaraqqi	م ترقّی	advanced, progressive
motarjem	م ترجم	translator, interpreter
motarjemi	م ترجمی	translation job
motasaddi	م تصدی	in charge
motašakker	م تشکر	thankful, grateful
motašannej	م تشنج	confused, disturbed
motavajjeh	م توجه	attentive, directed toward
motavajjeh šodan	م توجه شدن	to notice, to understand
motaväli	م توالی	continuous, successive
motavalled šodan	م تولد شدن	to be born
motavaqqe[3]	م توقع	expecting
motavaqqef šodan	م توقف شدن	to stop
motaväri šodan	م تواری شدن	to run away, to escapee
motavasset	م توسط	mean, average, ordinary
motaväze[3]	متواضع	humble, modest
motaväzi	م توازی	parallel
motaxasses	م تخصص	expert, specialist
motazäher	م تظاهر	pretentious
motezäd	م تضاد	opposed, antonym, adverse
moti[3]	مط یع	obedient, submissive
motlaq	مط لق	absolute, pure, definite
motlaqan	مط ل قا	absolutely
motma[3]enn	مطم نن	confident, certain, sure
motma[3]ennan	مطم ذ نا	certainly
motor	موت ور	engine, motorcycle
motori	موت وری	motorised, mechanised
motorsiklet	موتور سیکلت	motorcycle, motor bike
motreb	مطرب	musician
mottafeqin	م تفق ین	the allies
mottaham	م تهم	accused, charged, indicted
mottaham kardan	متهم کردن	to accuse
mottahed	م تحد	united, ally
mottahed šodan	م تحد شدن	to unite

mottaki budan	مـ تـکی بودن	to rely on, to depend on
mottale³	مطالـ عه	informed, aware, conscious
mottale³ kardan	مطالعه کردن	to study
mottasel	مـ تـصل	connected, joined, attached
moväfeq	موافـ ق	agree, congruent
moväfeq budan	موافـ قبودن	to agree
moväfeqat	موافـ قت	agreement, consent
moväfeqat kardan	موافـ قت کردن	to agree
moväfeqat näme	موافـ قت ذامه	contract
movaffaq	موفـ ق	successful, prosperous
movaffaq šodan	موفـ ق شدن	to succeed
movaffaqiyyat	موفـ قـ یت	success, prosperity
moväjeh	مواجه	facing, confronting
moväjeh šodan	مواجه شدن	to face, to confront
moväjehe	مواجهه	confrontation, encounter
movajjah	موجه	permitted, justified
movakkel	موکـ ل	client
movalled	مولـ د	generator, producer
movaqqat	موقـ ت	temporary, casual
movarrab	مورب	oblique, slant
movarrax	مورخ	dated
movarrex	مورخ	historian
moväzeb	مواظب	careful, heedful
moväzebat	مواظـ بت	care, heed, watching
moväzebat kardan	مواظـ بت کردن	to care, to protect
moväzene	موازذه	balance, equilibrium
moväzi	موازی	parallel
mox	مخ	brain, cerebrum
moxadder	مخدر	narcotic
moxaffaf	مخـ فف	abbreviated, short form
moxälef	مخالـ ف	opponent, opposite
moxälefat	مخالـ فت	objection, disagreement
moxallafät kardan	مخالـ فت کردن	to oppose, to disagree

moxammer	مخمر	fermented, yeast
moxarreb	مخرب	destructive, vandal
moxäteb	مخاطب	addressee
moxče	مخچه	cerebellum
moxles	مخلص	devoted, sincerely
moxtalef	مخـتـلف	various, different, diverse
moxtalet	مخـتـلط	mixed, bisexual
moxtall	مخـتـل	disturbed, disorganised
moxtare³	مخـترع	inventor
moxtasar	مخـتـصر	brief, short, abstract
moyassar	میسر	possible, feasible
moz	موز	banana
mozä³af	مضاعف	double, extra
mozäb	مذاب	melted, thawed
mozäf	مضاف	added
mozähem	مزاحم	troublesome, nuisance
mozähem šodan	مزاحم شدن	to annoy, to disturb
mozähemat	مزاحمت	nuisance, interruption
možak	مژک	cilia
mozäkere	مذاکره	discussion, negotiation
mozäkere kardan	مذاکره کردن	to discuss, to negotiate
mozakkar	مذکر	male, masculine
mozäre³	مضارع	tense for present and past
mozaxraf	مزخرف	absurd, nonsense
mozäyede	مزایده	auction, bid, tender
mozäyeqe	مضایقه	refraining, refusal
mozd	مزد	wage, pay
možde	مژده	good news
moždegäni	مژدگانی	reward for good news
mozdur	مزدور	hired worker, mercenary
može	مژه	eyelash
moze³	موضع	position, location, situation
moze³i	موضعی	local

mozerr	مضر	harmful, damaging
mozmen	مزمن	chronic
moztareb	مضطرب	anxious, restless, worried
mozu³	موضوع	subject, topic, issue
mozun	موزون	rhythmical, elegant
mu	مو	hair
mum	موم	wax
mumiyäyi	موه يابی	mummy
munes	مونس	companion, confident
murče	مورچه	ant
murmur	مورمور	creep (slang)
muryäne	موريانه	termite
muš	موش	mouse, rat
musä	موسی	moses
mušak	موشک	missile, rocket
mušekäfi	موشکافی	scrutiny, minuteness
musemi	موسمی	seasonal
musiqi	موسیقی	music
musiqidän	موسیقی دان	musician
muyrag	مويرگ	capillary
muze	موزه	museum
muzi	موذی	harmful, noxious
muzik	موزيک	music

N		
na	ﻧﻪ	no, neither, nor, not
nä amn	ﻧﺎ اﻣﻦ	unsafe, insecure, dangerous
nä javän mard	ﻧﺎﺟﻮاﻧﻤﺮد	unmanly, ungenerous
nä omid	ﻧﺎ اﻣﻴﺪ	hopeless, desperate
na³l	ﻧﻌﻞ	horseshoe
na³lbaki	ﻧﻌﻠﺒﻜﻰ	saucer
na³lband	ﻧﻌﻠﺒﻨﺪ	farrier
na³leyn	ﻧﻌﻠﻴﻦ	clergy slippers
na³nä	ﻧﻌﻨﺎ	spearmint, mint
na³re	ﻧﻌﺮه	yell, loud cry, roar
na³re zadan	ﻧﻌﺮه زدن	to yell
na³š	ﻧﻌﺶ	dead body, remains
na³uz belläh	ﻧﻌﻮذ ﺑﺎ ﻟﻠﻪ	we seek refuge in god
näb	ﻧﺎب	pure, clean
nabäb	ﻧﺎﺑﺎب	unfit
nabädä	ﻧﺎ ﺑﺎدا	never, beware
näbäleq	ﻧﺎﺑﺎﻟﻎ	immature, minor
nabaräbari	ﻧﺎﺑﺮاﺑﺮى	inequality
nabard	ﻧﺎ ﺑﺮد	fight, war, battle
nabät	ﻧﺎ ﺑﺎت	plant, rock sugar
nabäti	ﻧﺎ ﺑﺎﺗﻰ	related to plants
nabavi	ﻧﺎ ﺑﻮى	prophetic
näbehengäm	ﻧﺎﺑﻬﻨﮕﺎم	untimely, premature
näbejä	ﻧﺎﺑﺠﺎ	inappropriate, unwise
näbekär	ﻧﺎ ﺑﻜﺎر	wicked, useless
näbeqe	ﻧﺎﺑﻐﻪ	genius, gifted
näbesämän	ﻧﺎﺑﺴﺎﻣﺎن	disorganised, chaotic
nabi	ﻧﺎ ﺑﻰ	prophet, messenger
näbinä	ﻧﺎﺑﻴﻨﺎ	blind
näbinäyi	ﻧﺎﺑﻴﻨﺎﻳﻰ	blindness
nabš	ﻧﺒﺶ	exhumation, corner

näbud	ذ اب ود	extinct, vanished
näbudi	ذ اب ودی	destruction, extinction
nabz	ذ بض	pulse, beating
näčär	ذ اچار	helpless, inevitably
näčäri	ذ اچاری	helplessness, distress
näčiz	ذ اچ يز	trivial, petty
nädän	ذ ادان	ignorant, fool
nädäni	نادانی	ignorance, illiteracy
nädem	ذ ادم	regretful, sorry
näder	نادر	rare, scarce
nädorost	ذ ادر ست	incorrect, false, wrong
nädoxtari	نا دختری	step daughter
näf	ذ اف	umbilicus, centre
naf[3]	ذ فع	profit, benefit, interest
nafaqe	ذ ف قه	alimony, subsistence
nafar	ذ فر	individual, person
nafar bar	ذ فرب ر	personnel carrier
nafarät	ذ فرات	soldiers
näfarmäni	ذ اف رماذ ی	disobedience
nafas	ذ فس	breath, respiration, instance
nafis	ذ ف يس	exquisite, precious, costly
nafs	ذ فس	essence, self, soul
nafsäni	ذ ف ساذ ی	material, physical, bodily
naft	ذ فت	kerosene, petroleum, oil
nafte xäm	ذ فت خام	crude oil
naftkeš	ذ ف ت کش	oil tanker
nafty	ذ ف تی	oily, related to petroleum
nafx	ذ فخ	swelling, bloating, inflation
nafy	ذ فی	rejection, denial, negation
nägäh	ذ اگ اه	suddenly, all at once
nägahän	ذ اگ هان	suddenly, out of the blue
nägahäni	ذ اگ هاذ ی	unexpected, sudden
nagäštan(negär)	نگاشتن (نگار)	to write, to draw

nägofte	ذاگ ف ته	unsaid, unmentioned
nägovär	ذاگ وار	unpleasant, unpalatable
nägozir	ذاگ زیر ر	inevitable, indispensable
nahäd	ذهاد	subject, nature, disposition
nahäl	ذهال	twig, young tree or shrub
nähamvär	ذاهوار	uneven, rough
nahän	ذهان	hidden, concealed
nahang	ذهنگ	whale
nähanjär	ذاهنجار	abnormal, rough, coarse
nähaq	ذاحق	unjustified, unfair
nähär	ذاهار	lunch
nähär xori	نهار خوری	dining room
nahäyat	ذهایت	extreme, utmost, maximum
nähid	ذاهید	venus
nahif	ذ ح یف	weak, thin, frail
nähiye	ذاح یه	region, area, district
nahofte	ذه ف ته	hidden, covert, latent
nahr	ذهر	creek, river, stream
nahs	ذ حس	ominous, unlucky, sinister
nahv	ذ حو	syntax
nahve	ذ حوه	method, way, manner
nahy	ذهی	ban, restrain, forbidding
najes	ذ جس	unclean, filthy, polluted
näji	ذاجی	savoir, saver
najib	ذ ج یب	noble, decent, chaste
najjar	ذ جار	carpenter
najjari	ذ جاری	carpentry
näjur	ذاجور	ill-matched, incongruous
najvä	ذ جوا	whisper
näkäm	ذاک ام	unsuccessful, disappointed
nakare	ذ کره	indefinite
näkas	ذاک س	detestable, mean, coward
nälän	ذالان	groaning, moaning

näle	نا له	groan, whimper
nälidan(näl)	ناليدن (نال)	to moan, to groan
nam	نم	moisture, humidity
näm	نام	name, title
näm nevisi	نام نويسى	enrolment, registration
näm neveštan	نام نوشتن	to enrol, to register
namä	نما	sight, index, median
näma³lum	نامعلوم	unknown, undecided, vague
näma³qul	نامعقول	irrational, illogical
namad	نمد	felt
namäd	نماد	symbol
nämädari	نامادرى	step mother
nämafhum	نامفهوم	unintelligible, vague
nämahdud	نامحدود	infinite, unlimited
nämahram	نامحرم	stranger, not a close kin
namak	نمک	salt, charm
namak dän	نمک دان	saltshaker
namak päš	نمک پاش	saltshaker
namak zär	نمکزار	salt marsh
nämar³i	نامرئى	invisible
nämarbut	نامربوط	irrelevant, unrelated
nämard	نامرد	unmanly, coward
nämardi	نامردى	cowardliness, foul play
nämašru³	نامشروع	illegitimate, bastard, illegal
nämatbu³	نامطبوع	undesirable
namäya degi	نمايندگى	representation, agency
namäyän	نمايان	revealed, apparent
namäyande	نماينده	representative
namäyande gän	نمايندگان	representatives, delegates
namäyeš	نمايش	show, exhibition, play
namäyeš gäh	نمايشگاه	exhibit, fair
namäyeš näme	نمايشنامه	play
namäyeš nämenevis	نمايشنامه نويس	playwright

namäz	نماز	prayer
namäzxän	نمازخوان	prayer person
namäzxäne	نماز خانه	place for praying
nämborde	نامه برده	above-mentioned
nämdär	نامدار	popular, famous
näme	نامه	letter
näme fämil	نامه فامیل	family name
näme negäri	نامه نگاری	correspondence
näme rasän	نامه رسان	mailman, postman
nämehrabän	نامهربان	unkind, cold
namnäk	نمناک	damp, moist, muggy
namnam	نمنم	fine drops, drizzle
nämonäseb	نامناسب	improper, inappropriate
nämonazzam	نامنظم	irregular, unorganised,
nämorattab	نامرتب	clumsy, untidy, disorganised
nämus	ناموس	chastity, principle, reputation
nämzad	نامزد	fiancée, nominee, engaged
nämzadi	نامزدی	engagement, nomination
nän	نان	bread
nän ävar	نان آور	bread winner, supporter
nänajib	ناذجیب	unchaste, not noble
nänavä	ناذوا	baker
nänaväyi	ناذوایی	bakery
nane	ننه	mum, nanny
nang	ننگ	shame, disgrace, scorn
nang ävar	ننگ آور	disgraceful, shameful
nangin	ننگین	shameful, disgraceful
nanu	ننو	hammock
näpadid šodan	ناپدید شدن	to disappear
näpäk	ناپاک	dirty, unclean
näpasand	ناپسند	indecent
näpäydär	ناپایدار	transient, inconsistent
näpedari	ناپدری	stepfather

näpesari	ناپ سری	stepson
näpoxte	ناپ خ ته	raw, crude, uncooked
näqäbel	ناق اب ل	worthless, insignificant
naqb	ن قب	burrow, tunnel, shaft
naqd	ن قد	cash, ready money
naqdi	ن قدی	in cash
näqel	ناق ل	conductor, carrier
näqes	ناق ص	incomplete, defective
naqiz	ن ق يض	contradictory, contrary
naql	ن قل	narration, quotation
naql kardan	ن قل	to narrate, to quote
naqle qol	ن قل ق ول	citation, quotation
naqliye	ن ق ل يه	transport means, vehicles
naqme	ن غمه	song, melody
näqolä	ناق لا	naughty, cunning, clever
naqqäd	ن قاد	critic, reviewer
naqqäl	ن قال	narrator, storyteller
naqqäre	ن قاره	kettledrum
naqqäš	ن قاش	painter, portrayer
naqqäši	ن قا شی	painting, drawing, portraying
naqqäši kardan	ن قا شی کردن	to paint, to draw
naqs	ن قص	fault, deficiency, defect
naqš	ن قش	picture, design, painting
naqše	ن ق شه	map, plan, model
naqše kešidan	ن ق شه کشیدن	to map, to plan
naqše bardäri	ن ق شه ب رداری	topography, mapping
naqše keš	ن ق شه ک ش	draftsman, planner, drawer
naqše keši	ن ق شه ک شی	surveying, mapping
näqus	ناق وس	bell, chime
naqz	ن قض	violation, breach
naqz kardan	ن قض کردن	to violate, to breach
nar	ن ر	male, man, masculine
närähat	ناراحت	uncomfortable, sad

närähati	ناراحتى	discomfort, annoyance
näras	ناراس	immature, unripe, green
näräzi	ناراضى	dissatisfied, discontented
nard	نرد	backgammon
narde	نرده	fence, hedge
nardebän	نردبان	ladder
närej	نارنج	sour orange
närengi	نارنگى	mandarin
närenjak	نارنجک	grenade, shell
närenji	نارنجى	orange colour
narges	نرگس	daffodil
närgil	نارگيل	coconut
narm	نرم	soft, smooth, gentle
narmeš	نرمش	work out, warm up, softness
näru	نارو	double cross, foul play
närvan	نارون	elm tree
nasab	نسب	genealogy, lineage
nasabi	نسبى	consanguineous, ancestral
näšäyeste	ناشايسته	indecent, improper
näsäzgär	ناسازگار	maladjusted, unsuitable
nasb	نصب	planting, installing
nasb kardan	نصب کردن	to plant, to install, to set up
näšenäs	ناشناس	unknown, stranger
näšenavä	ناشنوا	deaf
näšenaväyi	ناشنوايى	deafness
näšer	ناشر	publisher
nasezä	ناسزا	swear, curse, coarse
nasezä goftan	ناسزاگفتن	to swear, to curse
näši	ناشى	naive, , novice, resulting
nasib	نصيب	share, portion, destiny
našib	نشيب	slope, descent
näši	ناشى	naive, clumsy
näšigari	ناشيگرى	inexperience, clumsiness

nasihat	نـ صـ يحت	advice, counsel
nasihat kardan	نصيحت كردن	to advise
nasim	نـ سـ يم	breeze
nasj	نـ سج	tissue, texture
nasl	نـ سل	race, generation, offspring
näšokr	ناشكر	ungrateful, unthankful
nasr	نـ ثر	prose
našr	نـ شر	publication, spreading
našriyyät	نـ شريات	publications
nassäji	نـ ساجى	weaving
našt	نـ شت	leak, seeping
našt kardan	نـ شت كردن	to leak
näštä	ناشـ تا	empty-stomach, breakfast
nastaran	نـ سـ ترن	sweetbrier
nasuz	نـ سوز	fireproof
našv	نشو	growth
nätamäm	ناتـ مام	incomplete, unfinished
natars	نترس	bold, fearless, brave
nätavän	ناتـ وان	weak, powerless, impotent
nätaväni	ناتـ وانى	weakness, impotence
näteq	نـ اطق	speaking, vocal
natije	نـ تـ يجه	result, consequence
näto	ناتـ و	charlatan
näv	نـ او	warship, vessel, frigate
näv dän	نـ او دان	drain pipe
näv ostovär	نـ او سـ توار	naval warrant officer
näv šekan	نـ او شـ كن	destroyer
navä	نـ وا	melody, tune, sustenance
navad	نـ ود	ninety
naväde	نـ واده	grand child
navadom	نـ ودم	ninetieth
navär	نـ وار	ribbon, cassette, tape, band
navär časb	نـ وارچ سب	adhesive tape

navasän	نوسان	fluctuation, vibration, sway
naväxtan(naväz)	نواختن (نواز)	to play music, to hit
naväzande	نوازنده	musical performer, musician
naväzandegi	نوازندگی	playing music
naväzeš	نوازش	patting, caress, fondling
naväzeš kardan	نوازش کردن	to pat, to fondle
naväzidan(naväz)	نوازیدن (نواز)	to play music, to pat
nävbän	ناوبان	lieutenant (navy)
nävbar	ناوبر	navigator
nävbari	ناوبری	navigation
nävče	ناوچه	small boat
nave	نوه	grandchild
näve haväpeymäbar	ناو هواپیمابر	aircraft carrier
navid	نوید	good news
navin	نوین	new, recent
nax	نخ	string, thread
nax risi	نخ ریسی	spinning
näxäste	ناخواسته	unwanted, uninvited
naxi	نخی	cotton
naxl	نخل	palm
naxlestän	نخلستان	palm grove
naxnomä	نخ نما	threadbare
näxodä	ناخدا	captain (of ship)
näxon	ناخن	nail, claw
näxon gir	ناخن گیر	nail clippers
näxonak	ناخنک	snitching, pilfering
näxoš	ناخوش	sick, ill
näxoši	ناخوشی	sickness, illness
naxost	نخست	first, foremost
naxost vazir	نخست وزیر	prime minister
naxostin	نخستین	the first
näy	نای	trachea
näyäb	نایاب	rare, extinct

näyeb	ناي ب	deputy, vice
näyeb ra³is	ناي ب رئ يس	vice president
näyel	ناي ل	achieving, attaining
näylon	ناي لون	plastic, nylon
näyže	ناي ژه	bronchus
näz	ناز	coyness, demurring
näz kardan	نازکردن	to cute-off
näz parvarde	ناز پرورده	pampered, spoiled
näzä	نازا	sterile, infertile, barren
näzäyi	نازایی	sterility, infertility
nazäkat	نزاک ت	elegance, courtesy
nazar	نظر	view, look, glance, opinion
nazar dädan	نظردادن	to comment
nazari	نظری	theoretical, speculative
nazarriye	نظریه	opinion, view, theory
nazarxähi	نظر خواهی	polling, opinion poll
nazd	نزد	near, by, among, by the side
nazdik	نزدیک	close, near, about
nazdik šodan	نزدیکشدن	to get closer, to approach
nazdikän	نزدی کان	relatives, kin
nazdikbin	نزدیک ب ین	near sighted, myopic
nazdikbini	نزدیک ب ینی	near-sightedness, myopia
nazdiki	نزدی کی	vicinity, intercourse
nazdiki kardan	نزدی کی کردن	to have intercourse
näzel šodan	نازلشدن	to descend, to fall
näzem	ناظم	regulator, assistant
näzer	ناظر	observer, supervisor
näzidan(näz)	نازیدن (ناز)	to boast of, to vaunt
nazir	نظ یر	match, equal, similar
nazm	نظم	order, regularity, discipline
nazm dädan	نظم دادن	to arrange, to sort
näzok	نازک	thin, tender, slim
näzok närenji	نازک نارنجی	fastidious

nazri	ذ ذری	vowed, oblatory
neᵉmat	ذ عمت	grace, blessing
nedä	ذ دا	call, evocation
nedämat	ذ دامت	regret, remorse
nefäq	ذ فاق	disunion, disharmony
nefrat	ذ فرت	hating, disgust, aversion
nefrat angiz	ذ فرت اذ گ يز	disgusting, repugnant
nefrin	ذ فرین ن	curse, evil words, damnation
nefrin kardan	ذ فرین کردن	to curse
negäh	ذ گاه	look, glance
negäh kardan	ذ گاه کردن	to look, to glance, to watch
negahbän	ذ گه بان	guard, watchman, keeper
negahbäni	نگهبانی	guarding, keeping, watching
negahdäri	ذ گهداری	keeping, taking care of
negahdäri kardan	نگهداری کردن	to keep, to take care of
negär xäne	ذ گار خاذه	gallery, painter's studio
negarän	ذ گران	worried, anxious, restless
negarän šodan	ذ گران شدن	to worry
negärande	ذ گارذ ده	author, writer
negaräni	ذ گراذ ی	worry, anxiety
negareš	ذ گرش	view point, opinion
negäreš	ذ گارش	writing, composing
negärestän	ذ گار س تان	picture's gallery, studio
negin	نگین	gem, of a ring, seal ring
nehzat	ذ هضت	movement, resurgence
nejäbat	ذ جاب ت	nobleness, nobility, chastity
nejät	ذ جات	salvation, rescue, relive
nejät dädan	ذ جات دادن	to rescue
nejät qariq	ذ جات غریق	life guard
nekäh	ذ کاح	marriage, matrimony, nuptial
nekbat	ذ ک بت	adversity, misery
nemudan(nemä)	نمودن (نما)	to do, to make, to perform
nemudär	ذ مودار	chart, table, diagram

nemune	ذموذه	sample, specimen, example
nemune bardäri	ذموذه برداری	sampling, biopsy
neqäb	ذ قاب	mask, veil
neqäbdär	دارذ قاب	veiled, masked
neqähat	ذ قاهت	ailment, indisposition
neqres	ذ قرس	gout
nerx	ذرخ	price, rate
nešä	ذ شا	seedling
nešädor	ذ شادر	sal ammoniac
nešän	ذ شان	mark, sign, brand, insignia
nešän dädan	نشان دادن	to show, to point out
nešäne	ذ شاذه	goal, target, mark, reminder
nešäne gereftan	ذ شاذه گرفتن	to aim
nešäne ravi	ذ شاذه روی	aiming
nešäni	ذ شاذی	address, sign, code word
nesär kardan	ذ ثاركردن	to bestow
nešast	ذ شست	meeting, sagging, subsiding
nešastan(nešin)	نشستن (نشين)	to sit, to sit down
nešäste	ذ شاسته	starch
nešät	ذ شاط	joy, freshness
nešät ävar	ذ شاط آور	joyful, cheerful, lively
nesbat	ذ س بت	relation, ratio, kinship
nesbatan	ذ س ب تا	relatively
nesbi	نسبی	relative, comparative
nesbiyat	ذ س ب یت	relativity
nesf	ذ صف	half
nesf onnahär	ذ صف ال نهار	line of longitude
nesfe	ذ صد فه	half-done
nešiman	ذ ش یمن	dwelling, lodging
nesye	ذ س یه	credit transaction
nevešt afzär	ذو شت اف زار	stationary
nevešt afzär foruši	نوشت افزار فروشی	stationary shop
neveštan (nevis)	سیون) نتشون)	to write, to put down

nevešte	ذوشته	written, manuscript
nevisande	ذویسنده	writer, author
nevisandegi	ذویسندگی	writing, authorship
ney	ذی	flute, bamboo
neyrang	ذیرذگ	deceit, trick, fraud
neyšakar	ذیشکر	sugar cane
neyzär	ذیزار	reed bed
nezä³	ذزاع	fight, war, quarrel
nežäd	ذژاد	race, tribe, ethnicity, breed
nežäd parast	ذژادپرست	racist
nežäd parasti	ذژادپرستی	racism
nežädi	ذژادی	racial, ethnic
nezäfat	ذظافت	cleanliness, neatness
nezäfat kardan	ذظافت کردن	to clean
nezäm	ذظام	order, regime
nezämi	ذظامی	limitary, martial
nezärat	ذظارت	supervision, inspection
nezärat kardan	ذظارت کردن	to supervise
nezäre	ذظاره	watching, looking
niku	ذیکو	good, excellent
nikukär	ذیکوکار	righteous, charity helper
nikukäri	ذیکوکاری	righteousness
nili	ذیلی	azure
nim	ذیم	half
nime	ذیمه	half, half size
nime afräšte	ذیمه افراشته	half mast
nime jän	ذیمه جان	half dead
nime käre	ذیمه کاره	incomplete, unfinished
nime nahäyi	ذیمه ذهایی	semi-final
nime šab	نیمه شب	midnight
nimkat	ذیمکت	bench, sofa
nimkore	ذیمکره	hemisphere
nimrox	نیمرخ	profile, vertical, silhouette

nimru	ن يمرو	scrambled egg
nimruz	ن يمروز	midday
nini	ن ی ن ی	baby
niru	ن يرو	power, strength, force
nirumand	ن يرومند	powerful, strong
niš	ن يش	a sting, prick
nist	ن يست	is not
ništar	نيشتر	lancet, stylet
nisti	ن ي س تی	non-existence
niyäbat	ن يابت	deputation, delegation
niyäkän	ن ياك ان	ancestors
niyäm	ن يام	sheath
niyäyeš	ن ياي ش	praise, praying
niyäz	ن ياز	need, requirement, exigency
niyäz däštan	نياز داشتن	to need, to require
niyäz mand	ن ياز مند	needy, in need
niyyat	نيت	intention, will, intent
niz	ن يز	also, too
nize	ن يزه	spear, dart
no	ن و	new, recent, modern
no ämuz	ن و آموز	novice, apprentice, beginner
no arus	ن وعروس	new bride
no ävari	ن وآوری	invention, innovation
no³	ن وع	type, kind
no³ dust	ن وعدوست	humanitarian
no³i	ن وعی	typical, specific
nobar	ن وب ر	first fruit, novel, rare
nobat	ن وب ت	turn, time, period
nobat gereftan	ن وب ت گرفتن	to take turn
nobati	ن وب تی	in turn, periodic
nobäve	ن وب اوه	child, youngster
nobe	نوبه	turn, intermittent
nobovvat	ن بوت	prophecy, prophetic mission

nobuq	نذ بوغ	talent, genius
noče	نوچه	novice, protégé
nofus	نذ فوس	population, lives
nofuz	نذ فوذ	influence, penetration
nofuz kardan	نذ فوذ كردن	to influence, to penetrate
noh	نذه	nine
nohe	نوحه	elegy, lament
nohexän	خوانذوحه	elegist, a hired mourner
nohom	نذهم	ninth
nojavän	نذوجوان	adolescent, teenager
nojaväni	نذوجوانی	adolescence, teenage
nojum	نذجوم	astrology, astronomy
nokar	نذوكر	servant, butler
nokte	نذ كته	point, pointer
nomovv	نذمو	growth
nomre	نذمره	number, grade, mark, point
nomre dädan	نذمره دادن	to number, to grade, to mark
nomre gozäri	نذمره گ ذاری	numbering, marking
noql	نذ قَل	a type of sweet
noqre	نذ قره	silver
noqreyi	نقره ای	of silver
noqsän	نذ قصان	shortage, lack, reduction
noqte	نذ قطه	point, dot, spot
noras	نذورس	fresh, young
noraside	نذور س يده	newborn, newcomer, fresh
noruz	نذوروز	the first day of Persian year
norvež	نذروژ	Norway
norveži	نذروژی	Norwegian
nosäxt	نذو ساخت	newly built
nosäzi	نذو سازی	renovation
nosäzi kardan	نوسازی كردن	to renovate, to rebuild
nošdäru	نذو شدارو	antidote
nosxe	نذ سخه	prescription, copy

notfe	نطفه	embryo, zygote
notq	نطق	speech, lecture
novämr	نوامبر	november
noxä³	نخاع	spine
noxäle	نخاله	sifting, rubbish
noxbe	نخبه	best part, chosen, the best
noxod	نخود	chickpea
noxodči	نخودچی	roasted pea
nozäd	نوزاد	baby, newborn
nozul	نزول	descent, fall, usury
nozul xär	نزول خوار	usurer
nozzär	نظار	spectators, watchers
nuh	نوح	noah
nuk	نوک	tip, nib, peak, top
nuktiz	نوک تیز	sharp-pointed
nur	نور	light, flash, beam
nurafkan	نورافکن	searchlight, limelight
nuräni	نورانی	sparkling, glittering, shinning
nurečešm	نورچشم	the apple of one's eye, dear
nušäbe	نوشابه	beverage, drink
nušidan(nuš)	نوشیدن (نوش)	to drink
nušidani	نوشیدنی	drink, beverage, drinkable
nuzdah	نوزده	nineteen
nuzdahom	نوزدهم	nineteenth

O		
obäš	اوب اش	lewd, rascals
obohhat	ابهت	dignity, glory
obur	ع بور	passing, passage, transit
obur kardan	ع بوركردن	to pass, to cross
ofoq	افق	horizon
ofoqi	افقى	horizontal
oft	افت	fall, shortage
oft kardan	افت كردن	to fall, to reduce
ofunat	ع فوذت	infection, stink
ofuni	ع فوذى	infectious, infected
ohde	عهده	responsibility, undertaking
oj	اوج	culmination, peak
ojäq	اجاق	oven, fireplace, stove
ojrat	اجرت	pay, earning
oksižen	اكسيژن	oxygen
oktobr	اكتبر	October
oläd	اولاد	children
oläq	الاغ	donkey
olgu	الگو	pattern, mould
oliyä	اوليا	saints
oltimätom	التيماتوم	ultimatum
olufe	ع لوف ه	forage, fodder
olyähazrat	ع ل ياحضرت	her majesty
omde	عمده	chief, main
omde foruš	عمده ف روش	wholesaler
omdeforuši	عمده ف رو شى	wholesale
omid	اميد	hope, expectation
omidvär	اميدوار	hopeful
ommat	امت	believers, followers
ommol	امل	old-fashioned
omq	عمق	depth, intensity

omr	عمر	life, lifetime, living
omr kardan	عمرکردن	to live
omrän	عمران	development, establishing
omum	عموم	all, the public, everyone
omumi	عمومی	universal, public, common
ons	انس	fellowship, acquaintance
ons gereftan	انس گرفتن	to get used to
onsor	عنصر	element, agent
onvän	عنوان	title, heading, topic
operä	اپرا	opera
operätor	اپراتور	operator
oqäb	عقاب	eagle, falcon
oqäf	اوقاف	charity, pious legacies
oqät	اوقات	times, hours
oqde	عقده	complex
oqiyänus	اقیانوس	ocean
oqiyänusiye	اقیانوسیه	Oceania
ordak	اردک	duck
ordangi	اردنگی	a kick on the back
ordibehešt	اردیبهشت	second Persian month
ordu	اردو	camp, urdu language
orf	عرف	tradition, custom
orib	اریب	diagonal
orkestr	ارکستر	orchestra
oryän	عریان	naked, nude, bare
orze	عرضه	capability, merit
osäre	عصاره	extract, essence, juice
osqof	اسقف	bishop
ostäd	استاد	professor, master, mentor
ostän	استان	province
oständär	استاندار	governor
ostexän	استخوان	bone
ostoväne	استوانه	cylinder

ostovär	استوار	warrant officer
otäq	اتاق	room, chamber
otäq xäb	اتاق خواب	bedroom
otriš	اتریش	austria
otriši	اتریشی	austrian
otubän	اتوبان	motorway (tollway)
otumobil	اتومبیل	car, motorcar
ozä³	اوضاع	conditions, situation
ozr	عذر	excuse, apology
ozr xähi	عذر خواهی	apology, apologising
ozr xästan	عذر خواستن	to apologise
ozv	عضو	organ, limb, member
ozv šodan	عضوشدن	to join
ozviyyat	عضویت	membership

P		
pä	پا	foot
pä dar havä	پا در هوا	groundless, uncertain
päče	پاچه	trotters
pädäš	پاداش	reward, bonus
pädäš dädan	پاداش دادن	to reward, to give bonus
pädegän	پادگان	barracks
pädešäh	پادشاه	king, shah, monarch
pädešähi	پادشاهی	royalty, kingdom
padide	پدیده	phenomenon
pädo	پادو	footboy, assistant
pädtan	پادتن	antibody
pädzahr	پادزهر	antidote
päfang	پافنگ	order arms
päfešäri	پافشاری	insistence, emphasis
päfešäri kardan	پافشاری کردن	to insist, to emphasis
pahlavän	پهلوان	hero, champion
pahlavän panbe	پهلوان پنبه	cardboard cavalier
pahlu	پهلو	side, near
pahn	پهن	wide, broad, extensive
pahnä	پهنا	width, extent
pahnävar	پهناور	extensive, vast
päk	پاک	clean, pure, innocent
päk kardan	پاک کردن	to clean
pakar	پکر	gloomy
päkat	پاکت	envelope, paper bag
päkize	پاکیزه	neat, clean
päkkon	پاکن	eraser, wiper, rubber
päknevis	پاکنویس	final draft, revised
palakidan(palak)	پلکیدن (پلک)	to hang out
pälän	پالان	packsaddle
palang	پلنگ	leopard

päläsidan(paläs)	پلاسیدن (پلاس)	to fade, to wither
päläyešgäh	پالایشگاه	refinery
palid	پلید	filthy, wicked
pälto	پالتو	coat
panäh	پناه	shelter, refuge, asylum
panähande	پناهنده	refugee, asylum seeker
panähgäh	پناهگاه	shelter
panbe	پنبه	cotton
panbe risi	پنبه ریسی	cotton spinning
pančari	پنچری	puncture
pand	پند	advice, guidance
pändol	پاندول	pendulum
panir	پنیر	cheese
panj	پنج	five
panj šanbe	پنج شنبه	thursday
panjäh	پنجاه	fifty
panjare	پنجره	window
panje	پنجه	claw, paw
panjul	پنجول	scratch, scrape
panke	پنکه	fan (hand-held)
pans	پنس	forceps, pin
pänsad	پانصد	five hundred
pänsemän	پانسمان	dressing, bandage
pänsiyon	پانسیون	boarding house, hostel
pänzdah	پانزده	fifteen
par	پر	feather
par kande	پرکنده	plucked(chicken)
päräf	پاراف	initialling
paräkande	پراکنده	scattered, dispersed
parande	پرنده	bird
parandegän	پرندگان	birds
parastär	پرستار	nurse
parastäri	پرستاری	nursing

parasteš	پرستش	worship, adoration
parastidan(parast)	پرستیدن (پرست)	to worship
parastu	پرستو	swallow
parčam	پرچم	flag, banner
pärče	پارچه	cloth, fabric
pärče bäfi	پارچه بافی	textile factory
parčin	پرچین	fence, hedge
pardäxt	پرداخت	payment, polish
pardäxtan(pardäz)	پرداختن (پرداز)	to pay
parde	پرده	curtain, screen, layer
pardepuši	پرده پوشی	secrecy
päre	پاره	torn, ragged
pare kardan	پاره کردن	to tear
pareš	پرش	jump
pargär	پرگار	calliper
parhiz	پرهیز	abstinence, avoidance
parhizkär	پرهیزکار	vitreous, godly
pari	پری	fairy
pari ruz	پریروز	day before yesterday
paridan(par)	پریدن (پر)	to fly, to jump, to fade
parišab	پریشب	the night before
parišän	پریشان	distressed. disturbed
pärk	پارک	a park, parking
pärs	پارس	barking, persia
pärsi	پارسی	Persian
pärsäl	پارسال	last year
part	پرت	remote, deviated
part kardan	پرت کردن	to throw
partäb kardan	پرتاب کردن	to throw, to shoot
partgäh	پرتگاه	crag; wall of rock
parto	پرتو	ray, beam, light
pärty	پارتی	connections, party
päru	پارو	snow-shovel, paddle

päru zadan	پارو زدن	to shovel, to paddle
parvande	پرونده	file, dossier, record
parväne	پروانه	butterfly, permit, propeller
parvär	پروار	fattened(animal)
parvardegär	پروردگار	god, nourisher
parvareš	پرورش	nurturing, breeding
parvareš dädan	پرورش دادن	to nurture, to breed
parvarešgäh	پرورشگاه	nursery, orphanage
parväz	پرواز	flight
parväz kardan	پرواز کردن	to fly
parxäš	پرخاش	protest, aggression
parxašgar	پرخاشگر	aggressive
pas	پس	then, after, thus
pas andäz	پس انداز	savings
pas andäz kardan	پس انداز کردن	to save money
pas fardä	پس فردا	day after tomorrow
pas mände	پس مانده	leftover, residue
pasand	پسند	admiration, approval
pasandidan(pasan)	پسندیدن (پسند)	to like, to approve
päsäž	پاساژ	shopping plaza
päsdär	پ ا سدار	islamic guard
paše	پشه	mosquito, fly
paše band	پشه بند	mosquito net
päsebän	پاسبان	policeman, guard
päsebäni	پاسبانی	guarding, patrolling
päsgäh	پاسگاه	rural police station
päšidan(päš)	پاشیدن (پاش)	to sprinkle
pašimän	پشیمان	regretful, remorseful
pašimän šodan	پشیمان شدن	to regret
pašm	پشم	wool
pašm čini	پشم چینی	sheep shearing
pašm risi	پشم ریسی	wool spinning
pašmak	پ شمک	cotton candy

pašmälu	پشمالو	hairy, shaggy
pašmi	پشمی	woollen
päšne	پاشنه	heel
päšne keš	پاشنه کش	shoe-horn
paso piš	پس وپیش	back and forth
päsox	پاسخ	answer, response
päsox dädan	پاسخ دادن	to answer
päsox gu	پاسخ گو	responsible, replier
past	پست	mean, inferior, low life
pästorize	پاستوریزه	posturised
pastu	پستو	closet
pasvand	پسوند	suffix
pätil	پاتیل	dead drunk
patu	پتو	blanket
pätuq	پاتوق	hang out, meeting place
pävaraqi	پاورقی	foot-article
paxme	پخمه	stupid, dumb
paxš	پخش	distribution, broadcast
paxš kardan	پخش کردن	to distribute, to broadcast
payäm	پیام	message
payämbar	پیامبر	prophet, messenger
päyän	پایان	end, finish
päyän yäftan	پایان یافتن	to end, to finish
päyän näme	پایان نامه	thesis, dissertation
päyäne	پایانه	terminal
päydär	پایدار	permanent, constant
päye	پایه	grade, pillar, basis
päygäh	پایگاه	base
päyiydan(päy)	پاییدن (پای)	to look out, to watch out
päyiyn	پایین	down, low, under
päyiyz	پاییز	fall, autumn
päytaxt	پایتخت	capital city
paziräyi	پذیرایی	reception, hospitality

pazireš	پذیرش	admission, reception
paziroftan(pazir)	پذیرفتن (پذیر)	to accept, to admit
pažmorde	پژمرده	faded, pale, sad
pažuheš	پژوهش	research, appeal
pečpeč	پچ پچ	whisper
pedar	پدر	father
pedar bozorg	پدربزرگ	grand father
pedar koši	پدرکشی	patricide
pedar šohar	پدر شوهر	father-in-law (husband)
pedar suxte	پدرسوخته	knavish, damn
pedar zan	پدرزن	father in law(wife's father)
pedaräne	پدرانه	fatherly
pedaro mädar	پدر و مادر	parents
pehen	پهن	dung, manure
pelästik	پلاستیک	plastic
pelk	پلک	eyelid
pelle	پله	stair, step
pellekän	پلکان	stairs, steps
penhän	پنهان	hidden, secret
penhän šodan	پنهان شدن	to hide
penisilin	پنی سیلین	penicillin
periyod	پریود	menstruation
pesar	پسر	boy, son
pesar amme	پسر عمه	son of paternal aunt
pesar amu	پسرعمو	son of paternal uncle
pesar bačče	پسر بچه	young boy
pesar däyi	پسر دایی	son of maternal uncle
pesar xäle	پسرخاله	son of maternal aunt
pesar xände	پسرخوانده	adopted son
pesarak	پسرک	little boy
pešgel	پشگل	sheep dung
pestän	پستان	beast, teat
pestänak	پستانک	nipple, pacifier

peständär	پستاندار	mammal
peste	پسته	pistachio
pey	پی	foundation, trace
pey dar pey	پی در پی	successive, continuous
peyäpey	پیاپی	successive, continuous
peydä	پیدا	visible, evident
peydä kardan	پیدا کردن	to find
peydäyeš	پیدایش	genesis, existence
peygard	پیگرد	prosecution
peykar taraš	پیکرتراش	sculptor
peykare	پیکره	sculpture
peymän	پیمان	contract, pact, treaty
peymän bastan	پیمان بستن	to make a treaty
peymäne	پیمانه	measure
peymänkär	پیمانکار	contactor
peyqäm	پیغام	message
peyqambar	پیغمبر	prophet
peyravi	پیروی	following, obeying
peyravi kardan	پیروی کردن	to follow, to obey
peyrizi	پی ریزی	founding
peyrizi kardan	پی ریزی کردن	to found
peyro	پیرو	follower, disciple
peyvand	پیوند	graft, union, relationship
peyvast	پیوست	appendix
peyvastan(peyvan)	پیوستن (پیوند)	to connect, to join
peyvaste	پیوسته	connected, continuous
pezešk	پزشک	physician, medical practicer
pezeški	پزشکی	medicine, medical practice
pežväk	پژواک	echo, reflection
pič	پیچ	twist, bend, screw
pič xordan	پیچ خوردن	to twist, to bend
pič xordegi	پیچ خوردگی	twist, bend
pičak	پیچک	ivy

pičidan (pič)	پیچیدن (پیچ)	to turn, to wrap
pičide	پیچیده	intricate, complicated
pičidegi	پیچیدگی	intricacy, twist
pile	پ یـ له	cocoon, abscess, gumboil
pine	پینه	patch, callous
pingpong	پینگ پونگ	table tennis
pip	پیپ	smoking pipe
pir česmi	پیرچشمی	presbyopia
pirähan	پیراهن	shirt, dress
pirämun	پیرامون	outskirts, around
piräste	پیراسته	trimmed, decorated
piräyeš	پیرایش	trimming, ornament
piri	پیری	old age
pir šodan	پیر شدن	to age
pirmard	پیرمرد	old man
piruzi	پیروزی	victory, triumph
piruz šodan	پیروز شدن	to win, to triumph
pirzan	پیرزن	old woman
piš	پیش	front, before, presence
piš ägahi	پیش آگهی	prognosis, warning
piš ähang	پیش آهنگ	scout, pioneer
piš ämad	پیشامد	event, accident
piš äpiš	پیشاپیش	beforehand
piš bahä	پیش بها	advance payment
piš band	پیش بند	apron, bib
piš bini	پیش بینی	forecast, anticipation
piš bini kardan	پیش بینی کردن	to forecast, to anticipate
piš darämad	پیش درآمد	prelude
piš dasti kardan	پیش دستی کردن	to forestall, to outreach
piš foruš kardan	پیش فروش کردن	to sell in advance
piš giri	پیشگیری	prevention
piš giri kardan	پیشگیری کردن	to prevent
piš guyi	پیشگویی	prediction, prophecy

piš guyi kardan	پیشگویی کردن	to predic
piš keš	پیشکش	present, gift
piš keš kardan	پیشکش کردن	to present
piš namäz	پیش نماز	prayer leader, chaplain
piš qadam	پیش قدم	leader, initiator
piš qadam šodan	پیش قدم شدن	to initiate, to volunteer
piš qest	پیش قسط	first instalment
piš xän	پیشخوان	counter
piš xarid	پیش خرید	advance purchase
piš xarid kardan	پیش خرید کردن	to buy in advance
piš xedmat	پیشخدمت	waiter, servant
pišäni	پیشانی	forehead
piše	پیشه	jib, trade, profession
pišfang	پیش فنگ	present arms
piši gereftan	پیشی گرفتن	to surpass
pišin	پیشین	former, previous
pišiniyän	پیشینیان	predecessors
pišine	پیشینه	background, file
pišnahäd	پیشنهاد	proposal, offer, suggestion
pišnahäd kardan	پیشنهاد کردن	to propose, to suggest
pišraft	پیشرفت	progress, improvement
pišraft kardan	پیشرفت کردن	to progress, to improvet
pišrafte	پیشرفته	progressed, advanced
pišravi	پیشروی	advancement
pišravi kardan	پیشروی کردن	to advance, to move ahead
pišro	پیشرو	forerunner, pioneer
pišvä	پیشوا	leader
pišvand	پیشوند	prefix
pišväz	پیشواز	welcoming
pišväz kardan	پیشواز کردن	to welcome
pit	پیت	tin, container
piyäde	پیاده	on foot, pedestrian, infantry
piyäde ravi	پیاده روی	walking, hiking

piyäde ravi kardan	پیاده روی کردن	to walk
piyäde ro	پیاده رو	side walk, footpath
piyäle	پیاله	cup, bowl, mug
piyäz	پیاز	onion, bulb
piyäzče	پیازچه	spring onion, bulbils
pläk	پلاک	plate, tag
pof	پف	puff, blowing out
pofyuz	پفیوز	crabbed, sullen
poker	پوکر	poker
pol	پل	bridge
polis	پلیس	police
poliver	پولیور	jumper (sweater)
polo	پلو	cooked rice
polomb	پلمب	seal
pomäd	پماد	ointment
por	پر	full, loaded, charged
por kardan	پر کردن	to fill, to load
por harf	پر حرف	talkative, yapping
por harfi	پر حرفی	loquacity
por saro seda	پرسروصدا	noisy
porčäne	پرچانه	talkative
porov	پرو	fitting, trying on
porov kardan	پرو کردن	to try on
porožoktor	پروژکتور	projector
porpošt	پرپشت	thick, dense
porru	پ ررو	rude
porruyi	پررویی	rudeness
porseš	پرسش	question, inquiry
porsidan(pors)	پرسیدن (پرس)	to ask a question
porteqäl	پرتقال	orange, portugal
porteqäli	پرتقالی	portugese
post	پست	post, mail, position
post kardan	پست کردن	to post, to mail

pošt	پشت	back, behind, wrong side
poštak	پشتک	somersault
postči	پستچی	postman
pošteväne	پشتوانه	backing
pošti	پشتی	cushion, pillow
poštibän	پشتیبان	supporter, patron
poštibäni	پشتیبانی	support, patronage
poštibäni kardan	پشتیبانی کردن	to support
poštkär	پشتکار	consistency, stamina
pošto ru	پشت و رو	inside out
postxäne	پستخانه	post office
potk	پتک	hammer, sledge
poxtan(paz)	پختن (پز)	to cook
poxte	پخته	cooked, experienced
poz	پز	show off
poz dädan	پز دادن	to show off
puč	پوچ	empty, blank, vain
puči	پوچی	, vainity, futility
pud	پود	woof
pudr	پودر	powder
puk	پوک	empty, hollow
pukiye ostoxän	پوکی استخوان	osteoprosis
puke	پوکه	cartridge-shell
pul	پول	money, currency
puli	پولی	paid
pul dädan	پول دادن	to pay
puläd	پولاد	steel
pulak	پولک	tinsel, fish-scale
pulaki	پولکی	money lover
puldär	پولدار	rich, wealthy
pure	پوره	puree, mash
pušak	پوشک	nappy
pušäk	پوشاک	clothing, dress

pušäl	پوشال	stuffing or packing material
pušäli	پوشالی	chaffy
puše	پوشه	file, folder
pušeš dädan	پوشش دادن	to cover
pušeš	پوشش	covering, wrap
pusidan(pus)	پوسیدن (پوس)	to decay, to rot
pušidan(puš)	پوشیدن (پوش)	to wear, to cover, to hide
pusidegi	پوسیدگی	decay, rottenness
pust	پوست	skin, peel, shell
pust kande	پوست کنده	frank, open
pust kandan	پوست کندن	to peel
pust koloft	پوست کلفت	tick-skinned
puste	پوسته	crust, scale
puster	پوستر	poster
putin	پوتین	boot
puyä	پویا	searcher
puze	پوزه	muzzle, chin
puze band	پوزه بند	a muzzle
puzeš	پوزش	apology, pardon
puzeš xästan	پوزش خواستن	to apologise
puzxand	پوزخند	sneer
puzxand zadan	پوزخند زدن	to sneer

Q		
qä³ede	قاعده	rule, base
qä³ede šodan	قاعده شدن	to menesturate
qä³edegi	قاعدگی	menstruation, period
qä³eme	قائمه	perpendicular
qäb	قاب	frame, case, knucklebone
qabä	قبا	cloak
qabähat	قباحت	hideousness, obscenity
qabäle	قباله	title deed, contract
qäbel	قابل	worthy, deserved
qäbele	قابله	midwife
qabih	قبیح	obscene, immoral, indecent
qabil	قبیل	kind, type
qabile	قبیله	clan, tribe
qabl	قبل	before, ago, previous
qäblame	قابلمه	stew pan, metal bowl
qablan	قبلا	beforehand, first of all
qabli	قبلی	previous, last, former
qabqab	غبغب	double chin, dewlap
qabr	قبر	grave, tomb
qabrestän	قبرستان	graveyard, cemetery
qabrkan	قبرکن	gravedigger
qabul	قبول	acceptance, consent
qabul kardan	قبول کردن	to accept, to admit
qabul šodan	قبول شدن	to pass, to succeed
qabuli	قبولی	acceptance, passing (test)
qabz	قبض	bill, receipt
qabze	قبضه	handle, clutch
qäčäq	قاچاق	smuggle, illicit
qäčäq kardan	قاچاق کردن	to smuggle
qäčäqči	قاچاقچی	smuggler
qad	قد	height, size, tallness

qadam	قدم	pace, footstep
qadam zadan	قدم زدن	to walk, to stroll
qadaqan	غدغن	forbidden
qadaqan kardan	غدغن کردن	to forbide
qadar	قدر	destiny
qadboland	قد بلند	tall
qäder	قادر	able, competent, capable
qadimi	قدیمی	old, ancient
qadr	قدر	value, worth, merit
qadrdäni	قدردانی	appreciation, gratitude
qafas	قفس	cage
qafase	قفسه	shelf, locker, bookcase
qäfel	غافل	negligent, ignorant
qäfele	قافله	caravan, convoy
qäfelgir	غافلگیر	blitzing, surprisal
qäfiye	قافیه	rhyme
qaflat	غفلت	negligence, carelessness
qaflat kardan	غفلت کردن	to neglect
qafqäz	قفقاز	caucasia
qahbe	قحبه	prostitute, whore
qahbegi	قحبه گی	prostitution
qahqahe	قهقهه	loud laugh
qahqahe zadan	قهقهه زدن	to laugh loaud
qahqarä	قهقرا	regression, retrogression
qahqarä raftan	قهقرا رفتن	to regress
qahr	قهر	not speaking with, angry at
qahr kardan	قهر کردن	to stop speaking with
qahramän	قهرمان	hero, champion
qahramäni	قهرمانی	championship
qahti	قحطی	famine, starvation
qahti zade	قحطی زده	famine-stricken
qahve	قهوه	coffee
qahveči	قهوه چی	tea house keeper

qahvexäne	قهوه خانه	tea house, bar, café
qahveyi	قهوه ای	brown
qäjär	قَاجار	the qajar dynasty
qal³	قَلع	tin
qal³e	قَلعه	fort, castle
qalabe	غَل به	dominance, victory, triumph
qalabe kardan	غَل به کردن	to dominate, to triumph
qaläf	غلاف	sheath, case cover
qalam	قَلم	pen, quill
qalam mu	قَلم مو	paintbrush
qalamro	قَلمرو	territory, domain
qalamzani	قلمزنی	engraving
qalat	غَلط	mistake, incorrect, wrong
qalatgiri	غلط گیری	proofreading
qalb	قَلب	heart, spirit, forged, fake
qalbi	قلبی	sincere, genuine, cordial
qäleb	غالب	victorious, most, dominant
qäleb	قَالب	mould, model, cast, matrix
qäleban	غالبا	frequently, often
qaliyän	قَلیان	hubble bubble, narghile
qalläde	قَلاده	collar(dog's), leash
qalle	غَله	corn, grain, cereals
qaltak	غَلتک	roller, coaster
qaltidan(qalt)	غلتیدن (غلت)	to roll, to tumble
qam	غم	sorrow, worry, sadness
qam xordan	غم خوردن	to worry, to be sad
qamangiz	غم انگیز	tragic, saddening
qambäd	غمباد	goitre
qame	قَمه	dagger
qamgin	غمگین	sad, gloomy, saddened
qanäri	قناری	canary
qand	قَند	sugar cube
qandän	قَندان	sugar bowl

qani	غنی	rich, wealthy
qanimat	غذ یمت	booty, windfall
qannädi	قنادی	confectionary, pastry shop
qänun	قانون	law
qänuni	قانونی	lawfull, legal
qänun gozäri	قانون گذاری	legislation
qäp	ق اپ	snatching
qapän	ق پان	steelyard, scale
qäpidan(qäp)	قاپیدن (قاپ)	to snatch, to grab
qär	غار	cave
qarämat	غرامت	indemnity, damage
qarantine	ق رنط ینه	quarantine
qarär	ق رار	appointment, date
qarär gozäštan	ق رار گذاشتن	to make an appointment
qarärdäd	ق رارداد	pact, treaty, contract
qarärdädi	قراردادی	conventional, contractual
qarärgäh	ق رارگ اه	headquarter
qärat	غارت	plunder, looting
qärat kardan	غارت کردن	to plunder, to loot
qarävol	ق راول	guard, patrol
qaraz	غرض	purpose, grudge, ill-will
qarb	غرب	west
qarbäl	غرب ال	sifter, riddle
qarbäl kardan	غرب ال کردن	to sift, to screen
qarbi	غربی	western
qärč	ق ارچ	mushroom, fungus
qäri	قاری	koran reader
qaribe	غریبه	alien, stranger, lonely
qarine	ق ری نه	symmetrical, match
qariye	ق ری ه	village
qarize	غری زه	instinct, nature
qarn	ق رن	centaury
qarniye	ق رذ یه	cornea

qarq šodan	غرق شدن	to drown, to sink
qärqär	قارقار	cawing
qarqare kardan	غرغره کردن	to gargle
qarqävol	قرقاول	pheasant
qärre	قاره	continent
qarz	قرض	debt, loan, borrowing,
qaš	غش	fit, coma, seizure
qaš kardan	غش کردن	to faint
qasam	قسم	oath, pledge, swear
qasam xordan	قسم خوردن	to make an oath, to swear
qašang	قشنگ	beautiful
qašanig	قشنگی	beauty
qasävat	قساوت	cruelty
qasb	غصب	usurpation, seizing
qasb kardan	غصب کردن	to usurpate, to seize
qasd	قصد	will, intension, purpose
qasd däštan	قصد داشتن	to intend
qasdi	قصدی	intentional
qäsed	قاصد	messenger, courier
qäsedak	قاصدک	dandelion
qäšoq	قاشق	spoon
qasr	قصر	palace
qassäb	قصاب	butcher
qassäbi	قصابی	butchery, butcher shop
qassäl	غسال	mortician
qassäl xäne	غسال خانه	mortuary
qat³	قطع	amputation, interruption
qat³ kardan	قطع کردن	to cut, to amputate
qat³an	قطعا	positively, definitely
qat³e	قطعه	piece, section, segment
qat³i	قطعی	definite, final, certain
qat³näme	قطعنامه	resolution, declaration
qatär	قطار	train, sequence

qatär barqi	قطار برقی	tram
qäte³	قاطع	decisive, clear-cut
qätel	قاتل	murderer, assassin
qäter	قاطر	mule
qäti	قاتی	mixed, mingled
qatl	قتل	murder, massacre
qatre	قطره	drop, drip
qatre čakän	قطره چكان	dropper
qatur	قطور	thick, bulky
qaväre	قواره	pattern, figure, cut
qavi	قوی	powerful, strong
qavväs	غواص	diver
qavväsi	غواصی	diving
qavväsi kardan	غواصی كردن	to dive
qäyeb	غایب	absent, hidden, missing
qäyem	قایم	firm, secure, strong, hidden
qäyem šodan	قایم شدن	to hide
qäyem mušak bäzi	قایم موشک بازی	hide-and-seek
qäyeq	قایق	boat
qäyeqräni	قایقرانی	sailing
qayy kardan	قی كردن	to vomit
qayyem	قیم	guardian
qäz	غاز	goose
qazä	غذا	food, meal
qazä xordan	غذا خوردن	to eat, to eat food
qazabnäk	غضبناک	angry, wrathful, infuriated
qazal	غزل	lyric, love poem
qazävat	قضاوت	judgement
qazävat kardan	قضاوت كردن	to judge
qazäyi	قضایی	judicial
qäzi	قاضی	judge, justice of peace
qaziyye	قضیه	case, proposition, clause
qeble	قبله	praying direction

qebres	قَ برس	Cyprus
qeddis	قديس	saint
qedmat	قَ دمت	antiquity, oldness
qelqelak kardan	قَ لَ قَ لک کردن	to tickle
qelzat	غ لظت	viscosity, density
qenä³at	قَ ناعت	continence, contentment
qerä³at	قَ رائ ت	reading, reciting
qermez	قَ رمز	red
qerqere	قَ رقَ ره	spool, pulley
qerqi	قرقی	sparrow hawk
qešä	غ شا	membrane, coat
qesäs	قصاص	retaliation, punishment
qesäs kardan	قَ صاص کردن	to retaliate, to punish
qešläq	قَ شلاق	winter quarters
qesm	قَ سم	kind, type, class
qesmat	قَ سمت	section, portion, fate
qešr	قَ شر	crust, layer, coating
qesse	قَ صه	story, tale
qessegu	قَ صه گ و	storyteller
qest	قَ سط	instalment, mortgage
qeyb	غ یب	invisible, mysterious
qeyb šodan	غ یبشدن	to disappear
qeybat	غ ی بت	backbiting, absence, gossip
qeybat kardan	غ ی بت کردن	gossiping, being abscent
qeybgu	غ ی ب گو	clairvoyant, oracle
qeybguyi	غیب گویی	prophecy, prognostication
qeyči	قیچی	scissors
qeyd	قَ ید	adverb, bond, limitation
qeymat	قَ یمت	price, fee, cost
qeymati	قیمتی	precious, costly
qeyme	قَ یمه	minced meat
qeymumat	قَ یمومت	guardianship
qeyr	غ یر	except, other than, without

qeyrat	غيرت	zeal, jealousy
qeyre addi	غير عادى	unusual, strange
qeyre amdi	غير عمدى	unintentional
qeyre herfeyi	غير حرفه اى	amateur , unprofessional
qeyre momken	غ ير ممكن	impossible
qeyre mostaqim	غ ير مستقيم	indirect
qeyre rasmi	غير رسمى	informal, unofficial
qeyre šar³i	غير شرعى	illegal, unlawful
qeyre tabiyi	غير طبيعى	unnatural
qeysi	قيسى	a type of apricot
qif	قيف	funnel
qir	قير	tar
qirät	قيراط	carat
qiyäb	غياب	absence, absenteeism
qiyäfe	قيافه	appearance, pose
qiyäm	قيام	revolt, rebellion, uprising
qiyäm kardan	قيام كردن	to revolt, to uprise
qiyämat	قيامت	resurrection day
qiyäs	قياس	analogy, comparison
qiyäs kardan	قياس كردن	to compare
qobär	غبار	dust, smog
qobärälud	غبار آلود	dusty, soiled
qodde	غده	gland, tumour, lump
qodrat	قدرت	power, strength
qofl	قفل	lock
qofl kardan	قفل كردن	to lock
qofle zanjir	قفل زنجير	padlock
qoflsäz	قفل ساز	locksmith
qol	قول	promise, vow
qol dädan	قول دادن	to promise, to vow
qoläm	غلام	servant, slave
qoldor	قلدر	bully, thug
qoldori	قلدرى	bullying

qolenj	قولنج	colic
qolläb	قلاب	hook, drag
qolläbduzi	قلاب دوزی	crocheting
qolläbi	قلابی	fake, phoney
qolle	قله	summit, peak, apex
qolovv	غلو	exaggeration, overstatement
qolovv kardan	غلو کردن	to exaggere, to overstate
qolve	قلوه	kidney
qom	قوم	tribe, nation, sect
qomär	قمار	gamble
qomärbäz	قمارباز	gambler
qomärbäzi	قماربازی	gambling
qomärbäzi kardan	قماربازی کردن	to gamble
qomärxäne	قمار خانه	casino
qomi	قومی	racial, ethnical
qomqome	قمقمه	flask, thermos bottle
qomri	قمری	ringdove
qonče	غنچه	bud, sprout, blossom
qondäq	قنداق	diapers, gunstock
qoqä	غوغا	disturbance, tumult
qor	غر	grumble, whinging
qor zadan	غرزدن	to grumble, to whing
qor³än	قرآن	koran
qor³e	قرعه	lottery, draw
qor³e kešidan	قرعه کشیدن	to draw
qorbäni	قربانی	sacrifice, victim
qorbäni kardan	قربانی کردن	to sacrifice
qorbat	غربت	away from home, nostalgia
qorbati	غربتی	gypsy
qorfe	غرفه	pavilion, booth, chamber
qormesabzi	قرمه سبزی	rice with vegetable stew
qoromsäq	قرمساق	pimp, cuckold
qoroq kardan	قرق کردن	to preserve, to restrict

qorreš	غرش	roaring, thundering
qorreš kardan	غرش کردن	to roar
qors	قرص	pill, tablet, loaf, firm
qors xordan	قرص خوردن	to take a tablet
qorse xäb	قرص خواب	sleeping pill
qorub	غروب	sunset, dusk
qorub kardan	غروب کردن	to set (sun)
qorur	غرور	pride, dignity, vanity
qos	قوس	bow, arch
qosl	غسل	ceremonial washing, bathing
qosl kardan	غسل کردن	to bath (religious)
qosqazah	قوس قزح	rainbow
qosse	غصه	sorrow, gloom, grief
qosse xordan	غصه خوردن	to be sad, to grief
qošun	قشون	troops, army
qotb	قطب	pole
qotbi	قطبی	polar
qotbnamä	قطب نما	compass
qotr	قطر	diameter
qovvat	قوت	power, strength, potency
qovve	قوه	power, energy
qozruf	غضروف	cartilage
qu	قو	swan
quč	قوچ	ram
qul	غول	giant
qurbäqe	قورباغه	frog, toad
qure	غوره	sour grape
quš	قوش	falcon, hawk
quti	قوطی	tin, can
quz	قوز	hunch, hump
qyre addi	غیر عادی	abnormal, unusual
qyre qäbele fahm	غیر قابل فهم	incomprehensible

R		
ra³d	رعد	thunder
ra³is	رئیس	chief, head, director, boss
ra³is jomhur	رئیس جمهور	president
ra³s	راس	head, head of (cattle)
ra³še	رعشه	tremor, trembling
ra³y	رای	poll, ballot, vote, opinion
ra³y dädan	رای دادن	to vote
ra³yyat	رعیت	inferior, farmer
rabb	رب	god, lord
räbet	رابط	connector, liaison
räbete	رابطه	relation, connection, link
rabt	ربط	connection, relation
radd	رد	refusal, disproval, trace
radd kardan	رد کردن	to reject, to refuse, to fail
radde pä	رد پا	footpath, track (footprints)
raddgiri	رد گیری	to trace, to track
rade	رده	category, row, line
rade bandi	رده بندی	classification
rade bandi kardan	رده بندی کردن	to classify
radif	ردیف	row, line, order
rädiyator	رادیاتور	radiator
rädiyo	رادیو	radio
rafiq	رفیق	friend, pale, mate, buddy
raftan(rav)	رفتن (رو)	to go
raftär	رفتار	behaviour, conduct, manner
rafto ämad	رفت و آمد	traffic, coming and going
rag	رگ	vein, artery, vessel
ragbär	رگبار	shower
räh	راه	road, route, way
räh raftan	راه رفتن	to walk
räh ähan	راه آهن	railway, rail road

räh bandän	راه بندان	traffic congestion
räh namä	راهنما	guide, directory, manual
räh namäyi	راهنمایی	guidance, direction
räh namäyi kardan	راهنمایی کردن	to guide, to lead
räh pelle	راه پله	stairway
räh peymäyi	راهپیمایی	walking, demonstration
räh peymäyi kardan	راهپیمایی کردن	to walk, to demonstrate
rahä	رها	freed, liberated
rahä kardan	رها کردن	to free, to abondon
rähat	راحت	comfortable, easy
rähati	راحتی	comfort, relaxation
rahäyi	رهایی	freedom, salvation
rahbar	رهبر	leader
rahbari	رهبری	leadership
räheb	راهب	monk
rähebe	راهبه	nun
rahem	رحم	uterus, womb
rahm	رحم	mercy, compassion
rahm kardan	رحم کردن	to have mercy
rahmat kardan	رحمت کردن	to bless (by God)
rahn	رهن	mortgage, renting by a bond
rahn kardan	رهن کردن	to rent by giving a bond
rahqozar	رهگذر	pedestrian, passer-by
rähro	راه رو	hall, corridor
rähzan	راهزن	bandit, highwayman
rähzani	راهزنی	highway rubbery
räked	راکد	stagnant, standstill
rakik	رکیک	obscene, indecent
ram kardan	رم کردن	to break away (of a kattle)
räm	رام	domestic, submissive, pet
räm kardan	رام کردن	to domesticate
ramaq	رمق	energy
ramazän	رمضان	fasting month

rammäl	رمال	fortune teller
ramz	رمز	code, secret, mystery
ramzi	رمزی	coded, secret, classified
rän	ران	thigh
ränande	راننده	driver
ränandegi	رانندگی	driving
ränandegi kardan	رانندگی کردن	to drive
rändan(rän)	راندن (ران)	to drive
rande	رنده	grater, shredder
rande kardan	رنده کردن	to grate
rang	رنگ	color, paint, hue
rang kardan	رنگ کردن	to color, to paint
rang ämizi	رنگ آمیزی	coloration
rang paride	رنگ پریده	pale, faded
rang zan	رنگ زن	painter
rang zadan	رنگ زدن	to paint
rangärang	رنگارنگ	multicolored, various
rangi	رنگی	colored, colour (film)
rangin kamän	رنگین کمان	rainbow
ranj	رنج	pain, suffering, agony
ranj kešidan	رنج کشیدن	to suffer
ranješ	رنجش	annoyance, irritation
ranjidan(ranj)	رنجیدن (رنج)	to be annoyed
raqam	رقم	figure, digit, number
raqbat	رغبت	desire, relish
räqeb	راغب	willing, keen
raqiq	رقیق	diluted, warty
raqqäs	رقاص	dancer
raqs	رقص	dancing
raqsidan(raqs)	رقصیدن (رقص)	to dance
rasad xäne	رصدخانه	observatory
rasänä	رسانا	conductor
rasändan(rasän)	رساندن (رسان)	to supply, to deliver

rasäne	رسانه	medium
rasid	رسید	receipt
rašid	رشید	brave
rasidan(ras)	رسیدن (رس)	to reach, to arrive
raside	رسیده	ripe, mature
rasidegi	رسیدگی	investigation, checking
rasm	رسم	custom, tradition
rasmi	رسمی	formal, official
rasmiyyat	رسمیت	formality
räst	راست	straight, true, right, upright
räst guyi	راست گویی	truthfulness
rästä	راستا	direction
rastäxiz	رستاخیز	resurrection
raste	رسته	class, rank
räste	راسته	fillet, row
rastegär	رستگار	saved, delivered
rästi	راستی	truth, honesty
räsu	راسو	weasel
rasul	رسول	prophet
ravä	روا	permissible, fair
ravädid	روادید	visa
raväj	رواج	currency, prevalence
ravän	روان	flowing, fluent, soul, spirit
ravän darmäni	روان درمانی	psychotherapy
ravän pezešk	روان پزشک	psychiatrist
ravän pezeški	روان پزشکی	psychiatry
ravän šenäs	روانشناس	psychologist
ravän šenäsi	روانشناسی	psychology
ravand	روند	process, procedure
ravāne	روانه	dispatched, sent
raväni	روانی	fluency, mental, psychic
raväyat	روایت	narrative
raveš	روش	method, procedure

raviyye	رویه	policy, tactic
raxt	رخت	clothes, garment
raxt äviz	رخت آویز	clothes hanger
raxt kan	رختکن	cloakroom, dressing room
raxt šuyi	رخت شویی	clothes washing, laundry
raxt xäb	رخت خواب	bed, bedding
räyegän	رایگان	free of charge
räyehe	رایحه	smell, odor, fragrance
räyej	رایج	current, customary
räz	راز	secret, mystery
räzdär	رازدار	confidant
räzi	راضی	satisfied, content
razl	رذل	mean, wicked
razm	رزم	fight, battle
razm näv	رزمناو	battleship, cruiser
razmande	رزمنده	fighter, combatant
re³äyat	رعایت	regard, consideration
re³äyat kardan	رعایت کردن	to observe, to consider
rebä	ربا	usury
rebä xär	ربا خوار	usurer
refäh	رفاه	welfare, convenience
rehlat	رحلت	death
rejäl	رجال	distinguished people
rekäb	رکاب	pedal, stirrup
reqäbat	رقابت	competition, rivalry
reqäbat kardan	رقابت کردن	to compete
resäle	رساله	thesis, dissertation
rešte	رشته	field, line, string
rešte kuh	رشته کوه	mountain range
resturän	رستوران	restaurant
rezäyat	رضایت	satisfaction
rezäyat dädan	رضایت دادن	to consent
rezäyat baxš	رضایت بخش	satisfactory

reže	رژه	parade
reže raftan	رژه رفتن	to march
rezerv	رزرو	booking
rezerv kardan	رزرو کردن	to book
ridan(rin)	ریدن (رین)	to shit, to defecate
rig	ریگ	pebble, sand, gravel
riš	ریش	beard
riš taraš	ریش تراش	razor, shaver
riše	ریشه	root, origin
riše kani	ریشه کنی	eradication
rismän	ریسمان	string, rope
ristan(ris)	ریستن (ریس)	to spin
rišu	ریش شو	bearded
rišxand	ریشخند	mocking, ridicule
rišxand kardan	ریشخند کردن	to mock, to ridicule
rixtan(riz)	ریختن (ریز)	to pour, to litter, to cast
rixtegar	ریخته گر	moulder
riyäkär	ریاکار	hypocritical
riyäl	ریال	riyal, Persian currency
riyäsat	ریاست	chairmanship, presidency
riyäzat	ریاضت	mortification, self discipline
riyäzidän	ریاضی دان	mathematician
riyäziyät	ریاضیات	mathematical
riye	ریه	lung
riz	ریز	tiny, little, detail
rizeš	ریزش	pouring, collapse
rob³	ربع	one fourth, quarter
robä³iyyät	رباعیات	quatrains
robäyande	رباینده	hijacker
robb	رب	tomato paste
robudan(robäy)	ربودن (ربای)	to kidnap, to hijack
roftgar	رفتگر	street sweeper
rofu kardan	رفو کردن	to darn, to mend

rofuze šodan	رفوزه شدن	to fail a test or a grade
roju³ kardan	رجوع کردن	to refer, to return
rok	رک	frank, open, blunt
rokud	رکود	stagnation, standstill
romän	رمان	novel (book)
roman nevis	رمان نویس	novelist
ronaq	رونق	success, prosperity
roqan	روغن	oil (cooking)
roqani	روغنی	oily, greasy
rošan	روشن	light, lit, bright
rošan kardan	روشن کردن	to lit, to turn on, to start
rošanäyi	روشنایی	light, brightness
rošandel	روشندل	blind
rošanfekr	روشنفکر	intellectual
rošd	رشد	growth, development
rošd kardan	رشد کردن	to grow, to develop
rosub	رسوب	sediment, dregs
rosub kardan	رسوب کردن	to deposit (materials)
rosvä šodan	رسوا شدن	to be exposed
rosväyi	رسوایی	scandal, stigma
rošve	رشوه	bribe, bribery
rošve dädan	رشوه دادن	to bribe
rošvexär	رشوه خوار	bribe taker
rotbe	رتبه	rank, grade, level
rotubat	رطوبت	moisture
rox	رخ	face, castel(in chess)
roy	روی	zinc
royä	رویا	dream
royat	رویت	sight, vision
rozan	روزن	hole, crack
roze	روضه	sermon
roze xändan	روضه خواندن	to give a sermon
rože lab	رژلب	lipstick

ru	رو	face, top, on
rubäh	روباه	fox
rubaleši	روبالشی	pillowcase
rubän	روبان	ribbon, band
ruband	روبند	veil, mask
ruberu	روبرو	face to face, opposite
ruberu šodan	روبرو شدن	to confront
rubusi	روبوسی	kissing each other
rud	رود	river, stream
rud xäne	رودخانه	river
rudarbäyesti	رودربایستی	bashfulness
rudarru šodan	رو در رو شدن	to confront
rude	روده	intestine, gut, bowel
rudel	رودل	upset stomach
ruh	روح	spirit, soul, ghost
ruh olqodos	روح القدس	holy spirit
ruhäni	روحانی	spiritual, holy, clergy
ruhäniyat	روحانیت	the clergy, spirituality
ruhiyye	روحیه	morale
rumizi	رومیزی	tablecloth
runevešt	رونوشت	copy
runevisi kardan	رونویسی کردن	to copy
rupuš	روپوش	cover, gown, uniform
rusari	روسری	scarf
rusiye	روسیه	Russia
rusi	روسی	Russian
ruspi	روسپی	prostitute, whore
ruspigari	روسپی گری	prostitution
rustä	روستا	village
rustäyi	روستایی	villager, rural
ruydäd	رویداد	event, incident
ruye	روی	over, above
ruy dädan	روی دادن	to happen, to occur

ruye ham rafte	روی هم رفته	altogether
ruyiydan(ruy)	روییدن (روی)	to grow
ruz	روز	day
ruzäne	روزانه	daily
ruze	روزه	fasting, fast
ruze xär	روزه خوار	fast breaker
ruzedär	روزه دار	one who fasts
ruzgär	روزگار	world, circumstance, time
ruzi	روزی	sustenance
ruzmarre	روزمره	daily, routine
ruzmozd	روزمزد	daily pay
ruznäme	روزنامه	newspaper
ruzname foruši	روزنامه فروشی	newsagency
ruznäme negär	روزنامه نگار	journalist
ruznäme negäri	روزنامه نگاری	journalism

S		
š³r	شعر	poem, poetry
sa³ädat	سعادت	luck, happiness
sä³at	ساعت	hour, time, watch
sä³ati	ساعتى	hourly
sä³at säz	ساعت ساز	watchmaker
sä³ed	ساعد	forearm
sä³eqe	صاعقه	lightening
šä³er	شاعر	poet
šä³eräne	شاعراذه	poetic, poetical
ša³n	شان	dignity, status
sa³y	سعى	attempt, trying, effort
sa³y kardan	سعى كردن	to attempt, to try
šab	شب	night, eve, evening
šab bexeyr	شب ب خ ير	good evening, good night
šab käri	شبكارى	night shift
šab nešini	شب نشينى	evening party
sabab	س بب	cause, reason
sabab šodan	س بب شدن	to cause
sabad	س بد	basket, hamper
šabah	ش به	phantom, ghost, spook
šabähat	ش باهت	similarity, resemblance
šabake	ش ب كه	net, network
šabakiyye	ش ب ك يه	retina
šabäne	ش باذه	nightly, overnight
šabäne ruz	ش باذه روز	day and night
šabäneruzi	شبانه روزى	all the time, boarding-house
sabbäbe	س باب ه	index finger
šabbu	شب ب و	wall flower
säbeq	سابق	former, old
säbeqe	سابقه	previous record, antecedent
säbeqe där	سابقه دار	experienced

säbet	ثابت	fixed, stable, proved
säbet kardan	ثابت کردن	to fix, to prove, to establish
šabih	شبیه	similar, alike
šabixun zadan	شبیخون زدن	to ambush
sabk	سبک	style
šabkuri	شبکوری	night blindness
šabnam	شبنم	dew
sabck	سبک	light, soft, undignified
sabr	صبر	patience, tolerance
sabr kardan	صبر کردن	to wait
sabt	ثبت	registration, record
sabt kardan	ثبت کردن	to register, to record
säbun	صابون	soap
sabur	صبور	patient, tolerant
sabus	سبوس	bran
sabz	سبز	green, greenery, growing
sabze	سبزه	dark complexion, brunet
sabzi	سبزی	vegetables, greenery
sabzi foruš	سبزی فروشی	greengrocer
sad	صد	hundred
šäd	شاد	happy, glad
šädi	شادی	happiness
sadaf	صدف	oyster, shell
sadame	صدمه	harm, injury, damage
sadame zadan	صدمه زدن	to harm, to injure
sadaqe	صدقه	charity
sadd	سد	dam, barrier, blockage
sadd kardan	سدکردن	to block
sade	سده	century
säde	ساده	simple, easy, naive
sädeq	صادق	sincere, honest
säder kardan	صادرکردن	to export, to issue
säder konande	صادرکننده	exporter

säderät	صادرات	exports
šadid	شديد	severe, intense
sadr	صدر	top, uppermost
šädravän	شادروان	the late, the deceased
saf	صف	queue
säf	صاف	clear, transparent, pure, flat
säf kardan	صاف کردن	to clear, to flatten
safä	صـفا	purity, serenity, clarity
šafä	شـفا	cure, remedy, recovery
šafähi	شفاهی	verbal, oral
safar	سـفر	travel, trip, cruise
safar kardan	سـفر کردن	to travel
safar bexeyr	سفر بخیر	bon voyage!
safarnäme	سـفرنامه	itinerary
šaffäf	شـفاف	transparent
šaffäfiyat	شفافيت	transparency, clarity
safhe	صـفحه	page, sheet, layer, record
safhe kelid	صفحه کلید	keyboard
safhebandi	صفحه بندی	pagination
säfi	صافی	strainer, sift, purity
safih	سـفيه	silly, lunatic
safine	سـفينه	space ship
safir	سـفير	ambassador, envoy
safsate	سـفسطه	fallacy
šaftälu	شـفتالو	peach
safte	سـفته	draft, exchange bill
sag	سگ	dog
šägerd	شاگـرد	student, pupil, apprentice
šägerdi	شاگردی	apprenticeship, training
šäh	شاه	king, shah
šahäb	شهاب	meteor
šahäb sang	شهاب سنگ	meteor
sahäbe	صحابه	companions(of prophet)

šahädat	شهادت	martyrdom, testimony
sahäm	سهام	shares, stocks
šahämat	شهامت	bravery, greatness
sahämi	سهامی	joint-stock
šähäne	شاهذه	kingly, royal
šähanšäh	شاهنشاه	king, emperor
sahar	سحر	dawn, twilight
šähdäne	شاهدانه	hempseed
säheb	صاحب	owner, possessor, proprietor
sähebxäne	صاحب خانه	landlord
šähed	شاهد	witness, testifier
sähel	ساحل	shore, beach, coast
säheli	ساحلی	coastal
säher	ساحر	magician
sahhäfi	صحافی	bookbinding
šähi	شاهی	kingship, cress
šahid	شهید	martyr
šahid šodan	شهیدشدن	to martyr
sahih	صحیح	correct, right, true
sahim šodan	سهیم شدن	to participate
šähkär	شاهکار	masterpiece
sahl	سهل	easy
sahl angär	سهل انگار	careless, negligent
sahl angäri	سهل انگاری	carelessness, negligence
sahm	سهم	share, stock
sahm däštan	سهم داشتن	to share, to be involved
sahn	صحن	courtyard
šähnäme	شاهنامه	An epic of Persian kings
sahne	صدنه	scene, theatre, stage
šähparast	شاه پرست	royalist
šahr	شهر	city, town
sahrä	صحرا	desert, wilderness
šährag	شاهرگ	carotid artery

šähräh	شاهراه	highway
sahränešin	صحرانشین	nomad, desert dweller
šahrdär	شهردار	mayor
šahrdäri	شهرداری	city council
šahrebäni	شهربانی	police headquarters
šahrestän	شهرستان	township
šahri	شهری	urban, metropolitan
šahrivar	شهریور	sixth Persian month
šahriye	شهریه	tuition fee, stipend
šahrnešin	شهرنشین	city dweller, citizen
šähtut	شاه توت	black mulberry
sahv	سهو	mistake, error
šahvat	شهوت	lust, passion
šahvat angiz	شهوت انگیز	lustful, sexy, arousing
šahvat parast	شهوت پرست	voluptuous, lustful
sahyonism	صهیونیسم	zionism
šähzäde	شاهزاده	prince, princess
šajarenäme	شجره نامه	genealogy
šajarenevis	شناس شجره	genealogist
sajde	سجده	bowing, prostration
šak	شک	doubt, suspicion, indecision
šak kardan	شک کردن	to doubt, to suspect
sakane	سکنه	inhabitants, residents
šakar	شکر	sugar
säken	ساکن	resident, inhabitant
säket	ساکت	quiet, silent
šäki	شاکی	suer, plaintiff
šakibäyi	شکیبایی	patience, tolerance
šakkäk	شکاک	sceptical, suspicious
sakku	سکو	platform
šakl	شکل	figure, shape, form, picture
šakl gereftan	شکل گرفتن	to form
säl	سال	year, annum

šal	شل	crippled, limp
šäl	شال	scarf
saläh	صلاح	goodness, advisable
salähiyat	صلاح يت	competency, merit, authority
saläm	سلام	hello, greeting
saläm aleykom	سلام ع ل ي كم	hello, greetings
salämati	سلامتى	health
salät	صلات	prayer
salavät	ص لوات	praise for God and prophet
šalaxte	شلخته	clumsy, sluttish
säleh	صالح	competent, decent
sälem	سال م	intact, healthy, safe
säles	ثالث	third
sälgard	سال گرد	anniversary
salib	ص ل يب	cross (religious)
salibi	صليبى	crusade, cross shaped
šalil	ش ل يل	nectarine
saliqe	س ل ي قه	taste, tact
salis	س ل يس	fluent
säliyäne	سال يانه	yearly, annual
šälizär	شال يزار	rice field
šalläq	شلاق	lash, whip
šalläq zadan	شلاق زدن	to lash, to whip
sälmand	سال م ند	aged, old
salmäni	سلمانى	barber, hairdresser
sälnäme	سال نامه	calendar
sälon	سال ن	hall, lounge
šalqam	ش ل غم	turnip
sälruz	سال گرد	anniversary
saltanat	س ل ط نت	kingdom, monarchy
saltanat talab	س ل ط نت ط لب	monarchist, royalist
saltanati	سلطنتى	royal
šalvär	ش لوار	pants, trousers

šalvarak	شلوارک	short
sälxorde	سال خورده	old, aged
šäm	شام	dinner, supper
šam³	شمع	candle
sam³ak	سمعک	hearing aid
šam³dän	شمعدان	chandelier
šam³däni	شمعدانی	geranium
sam³i basari	سمعی بصری	audio-visual
samar	ثمر	fruit, product, result
samar baxš	ثمربخش	useful, fruitful
šämel	شامل	including, containing
sämet	صامت	mute
samimi	صمیمی	sincere, intimate, genuine
samimiyat	صمیمیت	sincerity
samm	سم	poison, venom
šämme	شامه	sense of smell, olfactory
sammi	سمی	poisonous, toxic
šämpäyn	شامپاین	champagne
šampo	شامپو	shampoo
šamsi	شمسی	solar
šamšir	شمشیر	sword
šamšir bäzi	شمشیربازی	fencing
samt	سمت	side, direction
samur	سمور	sable
sän	سان	parade, march
san³at	صنعت	industry, craft
san³ati	صنعتی	industrial, industrialised
sanä	ثنا	eulogy, praise
sanad	سند	document, title
sanäye³e dasti	صنایع دستی	crafts, hand crafts
šanbe	شنبه	saturday
sandali	صندلی	chair, seat
sandaliye čarxdar	صندلی چرخدار	wheelchair

sanduq	صندوق	chest, safe, cash register
sanduqdär	صندوق دار	cashier
šäne	شانه	shoulder, comb
sänehe	سانحه	accident, casualty
sang	سنگ	stone, rock
sangak	سنگک	a type of bread
sangar	سنگر	trench, rifle pit
sangarbandi	سنگربندی	entrenchment, fortification
sangdel	سنگدل	cruel, stone-hearted
sangin	سنگین	heavy, massive
sangrize	سنگریزه	gravel
sangsär	سنگسار	stoning to death
sangtaräš	سنگ تراش	mason, stonecutter
säni	ثانی	secondary, second
šanidan(šenav)	شنیدن (شنو)	to hear, to listen
säniye	ثانیه	a second
sanjäb	سنجاب	squirrel
sanjäq	سنجاق	pin, hairpin
sanjäqak	سنجاقک	dragonfly
sanješ	سنجش	measurement, testing
sanjidan(sanj)	سنجیدن (سنج)	to measure, to test
šäns	شانس	luck, chance
šänsi	شانسی	random, accidentally
sänsor	سانسور	censorship
sänt	سانت	centimetre
säntimetr	سانتیمتر	centimetre
šänzdah	شانزده	sixteen
šappare	شب پره	bat
säq	ساق	leg
šaqäyeq	شقایق	corn poppy
säqduš	ساقدوش	groomsman
säqe	ساقه	stem, stalk
šäqel	شاغل	employed, incumbent

saqf	سـقف	roof, ceiling
šaqiqe	شـقـيـقه	forehead
saqir	صـغـیر	minor, underage
saqqez	سـقز	chewing gum
šäqul	شاقول	plumb line
sar	سر	head, top, end
sär	سار	starling
sar³	صرع	epilepsy, fits
šar³	شرع	religious law
šar³e	شرعی	lawful, legal
saräb	سـراب	mirage
šaräb	شراب	wine
šaraf	شرف	honour, dignity
šaräfat	شرافـت	dignity, honour
sarafkande	سـراف کـنده	ashamed, disgraced
sarafräz	سـراف راز	honoured
saräne	سـرانـه	per capita, per head
saranjäm	سـرانـجام	end, finally
šarärat	شرارت	wickedness, vice, vandalism
saräsar	سـرا سر	throughout, all over
saräšib	سـرا شـیب	slope, steep
saräsime	سـرا سـیمه	confused, in a hurry
saratän	سـرطان	cancer
saraxs	سـرخس	fern
šarayän	شریـان	artery
saräydär	سـرای دار	janitor, doorman
šaräyet (šart)	شرایـط (شرط)	conditions, terms
saräziri	سرازیری	slop, downhill, steep
sarbäläyi	سربالایـی	uphill
šarbat	شربـت	syrup, tonic
sarbäz	سربـاز	soldier, private
sarbäzi	سربازی	soldiering, military service
sarčešme	سرچشمه	source

sard	سرد	cold, frigid, discouraged
sard šodan	سرد شدن	to cool down
sardabir	سردبیر	editor, chief secretory
sardaftar	سردفتر	notary public
sardär	سردار	commander
sardard	سردرد	headache
sardaste	سردسته	group leader
sardi	سردی	coldness, frigidity
sardsir	سردسیر	cold region
sarduši	سردوشی	shoulder strap
säreq	سارق	robber, thief
sarf kardan	صرف کردن	to spend, to consume
sarfe	صرفه	benefit, economy, interest
sarfejuyi	صرفه جویی	economy, providence
sargardän	سرگردان	wanderer, vagabond
sargarm	سرگرم	busy, amused, preoccupied
sargarm konande	سرگرم کننده	entertaining
sargarmi	سرگرمی	hobby, amusement
sargije	سرگیجه	vertigo, dizziness
sargord	سرگرد	major
sargošäde	سرگشاده	open, open lid
sargozašt	سرگذشت	adventure, tale, narrative
šarh	شرح	description, explanation
šarh dädan	شرح دادن	to describe, to explane
sarhadd	سرحد	border, boundary
sarhang	سرهنگ	colonel
šarhe häl	شرح حال	biography
sariᵉ	سریع	fast, rapid, speedy
šariᵉat	شریعت	religious law, religion
šarif	شریف	noble, honourable
sarih	صریح	frank, explicit, precise
šarik	شریک	partner, associate
šarji	شرجی	sultry, muggy

sarjuxe	سرجوخه	corporal
sarkär	سرکار	honorific title in army
sarkarde	سرکرده	commander, leader
sarkärgar	سرکارگر	foreman
sarkeši kardan	سرکشی کردن	to inspect, to revolt
sarkoft	سرکوفت	taunt, scoff
sarkoft zadan	سرکوفت زدن	to taunt, to scoff
sarkonsul	سرکنسول	consulate general
sarkubi	سرکوبی	suppression, repression
šärlätän	شارلاتان	charlatan, quack
sarleškar	سرلشکر	major general
šarm	شرم	shame, timidity, pudency
sarmä	سرما	cold, coldness
sarmä xordan	سرماخوردن	to catch cold
sarmä xordegi	سرما خوردگی	a cold
šarmande	شرمنده	ashamed, embarrassed
šarmandegi	شرمندگی	embarrassment, shame
sarmaqäle	سرمقاله	editorial
sarmašq	سرمشق	copy, model
šarmävar	شرم آور	disgraceful, indecent
sarmäxordegi	سرما خوردگی	catching cold
sarmäye	سرمایه	capital
sarmäyedär	سرمایه دار	capitalist
sarmäyedäri	سرمایه داری	capitalism
šarmgäh	شرمگاه	pubis
šarmsär	شرمسار	ashamed, disgraced
sarnegun kardan	سرنگون کردن	to capsize, to topple
sarnešin	سرنشین	passenger, crew member
sarnevešt	سرنوشت	fate, destiny
sarnize	سرنیزه	bayonet
sarosedä	سروصدا	noise, commotion
sarparast	سرپرست	guardian, supervisor
sarpäyi	سرپایی	outpatient

sarpäyiyni	سر پایینی	slope, downhill
sarpiči kardan	سرپیچی کردن	to disoby, to revolt
šarq	شرق	east, orient
šarqi	شرقی	eastern
šarr	شر	evil, mischief
sarräfi	صرافی	currency exchange
sarsari	سرسری	carelessly
saršenäs	سر شناس	well known, famous
saršir	سر شیر	cream
saršomäri	سرشماری	census
šart	شرط	condition, bet, term
šart bastan	شرط بستن	to bet
sartäsar	سرتاسر	throughout, entire
šartbandi	شرط بندی	betting, bid
šarti	شرطی	conditional
sartip	سرتیپ	brigadier general
šarur	شرور	wicked, mischievous
sarv	سرو	cypress tree
sarvän	سروان	captain
sarvar	سرور	leader, master, lord
sarzade	سرزده	suddenly, unexpectedly
sarzamin	سرزمین	country, territory
sarzaneš	سرزنش	blame, scolding
sarzaneš kardan	سرزنش کردن	to blame, to scold
šäš	شاش	urine, piss, pee
šäšidan(šäš)	شاشیدن (شاش)	to urinate, to piss
šast	شست	thumb
šast	شصت	sixty
šäter	شاطر	baker
sath	سطح	surface, level
sathi	سطحی	shallow, superficial
satl	سطل	bucket
satr	سطر	line

šatranj	شطرنج	chess
sätur	ساطور	large knife
saväb	ثواب	spiritual reward
saväd	سواد	literacy
savär	سوار	rider, mounted, installed
savär šodan	سوارشدن	to ride, to mounted
saväre nezäm	سواره نظام	cavalry
savärkär	سوارکار	jockey
šäx	شاخ	horn
saxävat	سخاوت	generosity
saxävat mand	سخاوت مند	generous
šäxe	شاخه	branch, subdivision
saxre	صخره	rock, cliff
šaxs	شخص	individual, person
šaxsi	شخصی	personal, civilian, private
šaxsiyyat	شخصیت	personality, entity
saxt	سخت	difficult, hard, strict, rigid
säxt	ساخت	made, make, structure
säxtan(säz)	ساختن (ساز)	to build, to make
säxtär	ساختار	structure
säxtegi	ساختگی	artificial, forged
säxtemän	ساختمان	building, structure
saxtgir	سخت گیر	uncompromising, strict
šäyad	شاید	may, may be, possibly
säybän	سایبان	shade, sunshade
säye	سایه	shadow, shade
šäye³	شایع	prevalent, epidemic
šäye³e	شایعه	rumour, gossip
säyer	سایر	rest, other
säyeš	سایش	friction, abrasion
šäyeste	شایسته	worthy, deserving
šäyestegi	شایستگی	merit, worth, suitability
säyiydan(säy)	ساییدن (سای)	to grind, to erode

sayyäd	صیاد	hunter
šayyäd	شیاد	impostor, charlatan
sayyal	سیال	fluid, flowing
sayyar	سیار	mobile, wanderer
sayyäre	سیاره	planet
säz	ساز	musical instrument
säzande	سازنده	creative, builder
säzemän	سازمان	organization, institution
säzeš	سازش	compromise, reconciliation
säzeš kardan	سازش کردن	to compromise, to reconcile
se	سه	three
se čaharom	سه چهارم	three-quarters
šeʳr	شعر	poetry
šebh	شبه	likeness
sebil	سبیل	moustache, whiskers
seboʳdi	سه بعدی	tridimensional
sebqat	سبقت	overtaking, precedence
sebqat gereftan	سبقت گرفتن	to overtake
sečarxe	سه چرخه	tricycle
sedä	صدا	voice, sound, noise, call
sedä kardan	صدا کردن	to call
sedädär	صدا دار	voiced, noisy
sedäqat	صداقت	honesty, truthfulness
šeddat	شدت	intensity, severity
sefärat	سفارت	embassy
sefäreš	سفارش	order, advice
sefäreš kardan	سفارش کردن	to order, to recommend
sefäreši	سفارشی	registered, recommended
sefat	صفت	attribute, adjective
sefid	سفید	white, blank
sefid pust	سفید پوست	white skin, white
sefr	صفر	zero
seft	سفت	tight, stiff, hard

seft kardan	سفت کردن	to tighten
šegeft angiz	شگفت انگیز	surprising
šegefti	شگفتی	wonder, surprise
seguš	سه گوش	triangular
sehhat	صحت	health, well being
sehr	سحر	spell, magic
šekäf	شکاف	split, gap, cleavage
šekäftan(šekäf)	شکافتن (شکاف)	to split, to rip up, to analyse
šekam	شکم	tummy, stomach, belly
šekamu	شکمو	gluttonous
šekanande	شکننده	fragile
šekanje	شکنجه	torture, torment
šekanje kardan	شکنجه کردن	to torture, to torment
šekar	شکر	sugar
šekär	شکار	haunting, prey, hunt
šekär kardan	شکار کردن	to haunt
šekärči	شکارچی	hunter
šekärgäh	شکارگاه	haunting ground
šekast	شکست	defeat, failure
šekast dädan	شکست دادن	to defeat
šekast näpazir	شکست ناپذیر	invincible
šekastan(šekan)	شکستن (شکن)	to break, to crack
šekaste	شکسته	broken, sad
šekaste band	شکسته بند	bonesetter, orthopaedist
šekastegi	شکستگی	fracture, breakdown
šekäyat	شکایت	complaint, grievance
šekäyat kardan	شکایت کردن	to complain, to whin
sekke	سکه	coin
šekl	شکل	shape, form, figure
sekseke	سکسکه	hiccup
sekte	سکته	stroke, hear attack
šekve kardan	شکوه کردن	to complain
sel	سل	tuberculosis

seläh	سلاح	arms, armour
šelank	شلنگ	hose
self servis	سلف سرویس	self-service
šellik	شلیک	firing an arm, shooting
sellul	سلول	cell
selsele	سلسله	kingdom, dynasty
semäjat	سماجت	insistence, persistence
semäjat kardan	سماجت کردن	to insist, to persist
semat	سمت	position, designation
semej	سمج	persistent, cheeky
šemš	شمش	bullion
šemšäd	شمشاد	box tree
semsäri	سمساری	second hand store
šen	شن	sand, gravel
šenä	شنا	swimming
šenä kardan	شنا کردن	to swim
šenägar	شناگر	swimmer
šenäsäyi	شناسایی	recognition, identification
šenäsäyi kardan	شناسایی کردن	to identify, to recognise
šenäsnäme	شناسنامه	identity card, birth certificate
šenavande	شنونده	listener
šenävar	شناور	floating, buoyant
senaväyi	شنوایی	hearing
šenaväyi sanji	شنوایی سنجی	audiometry
šenäxt	شناخت	knowledge, recognition
šenäxtan(šenäs)	شناختن (شناس)	to know, to recognise
šenel	شنل	cloak, mantle
senf	صنف	trade union, class, trade
šeni	شنی	sandy
šenidan (šenav)	شنیدن (شنو)	to hear
senjed	سنجد	oleaster, wild olive
šenkeš	شنکش	rake
senn	سن	age

sepäh	سپاه	army
separ	سپر	shield, armour, bumper
sepas	سپس	then, afterwards
sepäsgozäri kardan	سپاس گزاری کردن	to thank
sepäye	سه پایه	tripod
šepeš	شپش	lice
sepordan(sepär)	سپردن (سپر)	to recommend, to give
seporde	سپرده	deposit
septämr	سپتامبر	September
seqolu	سه قلو	triplet
seqt	سقط	abortion, miscarriage
seqt kardan	سقط کردن	to abort, to miscarry
serähat	صراحت	frankness, bluntness
šeräkat	شراکت	partnership
šerakt	شرکت	company, particiapation
šerakt kardan	شرکت کردن	to particiape, to attend
serämik	سرامیک	ceramic
seräyat	سرایت	contagion, transmission
serf	صرف	pure, mere
serfan	صرفا	merely, purely
seri	سری	set, series
serial	سریال	episodic
seriš	سریش	glue
serke	سرکه	vinegar
serqat	سرقت	theft, robbery
serqat kardan	سرقت کردن	to steal, to rob
serri	سری	secret, classified
servat	ثروت	wealth, property
servat mand	ثروتمند	rich, wealthy
šeš	شش	six
šešlul	ششلول	revolver
šeššad	ششصد	six hundred
šetäb	شتاب	hurry, speed, rush, velocity

setäd	سـ تاد	headquarter
setam	سـ تم	cruelty, injustice, abuse
setamdide	سـ تمديـ ده	oppressed
setamgar	سـ تمـ گر	cruel, oppressor
setäre	سـ تاره	star, asterisk, fortune
setäre šenäs	سـ تاره شـ ناس	astronomer
setäregan	ستارگان	stars
setäyeš	سـ تايـ ش	praise, worship
setäyeš kardan	سـ تايـ ش كردن	to praise, to worship
setäyeš gar	سـ تايـ شـ گر	worshiper
setize	سـ تـ يزه	quarrel, dispute
sevvom	سوم	third
sevvomin	سومين	the third
šey³	شيىٔ	thing, object
šeyär	شـ يار	groove, fissure, cleft
seyd	صـ يد	hunt, prey, fishing
seyd kardan	صـ يد كردن	to hunt, to fish
seyfi	صيفى	summer crop
seyl	سـ يل	flooding
seyl zade	سـ يلزده	flood victim
seylän	سـ يلان	seri lanka
šeypur	شـ يـ پور	trumpet, horn
seyqal	صـ يـ قل	polish, shine
seyr	سـ ير	travel, tour, excursion
šeytän	شـ يطان	satan, devil, naughty
šeytanat	شـ يطـ نت	naughtiness, diabolism
šeytäni	شيطانى	satanic, diabolic, naughtiness
šeyx	شـ يخ	clergy, old man
seyyed	سـ يد	master
sezävär	سزاوار	deserving, worthy
si	سى	thirty
ši³e	شـ يـعه	shiites
sib	سـ يب	apple

sešanbe	سه شنبه	tuesday
šib	ش یب	slope, slant
sib zamini	سیب زمینی	potato
sidi	سی دی	cd
šifte	ش ی ف ته	fascinated, fond
sigär	س ی گار	cigarettes
sigär kešidan	س ی گار کشیدن	to smoke
sigäri	سیگاری	cigarette smoker
šihe	ش یهه	neighing
šik	ش یک	stylish, fashionable
šikpuš	ش یک پ وش	smartly dressed
sili	سیلی	slap
sili zadan	سیلی زدن	to slap
šili	شیلی	Chile
sim	سیم	wire, cable
sim pič	س یم پ یچ	armature winder
simä	سیما	face, vision, appearance
simän	س یمان	cement, concrete
šimi	شیمی	chemistry
šimidän	شیمی دان	chemist
šimiyäyi	شیمیایی	chemical
simkeš	س یم کش	wireman
sine	س ی نه	breast, chest, bosom
sine pahlu	سینه هلو	pneumonia
sineband	س ی نه ب ند	bra, bib
sinemä	سینما	cinema, movie
sini	سینی	tray, platter
siqe	صد یغه	temporary marriage
sir	س یر	full, satisfied, fed up, garlic
šir	ش یر	lion, milk, tap
šir dädan	ش یردادن	to breasfeed
siräb	س یراب	satisfied of drinking
siräbi	سیرابی	tripe

širbahä	شیربها	gift to bride's parents
širdän	شیردان	rennet stomach
širdeh	شیرده	milch
šire	شیره	syrup, extract, opium residue
širin	شیرین	sweet, succulent, attractive
širini	شیرینی	sweetness, confectionary
sirk	سیرک	circus
širväni	شیروانی	gable roof
širxärgäh	شیرخوارگاه	nursery
sisad	سیصد	three thundered
šiše	شیشه	glass, wind screen
šišebor	شیشه بر	glazier
šišegar	شیشه گر	glass blower
šivan	شیون	mourning, moaning
šive	شیوه	method, style
six	سیخ	skewer, stiff
šiyäf	شیاف	suppository
siyäh	سیاه	black
siyäh pust	سیاه پوست	black coloured
siyäh sorfe	سیاه سرفه	whooping cough
siyäh zaxm	سیاه زخم	anthrax
siyähat	سیاحت	tour, travel, excursion
siyähat näme	سیاحت نامه	tourist's itinerary
siyährag	سیاهرگ	vein
siyänor	سیانور	cyanide
siyäsat	سیاست	politics, policy
siyäsat madär	سیاستمدار	politician
siyäsi	سیاسی	political
sizdah	سیزده	thirteen
sizdahbedar	سیزده بدر	13th of new year's festivity
šo³ä³	شعاع	ray, radius, beam
so³äl	سئوال	question, inquiry
so³äl kardan	سئوال کردن	to ask, to inquire

šo³är	شعار	slogan, motto
šo³är dädan	شعار دادن	to chant slogan
šo³bade bäzi	شعبده بازی	magic
šo³bade bäz	شعبده باز	magician, juggler
šo³be	شعبه	branch, section
šo³le	شعله	flame, blaze
so³ud	صعود	climbing, ascending
šo³ur	شعور	intelligence, common sense
sobät	ثبات	stability, firmness
sobh	صبح	morning, am
sobh bexeyr	صبح بخیر	good morning
sobhäne	صبحانه	breakfast
šodan(šav)	شدن (شو)	to become
šodani	شدنی	possible, feasible
sodur	صدور	issuing, emission
sofäl	سفال	crockery, ceramic
sofälgari	سفال گری	pottery, crockery
sofre	سفره	tablecloth
sogand	سوگند	swear, oath
sogand xordan	سوگند خوردن	to swear, to make an oath
sogoväri	سوگواری	mourning, funeral
šogun	شگون	good omen
sohän	سوهان	file, a type of sweet
šohar	شوهر	husband
šohardär	شوهردار	married woman
sohbat	صحبت	speech, talk, chat
sohbat kardan	صحبت کردن	to speak, to talk, to chat
šohrat	شهرت	publicity, fame, reputation
sohulat	سهولت	easiness
šojä³	شجاع	brave, courageous
šojä³at	شجاعت	bravery, courage
sokkän	سکان	helm
sokkändär	سکان دار	helmsman

šokolät	شکلات	chocolate
šokr kardan	شکرکردن	to thank (to god), to appreciate
šokrgozäri	شکرگذاری	thanksgiving
šokufe	شکوفه	blossom, bud
sokuh	شکوه	magnificence, glory
sokunat	سکونت	residence, settlement
sokut	سکوت	silence, quiet
šol	شل	loose, soft, lenient
solh	صلح	peace, reconciliation
solhämiz	صلح آمیز	conciliatory, peaceful
solhtalab	صلح طلب	peace lover
sols	ثلث	third, one third
soltän	سلطان	king, sultan
solte	سلطه	dominance, control
šoluq	شلوغ	busy, crowded, noisy
šoluqi	شلوغی	noise, crowed, disturbance
som	سم	hoof
šomä	شما	you(pl)
šomäl	شمال	north
šomäli	شمالی	northern
somäq	سماق	sumac
šomäre	شماره	number, digit, issue
šomäregiri	شماره گیری	dialling
šomäreš	شمارش	counting, calculation
somäx	صماخ	tympan, eardrum
some³e	صومعه	monastery, convent
šomordan(šomär)	شمرن (شمار)	to count, to calculate
šomorde	شمرده	distinct, intelligible
sonbäde	سنباده	grindstone
sonbe	سنبه	ramrod
sonbol	سنبل	hyacinth
sonnat	سنت	tradition

sonni	سنّی	sunnite
šoq	شوق	keenness, desire, eagerness
šoqäl	شغال	jackal
soqät	سوغات	travel gift
šoql	شغل	job, employment, position
soqut	سقوط	fall, crash, decline
sor³at	سرعت	speed, rapidity
sorang	سرنگ	syringe
soräq	سراغ	clue, trace
sorb	سرب	lead
sorb dar	سرب دار	leaded (petrol; gas)
sorfe	سرفه	cough
sorfe kardan	سرفه کردن	to cough
sorme	سرمه	collyrium
sormeyi	سرمه ای	dark blue
šoršor	شر شر	flowing noise, splashing
sorsore	سرسره	skate
šoru³	شروع	beginning, start, outset
šoru³ kardan	شروع کردن	to begin, to start
sorud	سرود	song, lyric, nursery rhyme
sorur	سرور	happiness, joy
soruš	سروش	inspiration
sorx	سرخ	red
sorx kardan	سرخ کردن	to roast, to fry
sorx karde	سرخ کرده	roasted, browned, fried
sorxak	سرخک	measles
sorxje	سرخجه	rubella
sorxrag	سرخرگ	artery
sos	سوس	ketchup
šoš	شش	lung
sost	سست	weak, flabby, slow
šostan(šur)	شستن (شور)	to wash, to bathe
šostešu	شست و شو	washing, bathing

sosyal-domokrat	سوسیال دمکرات	social-democratic
sosyalist	سوسیالیست	socialist
sot	صوت	voice, sound
šotor	ش تر	camel
sotun	س تون	column, pillar
sotvän	س توان	lieutenant
šoväliye	شوال یه	cavalier
soxan	سخن	speech, talk
soxan paräkani	سخن پراکنی	broadcasting
soxančini	سخن چینی	gossip
soxangu	سخ ذ گو	spokesman, speaker
soxanrän	سخ نران	lecturer, speaker
soxanräni	سخنرانی	lecture, oration, speech
soxanräni kardan	سخنرانی کردن	to make a speech
šoxm zadan	شخم زدن	to plough
šoyu³	ش یوع	outbreak, prevalence
su	سو	direction, side
su³e häzeme	سوء هاضمه	indigestion
sud	سود	benefit, profit, interest
sud dehi	سود دهی	profitability
sudmand	سودم.ند	profitable, useful, helpful
sufi	صوفی	sufi
sug	سوگ	sorrow, mourning
šuluq	ش لوغ	busy, crowded
šum	شوم	bad omen, ominous
supäp	سوپ اپ	valve
supur	س پور	garbage man, street cleaner
sur	سور	party, feast
šur	شور	salty
šurä	شورا	assembly, council
šurangiz	شوراـگ یز	sensational
surat	صورت	face, form, list, manu
surat hesab	صورت حساب	bill (shopping)

surati	صورتی	pink
šuravi	شوروی	Soviet
suräx	سوراخ	hole, puncture, cavity
suräx kardan	سوراخ کردن	to dig a hole, to pierce
suräxkon	سوراخ ک ن	puncher
sure	سوره	a chapter of koran
šure	شوره	dandruff, flake, saltpetre
šureš	شورش	riot, revolt, uprising
šureš kardan	شورش کردن	to revolt, to uprise
šureši	شورشی	rebel
šuridan(šur)	شوریدن (شور)	to revolt, to rise
surutme	سورتُ مه	sledge
susan	سو سن	lily
šuse	سو سه	gravelled road
susk	سو سک	cockroach
susmär	سو سمار	lizard
sut	سوت	whistle, siren
sut zadan	سوت زدن	to whistle
suvis	سوی س	Switzerland
suvisi	سویسی	Swiss
šux	شوخ	funny, joker
šuxi	شوخی	joke, fun, humour, kidding
šuxi kardan	شوخی کردن	to joke, to kid
suxt	سوخت	fuel, combustion
suxtan(suz)	سوختن (سوز)	to burn, to flame, to grieve
suxtani	سوختنی	combustible, flammable
suxtegi	سوختگی	burn
suxtgiri	سوختگیری	fuelling
suzäk	سوزاک	gonorrheae
suzan	سوزن	needle, pin, injection
suzän	سوزان	burning, flaming, smarting
suzanbän	سوزن ب ان	switch man
suzeš	سوزش	burn, pain, twinge

T		
tä	تا	until, fold
ta³ädol	تعادل	balance, equilibrium
ta³ahhod	تعهد	commitment, liability
ta³ahhol	تاهل	marriage
ta³ajjob	تعجب	surprise, amazement
ta³ajjob ävar	تعجب آور	amazing, surprising
ta³ajjob kardan	تعجب کردن	to wonder, to be surprised
ta³äm	طعام	food
ta³ammol	تامل	hesitation, pause
ta³ärof	تعارف	compliment, offer, formality
ta³ärof kardan	تعارف کردن	to offer
ta³asof	تاسف	regret, remorse
ta³assob	تعصب	fanaticism, prejudice
ta³ävoni	تعاونى	cooperative
ta³bir	تعبیر	interpretation, paraphrasing
ta³bir kardan	تعبیرک ردن	to interpret
ta³kid	تاکید	emphasis, insistence
ta³kid kardan	تاکید کردن	to emphasise
ta³lif	تالیف	writing, composing
ta³m	طعم	taste, flavour
ta³mim	تعمیم	generalisation, extension
ta³min	تامین	securing, ensuring
ta³mir	تعمیر	repair, mend
ta³mir kardan	تعمیر ک ردن	to repair
ta³mirgäh	تعمیر گاه	repair shop, garage
ta³ne	طـعـنه	scoff, taunting, sarcasm
ta³ne zadan	طـعـنه زدن	to scoff, to taunt
ta³ne ämiz	طـعـنه آمـ یز	sarcastic, ironical
ta³qib	تعقیب	pursuit, chase, following
ta³qib kardan	تعقیب ک ردن	to follow, to chase
ta³refe	تعرفه	tariff, certificate

ta³rif	تعریف	praise, definition
ta³rif kardan	تعریف کردن	to define, to praise
ta³sir	تاثیر	influence, impression, effect
ta³sir kardan	تاثیر کردن	to influence, to affect
ta³sis	تاسیس	establishment, founding
ta³sis kardan	تاسیس کردن	to establish, to found
ta³sisät	تاسیسات	foundations, establishments
ta³til	تعطیل	cessation, holiday
ta³til kardan	تعطیل کردن	to close, to stop
ta³tilat	تعطیلات	holidays, vacation
ta³tili	تعطیلی	holiday
tä³un	طاعون	plague
ta³viz	تعویض	replacement, substitution
ta³viz kardan	تعویض کردن	to replace, to exchange
ta³xir	تاخیر	delay, pause
ta³xir kardan	تاخیر کردن	to be late
ta³yiyd	تایید	confirmation, verification
ta³yiyd kardan	تایید کردن	to confirm, to verify
ta³yiyn kardan	تعیین کردن	to assign, to appoint
tab	تب	temperature (fever)
täb	تاب	curl, twist, resistance
tab³id	تبعید	exile
tab³iz	تبعیض	prejudice, bias, discrimination
taba³e	تبعه	national, citizen
tabädol	تبادل	exchange
tabäh	تباه	ruined, demolished
tabah kär	تبهکار	criminal, convict
tabahhor	تبحر	mastery, skill
täbän	تابان	shiny, glowing, brilliant
tabäni	تبانی	conspiracy, compact
tabaqe	طبقه	class, layer, category, floor
tabaqebandi	طبقه بندی	classification, ranking
tabaqebandi kardan	طبقه بندی کردن	to classify, to rank

tabar	تبر	axe
tabassom	تبسم	smile
tabbäxi	طباخی	cooking
tabdil	تبدیل	change, exchange
tabdil kardan	تبدیل کردن	to change, to exchange
täbe	تابه	frying pan
täbe³	تابع	dependent, follower, citizen
täbe³iyat	تابعیت	citizenship, nationality
täbeš	تابش	radiation
täbestän	تابستان	summer
tabi³at	ط ب ی عت	nature, temper
tabi³i	طبیعی	natural, normal, typical
tabib	ط ب یب	doctor, physician
täbidan(täb)	تابیدن (تاب)	to shine, to curl
tabl	ط بل	drum
tabliq	تبلیغ	propaganda, advertisement
täblo	تابلو	board, painting
tabrik	تبریک	congratulation, good wishes
tabrik goftan	تبریک گفتن	to congratulate
täbut	تابوت	coffin
tabxäl	تبخال	herpes
tabxir	تبخیر	evaporation, steaming
tabxir šodan	تبخیر شدن	to evaporate
tadfin	ت دف ین	burial
tadriji	تدریجی	gradual
tadris	تدریس	teaching, instruction
tadris kardan	تدریس ک ردن	to each
tafähom	تفاهم	mutual agreement
tafakkor	تفکر	thought, deliberation
tafävot	تفاوت	difference, diversity
tafraqe	تفرقه	division, dispersion
tafrih	تفریح	recreation, fun
tafrih kardan	تفریح کردن	to have fun

tafsir	تفسیر	interpretation, commentary
tafsir kardan	تفسیر کردن	to interpretate
taftiš	تفتیش	inspection, interogation
taftiš kardan	تفتیش کردن	to inspect, to interogate
tagarg	تگرگ	hail
tah	ته	bottom, base
tah mande	ته مانده	leftover
tah nešin	ته نشین	sediment, deposit
tah sigär	ته سیگار	cigarettes butt
tahäjom	تهاجم	attack, offensive
tahäl	طحال	spleen
tahammol	تحمل	endurance, tolerance
tahammol kardan	تحمل کردن	to endure, to tolerate
tahavvo³	تهوع	nausea, vomiting
tahavvol	تحول	change, transformation
tahavvol yaftan	تحول یافتن	to change, to transform
tahdid	تهدید	threat, intimidation
tahdid kardan	تهدید کردن	to threaent, to intimidate
tahiyye	تهیه	preparation, provision
tahiyye kardan	تهیه کردن	to prepare, to provide
tahlil raftan	تحلیل رفتن	to exhaust, to detoriate
tahlil kardan	تحلیل کردن	to analyse
tahmil	تحمیل	imposition
tahmil kardan	تحمیل کردن	to impose
tahniyat	تهنیت	congratulations
tahniyat goftan	تهنیت گفتن	to congratulate
tahqiq	تحقیق	research, investigation
tahqiq kardan	تحقیق کردن	research, investigation
tahqir	تحقیر	humiliation, belittling
tahqir kardan	تحقیر کردن	humiliation, belittling
tahrif	تحریف	distortion, alteration
tahrif kardan	تحریف کردن	to distort
tahrik	تحریک	instigation, stimulation

tahrik kardan	تحریک کردن	to instigate, to stimulate
tahrim	تحریم	sanction, prohibition
tahrim kardan	تحریم کردن	to prohibit, to bycott
tahsil	تحصیل	education, study
tahsil kardan	تحصیل کردن	to study
tahsin	تحسین	admiration
tahsin kardan	تحسین کردن	to admire
tahvil dädan	تحویل دادن	to give, to hand over
tahviye	تهویه	ventilation
täj	تاج	crown, crest
täj gozäri	تاج گذاری	crowning, coronation
tajärob	تجارب	experiences
tajävoz	تجاوز	rape, aggression, invasion
tajävoz kardan	تجاوز کردن	to rape, to invade
täjer	تاجر	businessman, trader
tajrobe	تجربه	experience
tajrobe kardan	تجربه کردن	to experience
tajrobi	تجربی	experimental
tajviz	تجویز	prescription, recommendation
tajviz kardan	تجویز کردن	to prescribe
tajziye	تجزیه	analysis, decomposition
tajziye kardan	تجزیه کردن	to analysis, to decompose
tak	تک	single, alone, unique
tak xäl	تک خال	ace
takabbor	تکبر	pride, vanity
takälif	تکالیف	duties, responsibilities
takallom	تکلم	conversation, speaking
takämol	تکامل	evolution
takän	تکان	shaking, movement, motion
täkestän	تاکستان	vineyard
takfir	تکفیر	excommunication
takfir kardan	تکفیر کردن	to excommunicate
taklif	تکلیف	duty, assignment

takmil	تكميل	completion, full
takmil kardan	تكميل كردن	to complete
täksi	تاكسى	taxi
taksir	تكثير	multiplication, reproduction
taksir kardan	تكثير كردن	to multiplicate, to reproduce
takye	تكيه	reliance, leaning
takye kardan	تكيه كردن	to rely, to lean
takzib	تكذيب	denial, refusing
takzib kardan	تكذيب كردن	to deny, to refuse
talä	طلا	gold
talab	ط لب	loan, search, claim
täläb	تالاب	pond pool
talabe	طلبه	theology student
talabidan(talab)	طلبيدن (طلب)	to call, to summon, to invite
talabkär	ط ل ب كار	creditor
talaf	تلف	waste, loss, casualty
talaf kardan	تلف كردن	to waste
talafät	تلفات	casualty, fatalities
talaffoz	تلفظ	pronunciation
talaffoz kardan	تلفظ كردن	to pronunce
taläfi	تلافى	retaliation, revenge
taläfi kardan	تلافى كردن	to retaliate
taläkub	طلاك وب	inlaid with gold
talangor	تلنگر	fillip
taläq	طلاق	divorce
taläq dädan	طلاق دادن	to divorce (by male)
taläq gereftan	طلاق گرفتن	to divorce (by female)
tälär	تالار	auditorium, hall
taläš	تلاش	effort, struggle
taläš kardan	تلاش كردن	to make effort, to struggle
talayi	طلايى	golden
täle[3]	طال ع	fortune, star, destiny
täle[3]bin	طال ع ب ين	fortune-teller

täleb	طالب	seeker, wiling
tälebi	طالبی	cantaloupe
talqin	تلقین	suggestion
talqin kardan	تلقین کردن	to suggest
talx	تلخ	bitter
tama³	طمع	greed
tama³kär	طمع ک ار	greedy
tamaddon	تمدن	civilization
tamalloq	تملق	flattery, sycophancy
tamäm	تمام	whole, full, complete
tamäm kardan	تمام کردن	to complete, to finish
tamannä kardan	تمنا کردن	to request
tamarkoz	تمرکز	centralization, concentration
tamarkoz kardan	تمرکز کردن	to concentrate, to focus
tamäs	تماس	contact, impact
tamäs gereftan	تماس گرفتن	to contact
tamäšä	تماشا	sightseeing, watching
tamäšä kardan	تماشا کردن	to sightsee, to watch
tamäšäči	تماشاچی	spectator, viewer
tamasxor	تمسخر	ridicule, mocking
tamasxor kardan	تمسخر کردن	to ridicule, to mock
tamäyol	تمایل	inclination, tendency
tamäyol däštan	تمایل داشتن	to tend, to desire
tambr	تمبر	stamp
tamcid	تمدید	extension, prolongation
tamcid kardan	تمدید کردن	to extend
tamešk	تمشک	raspberry
tamiz	تمیز	clean, distinction
tamiz kardan	تمیز کردن	to clean
tamkin kardan	تمکین کردن	to obey, to submit
tampän	تمپان	tampons
tamrin	تمرین	exercise, drill
tamrin kardan	تمرین کردن	to exercise

tan	تن	body
tanäb	طناب	rope, cord
tanaffor	تنفر	aversion, dislike
tanaffos	تنفس	breathing, respiration
tanaffos kardan	تنفس کردن	to breath
tanägoz	تناقض	contradiction, inconsistency
tanäsob	تناسب	proportion, ratio, symmetry
tanäsoli	تناسلی	genital
tanäsox	تناسخ	metempsychosis
tanävob	تناوب	alternation, recurrence
tanavvo³	تـنوع	variety, diversity
tanazzol	تنازل	decrease, reduction
tanbäku	تنباکو	tobacco
tanbal	تنبل	lazy, idle
tanbali	تنبلی	laziness
tanbih	تنبیه	punishment
tanbih kardan	تنبیه کردن	to punisht
tandis	تندیس	statue
tandorost	تندرست	healthy
tane	تنه	trunk, body
tanfiz kardan	تنفیض کردن	to authorize, to confirm
tang	تنگ	tight, narrow
tange	تنگه	strait, narrow pass
tanhä	تنها	alone, lonely, sole
tanhäyi	تنهایی	loneliness
tanin	طنین	echo, tone, intonation
tanparvar	تن پرور	self indulgent
tanqiye	تنقیه	enema
tanur	تنور	furnace, oven
tanxäh	تنخواه	capital, funds
tanz	طنز	satire, joke
tanzim kardan	تنظیم کردن	to arrange, to adjust
tanznevis	طنز نویس	satirist

tapänče	طپانچه	revolver, pistol
tapeš	تپش	palpitation, beating
tapidan(tap)	تپیدن(تپ)	to beat, to pulsate
tappe	تپه	hill
täq	طاق	arch, roof, odd
taqaddom	تقدم	priority, precedence
taqallä	تقلا	struggle, strife
taqallob	تقلب	cheating, falsification
taqallob kardan	تقلب کردن	to cheat
taqallobi	تقلبی	forged, false
täqat	طاقت	power, endurance
taqäto³	تقاطع	intersection, junction
taqäzä	تقاضا	request, demand
taqäzä kardan	تقاضا کردن	to request, to demand
täqče	طاقچه	mantel, rack, shelf
taqdim kardan	تقدیم کردن	to present, to offer
taqdir	تقدیر	destiny, fate, praise
taqdir kardan	تقدیر کردن	to praise
taqlid	تقلید	imitation, mimicry
taqlid kardan	تقلید کردن	to imitate, to mimic
taqriban	تقریبا	approximately, almost, about
taqsim	تقسیم	division, distribution
taqsim kardan	تقسیم کردن	to divide, to distribute
taqsir	تقصیر	guilt, fault
taqtir	تقطیر	distillation
täqut	طاغوت	devil, evil force
taqvä	تقوا	virtue
taqvim	تقویم	calendar
taqviyat	تقویت	strengthening, fortification
taqviyat kardan	تقویت کردن	to strengthen
taqyiyr	تغییر	change, alteration
taqyiyr kardan	تغییر کردن	to change
taqziye	تغذیه	eating, feeding

taqziye kardan	تغذیه کردن	to eat, to feed
tar	تر	wet, moist, damp
tar kardan	تر کردن	to wet, to moisten
tär	تار	cord, blurred
taraddod	تردد	traffic
taraf	طرف	side, direction, opponent
tarafdär	طرف دار	supporter, fan, follower
tarafdäri	طرفداری	supporting, taking side
taräh	طراح	designer, sketcher
taräihi	طراحی	designing, planning
täräj	تاراج	plunder
tarak	ترک	crack, split
tarakidan(tarak)	ترکیدن (ترک)	to burst, to explode, to crack
taräkom	تراکم	accumulation, congestion
taräne	ترانه	song
taraqqe	ترقه	firecracker
taraqqi	ترقی	progress, improvement
taraqqi kardan	ترقی کردن	to progress, to improve
taräšidan(taräš)	تراشیدن (تراش)	to shave, to scrape
taraššoh	ترشح	excretion, discharge
taraššoh kardan	ترشح کردن	to excrete, to discharge
taräxom	تراخم	trachoma
taräzu	ترازو	scale
tarbiyat	تربیت	training, cultivation
tarbiyat kardan	تربیت کردن	to train, to nurture
tarbiyat badani	تربیت بدنی	physical training
tard	طرد	rejection, expulsion
tard kardan	طرد کردن	to reject
tardid	تردید	doubt, skepticism
tardid kardan	تردید کردن	to doubt
tare	تره	leek
tarh	طرح	design, plan, sketch, project
tarh kardan	طرح کردن	to design, to plan

tarhim	ترحیم	funeral
tarhrizi	طرح ریزی	planning, designing
tärik	تاریک	dark, gloomy
tärik xäne	تاریک خانه	darkroom
täriki	تاریکی	darkness
tariq	طریق	means, manner, via
tärix	تاریخ	history, date
tärixče	تاریخچه	diary, account
tärixi	تاریخی	historical
tärixnevis	تاریخ نویس	historian
tarjih dädan	ترجیح دادن	to prefer
tarjome	ترجمه	translation
tarjome kardan	ترجمه کردن	to translate
tark kardan	ترک کردن	to abandon, to leave, to quit
tarkeš	ترکش	quiver
tarkib	ترکیب	form, shape, combination
tarmim	ترمیم	repair, amendment
tarrähi	طراحی	designing, sketching
tars	ترس	fear, fright, panic
tarsidan(tars)	ترسیدن (ترس)	to be scared, to be afraid
tarsim	ترسیم	drawing
tarsnäk	ترسناک	horrible, scary
tarsu	ترسو	coward
tartib	ترتیب	order, arrangement
tarvij	ترویج	propaganda, promotion
tarz	طرز	manner, method, mode
täs	طاس	bald, dice, bowl
tašäboh	تشابه	similarity, resemblance
tasädof	تصادف	accident, coincidence
tasädofan	تصادفا	accidentally, by chance
tašakkor	تشکر	gratitude, thanking
tašannoj	تشنج	convulsion, fit
tasarrof	تصرف	occupation, seizure

tasarrof kardan	تصرف کردن	to occupay, to seize
tasävi	تساوی	equality
tasävir	تصویر	pictures
tasavvof	تصوف	sufism
tasavvor	تصور	imagination, conception
tasavvor kardan	تصور کردن	to imagine
tašayyo³	تشیع	shiism
tasbit	تثبیت	stabilization, establishment
tasbit kardan	تثبیت کردن	to stabilise, to establish
tašdid	تشدید	aggravation, intensification
tašdid kardan	تشدید کردن	to aggravate, to intensify
tasdiq	تصدیق	confirmation, license
tasdiq kardan	تصدیق کردن	to confirm, to certify
tasfiye	تصفیه	filtration, purification
tasfiye kardan	تصفیه کردن	to cleanse, to purify
tasfiye šode	تصفیه شده	filtered
tashih	تصحیح	correction, proof reading
tashih kardan	تصحیح کردن	to correct, to proof read
tashilät	تسهیلات	facilities
taškil	تشکیل	formation, establishment
taškil dädan	تشکیل دادن	to form, to establish
taškilät	تشکیلات	organization, institution
taskin	تسکین	soothing, alleviation
taskin dädan	تسکین دادن	to sooth, to alleviate
taslihät	تسلیحات	ammunitions, armaments
taslim	تسلیم	submission, surrender
taslim kardan	تسلیم کردن	to submit, to surrender
taslis	تثلیث	trinity
tasliyat	تسلیت	condolence, sympathy
tasliyat goftan	تسلیت گفتن	to give condolence
tasmim	تصمیم	decision, determination
tasmim gereftan	تصمیم گرفتن	to decide, to determine
tašrifät	تشریفات	ceremonies, formalities

tašrih	تشریح	description, explanation
tašrih kardan	تشریح کردن	to describe, to explane
tasvib	تصویب	approval, confirmation
tasvib kardan	تصویب کردن	to approve, to confirm
tašviq	تشویق	encouragement
tašviq kardan	تشویق کردن	to encourage
tasvir	تصویر	picture, illustration
tasxir kardan	تسخیر کردن	to conquer, to captivate
tašxis	تشخیص	distinction, diagnosis
tašxis dädan	تشخیص دادن	to distinguish, to diagnose
tatbiq	تطبیق	comparison, checking
tatbiq kardan	تطبیق کردن	to match, to adjust
taväfoq	توافق	agreement, mutual consent
taväfoq kardan	توافق کردن	to agree, to consent
tavahhom	توهم	imagination, illusion
tavahhoš	توحش	savagery, wildness
tavajjoh	توجه	attention
tavajjoh kardan	توجه کردن	to pay attention
tavakkol kardan	توکل کردن	to rely, to trust
täval	تـ ـاول	blister
tavallod	تولد	birth
tavän	توان	strength, power
tävän	تاوان	indemnity, compensation
tavänäyi	توانایی	ability
tavänestan(tavän)	توانستن (توان)	to be able, can
tavaqqo³	توقع	expectancy, anticipation
tavaqqo³ däštan	توقع داشتن	to expect
tavaqqof	توقف	stop, pause, halt
tavaqqof kardan	توقف کردن	to stop, to pause
tavarrom	تورم	inflation, edema
tavassol	توسل	resort, recourse
tavassot	توسط	by, via, by means of
täve	تاوه	pan

tavil	طویل	long, lengthy
tavile	طویله	stable, stall
tävus	طاووس	peacock
taxallof	تخلف	violation, infringement
taxassos	تخصص	specialty, expertise
taxayyol	تخیل	imagination, fantasy
taxfif	تخفیف	discount, reduction
taxliye	تخلیه	evacuation
taxliye kardan	تخلیه کردن	to evacuate
taxmin	تخمین	estimate
taxmin kardan	تخمین کردن	to estimate
taxmir	تخمیر	fermentation
taxrib	تخریب	demolition, destruction
taxrib kardan	تخریب کردن	to demolish, to destroy
taxt	تخت	bed, throne
taxte	تخته	board, wooden piece
taxte nard	تخته نرد	backgammon, dice, die
taxtesiyäh	تخته سیاه	blackboard
täxto täz	تاخت و تاز	invasion
taxtxab	تخت خواب	bed
täyefe	طایفه	tribe, clan, sect
täyp	تایپ	typing
taz³if kardan	تضعیف کردن	to weaken, to reduce
tazäd	تضاد	contrast, contradiction
tazähorät	تظاهرات	demonstrations
tazakkor	تذکر	reminding, warning
tazakkor dädan	تذکر دادن	to remind, to warn
täze	تازه	new, fresh
täze väred	تازه وارد	new comer
täzekär	تازه کار	inexperienced, novice
täzi	تازی	haunting dog
täziyäne	تازیانه	whip, lash
tazmin	تضمین	guarantee, warranty

tazmin kardan	تضمین کردن	to guarantee
tazriq	تزریق	injection
tazriq kardan	تزریق کردن	to inject
tazyiyn kardan	تزیین کردن	to decorate
tazyiyn	تزیین	decoration, ornament
te³ätr	تناتر	theatre
te³däd	تعداد	number
tebb	طب	medicine, medical practice
tebbi	طبی	medical
tebqe	ط بق	according to
tefl	ط فل	kid, child
teflak	طفلک	little kid, poor thing
tehrän	تهران	Tehran
tejärat	تجارت	business, commerce
tejäri	تجاری	commercial
tekke	تکه	piece, fragment
tekrär	تکرار	repetition, recurrence
tekrär kardan	تکرار کردن	to repeat, to rehearse
tekräri	تکراری	repetitious
telävat	تلاوت	recital (of koran)
telävat kardan	تلاوت کردن	to recit (of koran)
telefon	تلفن	telephone
telefon kardan	تلفن کردن	to call to telephone
telefon či	تلفن چی	operator
telefone hamräh	تلفن همراه	mobile phone
telegeräf	تلگراف	telegram
teleskop	تلسکوپ	telescope
telesm	ط ل سم	spell, charm
televiziyon	تلویزیون	television
temsäh	تمساح	crocodile
tenis	تنیس	tennis
teribun	تریبون	lectern
terminäl	ترمینال	bus station

teryäk	تریاک	opium
teryäki	تریاکی	addicted to opium
tešne	تشنه	thirsty
test	تست	test
test kardan	تست کردن	to test
teyf	طیف	spectrum
teyye	طی	during
teyy kardan	طی کردن	to pass
tile	تیله	marble
tim	تیم	team
timärestän	تیمارستان	mental hospital
timsär	تیمسار	high rank military officer
tinat	طینت	instinct, nature, disposition
tip	تیپ	type, brigade
tiq	تیغ	razor, blade
tiqe	تیغه	lamella, edge, ridge
tir	تیر	bullet, fourth Persian month
tir xordan	تیر خوردن	to get shot
tir zadan	تیر زدن	to shoot
tirandäzi	تیراندازی	shooting, gunfire
tiräž	تیراژ	circulation (newspaper)
tirbärän	تیرباران	a shower of shots, execution
tire	تیره	dark, dim, dash
tiše	تیشه	chip-axe
tiz	تیز	sharp, keen
tizhuš	تیزهوش	genius, very intelligent
to	تو	you(singular)
to³am	توام	linked, joint
to³me	طعمه	bait, prey, victim
tobe	توبه	remorse, penitence
tobe kardan	توبه کردن	to repent
tobix	توبیخ	reproof, reprimand
tobix kardan	توبیخ کردن	to reprimand, to warn

tof	تف	spit, saliva
tof kardan	تف کردن	to spit
tofäle	تفاله	scum, refuse
tofang	تفنگ	rifle, gun
tohfe	تحفه	gift, souvenir
tohidast	تهیدست	poor, empty-handed
tohin	توهین	offence, insult
tohin kardan	توهین کردن	to offend, to insult
tohmat	تهمت	false accusation,
tohmat	تهمت زدن	to accuse falsely
tojih	توجیه	accounting for, justification
tojih	توجیه کردن	to justify
tojjär	تجار	merchants, businessmen
tolid	تولید	production, generation
tolid	تولید کردن	to produce, to generate
tolid konande	تولید کننده	producer
tolide mesl	تولید مثل	reproduction
tolide mesl kardan	تولید مثل کردن	to reproduce
tolombe	تلمبه	pump
tolu³	ط لوع	sunrise
ton	تن	metric ton
tonbak	تنبک	tambourine
tonbän	تنبان	loose pants
tond	تند	fast, spicy, hot, quick
tondar	تندر	thunder
toqif	توقیف	arrest, custody
toqif kardan	توقیف کردن	to arrest, to sieze
toqyän	طغ یان	overflowing, rebellion
toqyän kardan	طغ یان کردن	to overflow, to rebel
tor	طور	manner, method, kind
torät	تورات	torah
tord	ترد	crisp, frail
tormoz	ترمز	brake

torob	ترب	radish
torš	ترش	sour
torši	ترشی	sourness, pickles
tošak	تشک	mattress
tose³e	توسعه	expansion, extension
tose³e dädan	توسعه دادن	to expand, to extend
tosif	توصیف	description
tosif kardan	توصیف کردن	to describe
tosiye	توصیه	recommendation, advice
tosiye kardan	توصیه کردن	to recommend, to advise
tote³e	توطئه	plot, conspiracy
tote³e kardan	توطئه کردن	to plot, to conspire
toxm	تخم	seed, egg, sperm, testicle
toxm gozäštan	تخم گذاشتن	to lay eggs
toxm ozär	تخم گذار	oviparous
toxmak	تخمک	ovum
toxmdän	تخمدان	ovary
toxme	تخمه	roasted seeds
toxme morq	تخم مرغ	egg
tozi³	توزیع	distribution, division
tozi³ kardan	توزیع کردن	to distribute, to divide
tozi³konande	توزیع کننده	distributor
tozih	توضیح	explanation
tozih dädan	توضیح دادن	to explane
tu	تو	inside, within, in
tu rafte	تورفته	indented
tubre	توبره	feed bag
tudamäqi	تودماغی	nasal
tude	توده	mass, heap, pile
tufän	طوفان	typhoon, storm
tul	طول	length, duration
tuläni	طولانی	long, lengthy
tule	توله	puppy

tule sag	توله سگ	puppy
tuli	طولی	longitudinal
tulu³	طلوع	sunrise
tumär	طومار	scroll, roll
tup	توپ	ball, cannon, piece
tup bäzi	توپ بازی	playing game
tupxäne	توپخانه	artillery
tur	تور	net
tusari	توسری	a blow on the head
tuše	توشه	provisions
tusi	طوسی	dark grey
tut	توت	berry
tut ferangi	توت فرنگی	strawberry
tuti	طوطی	parrot
tutivär	طوطی وار	parrot-like
tutun	توتون	tobacco
tuvälet	توالت	toilet

U		
u	او	he, she
ulteräsänd	اولتراساند	ultrasound
ulum	علوم	sciences
umumi	عمومی	general
umur	امور	affairs, matters
urupä	اروپا	Europe
urupäyi	اروپایی	European
usul	اصول	principles
ut	اوت	august
utu	اطو	iron
utubus	اتوبوس	bus
utušuyi	اطوشویی	dry cleaner

V		
va	و	and
va ellä	و الا	otherwise, or else
va³de	وعده	promise, vow
va³degäh	وعده گاه	meeting place
vä³ez	واعظ	preacher
vabä	وبا	cholera
vabäl	وبا ل	trouble, bother
väbaste	وابسته	related, dependent, relative
väbaste budan	وابسته بودن	to depend
väbastegi	وابستگی	affiliation, connection, linkage
vädär	وادار	made, persuaded, led
vädär kardan	وادار کردن	to make, to persuade
vädi	وادی	valley, desert
vadi³e	ودیعه	deposit, bond
vafä	وفا	loyalty, fidelity
vafädär	وفادار	loyal, trusty
vafädäri	وفاداری	loyalty, fidelity
väfer	وافر	abundant, plentiful
väfi	وافی	adequate, sufficient
väfur	وافور	opium smoking pipe
vagarna	وگرنه	otherwise
vägerä	واگرا	divergent
vägeräyi	واگرایی	divergence
vägirdär	واگیردار	contagious
vägon	واگن	wagon, railway coach
vägozär kardan	واگذار کردن	to hand over, to transfere
vah	واه	oh, alas
vahdat	وحدت	unity, solitude, union
vähed	واحد	one, single, unit, credit
väheme	واهمه	fear, fright
vähi	واهی	futile, vain, groundless

vahle	وهله	step, period, stage
vahm	وهم	illusion, imagination
vahš	وحش	wild, wilderness
vahšat	وحشت	dread, fright, panic
vahšatnäk	وحشتناک	horrible, terrifying, frightful
vahšatzade	وحشتزده	frightened, terrified
vahši	وحشی	savage, uncivilised, wild
vahšigari	وحشیگری	cruelty, barbarity, savagery
vahšiyäne	وحشیانه	savage, cruel
vahy	وحی	inspiration, revelation
vajab	وجب	span
vajd	وجد	ecstasy, excessive joy
väjeb	واجب	compulsory, necessary
väjebät	واجبات	religious precepts
väjebi	واجبی	depilatory cream
väjed	واجد	possessing, having
vajh	وجه	fund, money, face, surface
väkdär	واکدار	voiced
väke	واکه	vowel
vakil	وکیل	parliament member, attorney
väkoneš	واکنش	reaction
väks	واکس	polish
väksan	واکسن	vaccine
väksi	واکسی	shoeblack
väksinäsyon	واکسیناسیون	vaccination
väl	وال	whale
välä	والا	exalted, eminent, highness
vala³	ولع	voracity, greed
valadozzenä	ولدزنا	bastard
välähazrat	والاحضرت	royal highness
välede	والده	mother
väledeyn	والدین	parents
väleh	واله	distracted, dazzled

vali	ولی	but, guardian, parent
väli	والی	governor-general
vali³ahd	ولیعهد	crown prince
valikan	ولیکن	but, however
valläh	والله	by god
valo	ولو	even though
väm	وام	debt, loan
vämändan(vä män)	واماندن (وا مان)	to be exhausted, to liger
vämände	وامانده	exhausted, helpless, worn out
vän	وان	bathtub
vänemud kardan	وانمود کردن	to pretend
vänet	وانت	van
vang	ونگ	cry
vängahi	وانگهی	furthermore, besides
vänil	وانیل	vanilla
väpas	واپس	back
väpasin	واپسین	last
väqe³	واقع	placed, situated, located
väqe³an	واقعا	really, indeed
väqe³e	واقعه	event, happening, event
väqe³i	واقعی	real, actual
väqe³iyat	واقعیت	reality, truth, fact
väqef	واقف	aware, informed, conscious
vaqf	وقف	pious legacy, endowment
vaqfe	وقفه	standstill, pause, delay
vaqfi	وقفی	endowed, dedicated
vaqih	وقیح	impudent, shameless
vaqt	وقت	time, occasion
vaqt koši	وقت کشی	killing time, idling
vaqti	وقتی	when, once, whenever
vaqtšenäs	وقت شناس	punctual, tactful
var ämadan(var äy)	ور آمدن (ور آی)	to ferment, to rise, to come off

var raftan(var rav)	ور رفتن (ور رو)	to tamper, to manipulate
varä[3]	ورا	behind, beyond
väraftan(värav)	وارفتن (وارو)	to loosen, to become flabby
värafte	وارفته	loose, relaxed, mushy
varam	ورم	inflammation, swelling
varam kardan	ورم کردن	to inflamm, to swell
varandäz kardan	ورانداز کردن	to measure, to look over
varaq	ورق	leaf, sheet, page, game card
varaqbäz	ورق باز	card player, gambler
varaqbäzi	ورق بازی	card playing, gambling
varaqe	ورقه	paper, sheet, coat, lamina
varaqpäre	ورق پاره	scrap of paper
värasi kardan	وارسی کردن	to investigate, to inspect
väraste	وارسته	free, librated
vardäštan(var där)	ورداشتن (وردار)	to take, to pick up
väred	وارد	entered, aware, expert
väred kardan	وارد کردن	to import
väredät	واردات	imports
väredäti	وارداتی	imported
värede	وارده	received, imported, recorded
väres	وارث	heir, heiress
varid	ورید	vein
varšekast(e)	ورشکسته	bankrupt, broke
varšekastegi	ورشکستگی	bankruptcy
väru	وارو	reversed, upside down
värune	وارونه	upside down, inside out
varzeš	ورزش	exercise, sport, athletics
varzeš kardan	ورزش کردن	to exercise
varzešgäh	ورزشگاه	stadium, sports arena
varzeši	ورزشی	related to sport
varzeškär	ورزشکار	sportsman, athlete
varzide	ورزیده	trained, skilled
varzidegi	ورزیدگی	dexterity, being well trained

vasat	وسط	middle, centre, between
vasati	وسطى	central, middle
väsete	واسطه	mediator, broker, agent
vasf	وصف	explanation, descrption
vasfi kardan	وصف کردن	to explane, to describe
vasfi	وصفى	explanatory, participial
vasi	وصى	guardian, representative
vasi³	وسیع	large, wide, extensive
vasile	وسیله	equipment, medium, means
vasiqe	وثیقه	deposit, bond
vasiyyat	وصیت	will, testament
vasiyyat näme	وصیت نامه	written will
vasl	وصل	connecting, joining, link
vasl kardan	وصل کردن	to connect, to join, to link
vaslat	وصلت	matrimony, wedlock
vaslat kardan	وصلت کردن	to marry
vasle	وصله	patch, repair, mending
vasväs	وسواس	obsession, fuss
vasvase	وسوسه	temptation, seduction
vasvase kardan	وسوسه کردن	to tempt, to seduce, to entice
vasväsi	وسواسى	obsessive, fussy
vatan	وطن	motherland, native country
vatan parast	وطن پرست	patriot
vatandust	وطن دوست	patriot
vatanparasti	وطن پرستى	patriotism
väveylä	واویلا	alas, woe
väx	واخ	ouch
vaxim	وخیم	bad, critical
väy	واى	ah, alas, woe
väyistädan(väyist)	وایستادن (واى)	to stand, to wait, to stop
väz	وعظ	preaching, sermon
vaz³	وضع	condition, state, position
vaz³e haml	وضع حمل	labour, childbirth, deliver

vaz³e haml kardan	وضع حمل کردن	to give birth
vaz³yyat	وضعیت	condition, situation, position
vazaq	وزغ	frog, toad
väže	واژه	word, term
väžegän	واژگان	vocabulary
väžegun	واژگون کردن	to capsize, to overturn
väzeh	واضح	obvious, apparent
väženäme	واژه نامه	dictionary
vazidan (vaz)	وزیدن (وز)	to blow, to breeze
vazife	وظیفه	duty, task, obligation
vazife šenäs	وظیفه شناس	dutiful
vazin	وزین	heavy, dignified
vazir	وزیر	minister
väzlin	وازلین	vaseline
vazn	وزن	weight, tonnage, load
vazn kardan	وزن کردن	to weigh
vazne	وزنه	weight, counter weight
vazne bardär	وزنه بردار	weight lifter
vazne bardäri	وزنه برداری	weight lifting
vedä³ kardan	وداع کردن	to farewell
vefq dädan	وفق دادن	to conform, to adjust
vejdän	وجدان	conscience
vejdänan	وجدانا	conscientiously, justly
vejhe	وجهه	popularity, esteem
vejin	وجین	weeding
vekälat	وکالت	proxy, power of attorney
vekälat näme	وکالت نامه	a proxy, a mandate
vel	ول	loose, free, unrestrained
vel kardan	ول کردن	to leave alone, to release
velädat	ولادت	birth
velarm	ولرم	tepid, mild
veläyat	ولایت	province, state, guardianship
velgard	ولگرد	vagabond, tramp, wanderer

velo	ولو	spread wide, scattered
velvele	ولوله	noise, brawl
veqähat	وقاحت	shame, impudence
veqär	وقار	dignity, poise
ver zadan	ور زدن	to chatter, to gabble
veräsat	وراثت	heredity, inheritance
verd	ورد	spell, incantation
verd xändan	ورد خواندن	to cast a spell
verräj	وراج	talkative, verbose
verräji	وراجی	talkativeness, verbosity
verräji kardan	وراجی کردن	to talk nonstop
vesätat	وساطت	mediation, intervention
vesätat kardan	وساطت کردن	to mediate, to intervene
vesileye naqliye	وسیله نقلیه	means of transport, vehicle
vexämat	وخامت	badness, critical situation
veylän	ویلان	wandering, vagrant
vezärat	وزارت	ministry, department
vezärati	وزارتی	ministerial
vezäratxäne	وزارتخانه	ministry, department
vezvez	وز وز	buzzing, humming
vezvez kardan	وز وز کردن	to buzz, to humm
virän	ویران	destroyed, ruined
virän kardan	ویران کردن	to destroy, to ruine
viräne	ویرانه	ruin
viräni	ویرانی	destruction, demolition
virästär	ویراستار	editor
viräyeš	ویرایش	edition
viräyeš kardan	ویرایش کردن	to edit
virus	ویروس	virus
vitämin	ویتامین	vitamin
viyär	ویار	pica, longing
viyolon	ویولون	violin
vizä	ویزا	visa

viže	ویژه	special, specific
vižegi	ویژگی	speciality
vofur	وفور	abundance, plenitude
vojud	وجود	being, entity, existence
vojud dāštan	وجود داشتن	to exist, to be
voqu[3]	وقوع	happening, occurrence
vorud	ورود	entrance, arrival, entry
vorudi	ورودی	entrance, admission fee
vos[3]	وسع	ability, capacity
vos[3]at	وسعت	breadth, extent, width
vostā	وسطی	medieval, middle
vosul	وصول	reception, arrival, collection
vozu	وضو	ablution before prayer
vozu gereftan	وضو گرفتن	to have ablution
vozuh	وضوح	clarity, lucidity
vul xordan	ول خوردن	to wiggle, to toss

X		
xä³en	خائن	traitor, betrayer
xäb	خواب	sleep
xäb älud	خواب آلود	to sleepy
xäb gardi	خواب گردی	sleepwalking
xabar	خبر	news, notice
xabar dädan	خبر دادن	to inform
xabar gozäri	خبر گذاری	news agency
xabarčin	خبرچین	informer
xabardär	خبردار	alert, attention, aware
xabarnegär	خبرنگار	correspondent, reporter
xäbgäh	خوابگاه	dormitory, mess
xäbidan(xäb)	خوابیدن (خواب)	to sleep
xabis	خبیث	malicious, wicked
xadamät	خدمات	services (assistance)
xadame	خدمه	crew, servants, attendants
xädem	خادم	servant, server
xafe	خ فه	stuffy, choked
xafe kardan	خ فه کردن	to choke, to strangle
xafeqän	خفقان	suffocation, oppression
xafif	خفیف	mild, light
xägine	خاگینه	omelet
xähar	خواهر	sister
xähar šohar	خواهر شوهر	husband's sister
xähar xände	خواهر خوانده	adopted sister
xähar zäde	خواهر زاده	nephew or niece
xähar zan	خواهر زن	wife's sister
xäheš kardan	خواهش کردن	to request, to beg
xäje	خواجه	eunuch, master
xäk	خاک	soil, earth, land
xäk älud	خاک آلود	soiled, dusty
xäk andäz	خاک انداز	dustpan

xäk sepäri	خاک سپاری	funeral
xäke	خاک ه	powder, dust
xäkestar	خاکستر	ash
xäkestari	خاکستری	gray
xäki	خاکی	soiled, earthly
xäkriz	خاکریز	embankment, bund
xäl	خال	mole
xäl kubi	خال کوبی	tattooing
xal³ kardan	خلع کردن	to depose, to sack
xalabän	خلبان	pilot
xäldär	خالداز	spotted
xäle	خاله	maternal aunt
xäleq	خالق	creator, maker
xäles	خالص	pure, unalloyed
xäli	خالی	empty, void, vacant
xäli kardan	خالی کردن	to empty, to vacate
xalife	خلیفه	caliph
xalij	خلیج	gulf, bay
xälq	خلق	people, creation
xälq kardan	خلق کردن	to create
xalse	خلسه	ecstasy
xalvat	خلوت	privacy, seclusion
xam	خم	curve, bend
xam kardan	خم کردن	to bend
xäm	خام	raw, crude, naïve
xäme	خامه	cream
xamide	خمیده	curved, bent
xamir	خمیر	paste, dough
xamir dandän	خمیر دندان	toothpaste
xämuš	خاموش	quiet, silent, extinct
xämuš kardan	خاموش کردن	to turn off
xämuši	خاموشی	black out, silence
xamyäze	خمیازه	yawn

xän	خان	tribal chief
xänä	خوانا	readable, legible
xänande	خواننده	singer, reader
xänaväde	خانواده	family, household
xänavädegi	خانوادگی	familial
xändan(xän)	خواندن (خوان)	to read, to sing, to study
xandaq	خندق	moat, ditch
xande	خنده	laughter
xande där	خنده دار	funny, ridiculous
xandidan(xand)	خندیدن	to laugh
xäne	خانه	house, home
xäne där	خانه دار	housewife
xäne nešin	خانه نشین	retired, staying at home
xänedän	خاندان	dynasty, family
xänegi	خانگی	domestic, house-made
xänemän	خانمان	household
xäneqäh	خانقاه	monastery
xänevär	خانوار	family
xanjar	خنجر	dagger
xänom	خانم	lady, mrs. mistress
xänom bäz	خانم باز	whoremonger
xär	خار	thorn, bristle
xärä	خارا	granite
xaräb	خراب	broken, out of order, faulty
xaräb kardan	خراب کردن	to break, to destroy
xaräbe	خرابه	ruins
xarboze	خربزه	melon
xarčang	خرچنگ	crab, lobster
xardal	خردل	mustard
xärej	خارج	outside, abroad, away
xärej kardan	خارج کردن	to take out
xäreje	خارجه	abroad, foreign country
xäreji	خارجی	external, foreigner

xäreq oläde	خارق العاده	extraordinary
xäreš	خارش	itching, scratching
xarguš	خرگوش	hare, rabbit, bunny
xäri	خواری	despise, degradation
xarid	خرید	purchase, buying
xaridan(xar)	خریدن (خر)	to buy
xäridan(xär)	خاریدن (خار)	to scratch
xaridär	خریدار	buyer, customer
xariyyat	خریت	stupidity, silliness
xarj	خرج	cost, expense
xarj kardan	خرج کردن	to spend
xarji	خرجی	allowance, budget
xarmagas	خرمگس	horsefly, gadfly
xarman	خرمن	stack, harvest, yield
xarmast	خرمست	dead drunk
xärobär	خوار و بار	grocer
xärobär foruši	خوار و بار فروشی	grocery
xäs	خاص	special, proper
xašäb	خشاب	loader of rifle magazine
xäšäk	خاشاک	motes, stalks
xašen	خشن	rough, coarse
xasis	خسیس	stingy
xäsiyat	خاصیت	property, use, virtue
xašm	خشم	anger, wrath
xasmäne	خصمانه	hostile
xašmgin	خشمگین	angry, furious
xäst	خواست	will, desire
xästan(xäh)	خواستن (خواه)	to want, to ask
xaste	خسته	tired, worn out, bored
xäste	خواسته	wish, desire
xaste konande	خسته کننده	boring, tiresome
xästegäri	خواستگاری	proposing (marriage)
xašxäš	خشخاش	opium poppy

xat	خط	line, lane, hand writing
xat zadan	خط زدن	to cross out
xatä	خطا	mistake, offence
xätam käri	خاتم کاری	inlaid work
xatar	خطر	danger, risk, jeopardy
xatarnäk	خطرناک	dangerous
xäteme	خاتمه	conclusion, end
xäteme yäftan	خاتمه یافتن	to conclude, to end
xäter	خاطر	mind, sake, memory
xäter jam³	خاطر جمع	sure, tranquil
xäter xäh	خاطر خواه	fond, lover
xäterät	خاطرات	memories
xätere	خاطره	memory, memento
xatkeš	خط کش	ruler
xatkeši	خط کشی	delineation, drawing lines
xatm	ختم	termination, funeral service
xatne	ختنه	circumcision
xattät	خطاط	calligraphist
xätun	خاتون	lady
xävare dur	خاور دور	far east
xävare miyäne	خاور میانه	Middle East
xäviyär	خاویار	caviar
xäxäm	خاخام	rabbi
xäye	خایه	testicle, balls
xäye mäli	خایه مالی	flattery, servile
xayyät	خیاط	tailor
xayyäti	خیاطی	sewing, tailoring
xayyer	خیر	benevolent
xayyeriye	خیریه	charity
xaz	خز	fur
xazän	خزان	fall, autumn
xazande	خزنده	reptile
xazäne	خزانه	treasury, reservoir

xazäne där	خزانه دار	treasurer
xazar	خزر	caspian
xaze	خزه	algae
xäzen	خازن	condenser, capacitor
xazidan(xaz)	خزیدن (خز)	to crawl
xebre	خبره	expert
xedmat	خدمت	service
xedmat kardan	خدمت کردن	to serve
xedmatkär	خدمتکار	servant, waiter
xeffat	خفت	disgrace, humiliation
xejälat	خجالت	shyness, embarrassment
xejälat kešidan	خجالت کشیدن	to be embarrassed
xejälat ävar	خجالت آور	shameful, embracing
xejälat zade	خجالت زده	embarrassed
xejälati	خجالتی	shy, coy
xejel	خجل	ashamed, embarrassed
xeläf	خلاف	offence, violation
xeläf kär	خلاف کار	offender
xeläfat	خلافت	caliphate
xeläl	خلال	interval
xeläs kardan	خلاص کردن	to release, to save
xelqat	خلقت	creation
xelt	خلط	mucus
xepel	خپل	chubby
xerad mand	خردمند	wise
xers	خرس	bear
xerto pert	خرت وپرت	junk
xerxere	خرخره	larynx, throat
xesärat	خسارت	damage, loss
xeslat	خصلت	character, feature
xešt	خشت	mud brick
xeyli	خیلی	many, very, more
xeyr	خیر	benefit, good

xeyrät	خیرات	charity
xeyriyye	خیریه	charity, relief
xiki	خیکی	fat, flabby
xire	خیره	dazzled, gazed
xis	خیس	wet, drenched
xiš	خیش	ploughshare
xiš	خویش	relative, oneself
xišävand	خویشاوند	kin, relative
xištan	خویشتن	self
xit šodan	خیط شدن	to loss face
xiyäbän	خیابان	street, avenue
xiyäl	خیال	fancy, imagination
xiyäl kardan	خیال کردن	to imagine, to think
xiyäl bäfi	خیالبافی	daydreaming
xiyäli	خیالی	imaginary, visionary, fiction
xiyänat	خیانت	treason
xiyänat kardan	خیانت کردن	to betray, to cheat
xiyänat kär	خیانت کار	traitor
xiyär	خیار	cucumber
xod	خود	self, oneself
xod ämuz	خود آموز	self-learner
xod bini	خودبینی	self-conceit
xod koši	خودکشی	suicide
xod koši kardan	خودکشی کردن	to commit suicide
xod nevis	خودنویس	fountain pen
xod suzi	خودسوزی	self burning
xodä	خدا	god, the lord
xodä biyämorz	خدابیامرز	god bless his soul
xodä häfez	خداحافظ	good bye, farewell
xodä häfezi	خداحافظی	farewell, good bye
xodä parasti	خداپرستی	theism, godliness
xodä šenäs	خداشناس	theist
xodam	خودم	myself

xodävand	خداوند	god, the lord
xodäyä	خدایا	o' god
xodbexod	خودبخود	automatically
xoddäri	خودداری	self-control, continence
xodemäni	خودمانی	intimate
xodforuš	خودفروش	prostitute, whore
xodforuši	خودفروشی	prostitution
xodkär	خودکار	pen (ballpoint), automatic
xodmoxtäri	خودمختاری	autonomy
xodnamäyi	خودنمایی	showing off
xodnamäyi kardan	خودنمایی کردن	to show off
xodpasandi	خودپسندی	selfishness
xodra³y	خودرای	stubborn, wilful
xodro	خودرو	car, automobile
xodxäh	خودخواه	selfish
xodxähi	خودخواهی	selfishness
xof	خوف	fear, phobia
xoffäš	خفاش	bat
xofnäk	خوفناک	fearful, dreadful
xol	خل	crazy
xoläse	خلاصه	summery, brief
xolq	خلق	temper, temperament
xompäre	خمپاره	mortar shell
xoms	خمس	one fifth
xonak	خنک	cool, chilly
xonsä	خنثی	neutral, sexless
xonsä kardan	خنثی کردن	to neutralise
xoräfät	خرافات	superstitions
xord	خرد	small, tiny, minced
xord kardan	خرد کردن	to dice, to cut in pieces
xordäd	خرداد	third Persian month
xordan(xor)	خوردن (خور)	to eat, to drink
xorde	خرده	bit, fragment

xorde foruš	خرده فروش	retailer
xordsäl	خردسال	child, infant
xore	خوره	leprosy
xoreš	خورش	stew
xorjin	خورجین	saddlebag
xormä	خرما	date (edible)
xormälu	خرمالو	persimmon
xornäs	خرناس	snort
xorsand	خرسند	satisfied, content
xoršid	خورشید	sun
xoršidi	خورشیدی	solar
xortum	خرطوم	elephant's trunks
xoruj	خروج	exit
xorxor	خرخر	snoring
xorxor kardan	خرخر کردن	to snore
xoš	خوش	happy, pleasant
xoš axläq	خوش اخلاق	good-tempered, cheerful
xoš gozaräni	خوشگذرانی	living in pleasure
xoš qiyäfe	خوش قیافه	handsome
xoš šans	خوش شانس	lucky
xošämad	خوشامد	welcome
xošbaxt	خوشبخت	lucky, fortunate
xošbaxti	خوشبختی	prosperity, luck, fortun
xošbaxtäne	خوشبختانه	luckily, fortunately
xošbin	خوش بین	optimistic
xošbini	خوش بینی	optimism
xošbu	خوشبو	fragrance, aroma
xošgel	خوشگل	beautiful, handsome
xošhäl	خوشحال	glad, happy
xošhäli	خوشحالی	happiness
xoši	خوشی	joy, happiness
xošk	خشک	dry, dried
xoškbär	خشکبار	dried fruits

xoški	خشکی	land, ground, dryness
xošksäli	خشکسالی	draught
xošmaze	خوشمزه	tasty, delicious
xošnud	خوشنود	happy, pleased
xotbe	خطبه	sermon, exhortation
xub	خوب	good, ok, well, nice
xubi	خوبی	goodness, kindness
xud	خود	helmet, headgear
xuk	خوک	pig, boar
xukčeye hendi	خوکچه هندی	guinea pig
xun	خون	blood, kinship
xun älud	خون آلود	bloody, blood stained
xun äšäm	خون آشام	blood sucker
xun bahä	خون بها	blood money
xun damäq	خون دماغ	nose bleeding
xun garm	خون گرم	warm-blooded, kind
xun mordegi	خون مردگی	ecchymosis
xun xär	خون خوار	blood thirsty, cruel
xunäbe	خونابه	serum, bitter tears
xunin	خونین	bloody
xunrizi	خون ریزی	haemorrhage, murder
xunsard	خونسرد	cold-blooded
xuräk	خوراک	food, meal
xuräki	خوراکی	edible, food
xurd	خرد	change (coins)
xurus	خروس	rooster, cock
xurušän	خروشان	roaring
xuše	خوشه	bunch, cluster
xusuf	خسوف	lunar eclipse
xusumat	خصومت	hostility
xušunat	خشونت	coarseness, hostility
xususan	خصوصا	especially, in particular
xususi	خصوصی	private, personal, special

xususi säzi	خصوصی سازی	privatisation
xususiyyät	خصوصیت	characteristics, particulars

Y		
yä	یا	either, or, oh
yä³ese	یائسه	menopausic
yä³esegi	یائسگی	menopause
ya³ni	یعنی	meaning, namely, it means
ya³s	یاس	despair, disappointment
yäbu	یابو	pony, nag, hack
yäd	یاد	memory, recall
yäd dädan	یاد دادن (یاد ده)	to teach, to instruct
yäd gereftan	یاد گرفتن (یاد گیر)	to learn
yadak	یدک	towing
yadak kešidan	یدک کشیدن	to tow
yadak keš	یدک کش	towboat
yadaki	یدکی	spare part
yädäv ardan	یاد آوردن (یاد آور)	to remember, to remind
yädävari	یاد آوری	remembrance, reminding
yädävari kardan	یاد آوری کردن	to remind
yädbud	یادبود	remembrance, memorial
yäddäšt	یادداشت	note, reminder
yäddäšt kardan	یادداشت کردن	to take note
yädgär	یادگار	a souvenir, a keepsake
yädgiri	یادگیری	learning, instruction
yäftan(yäb)	یافتن (یاب)	to find, to obtain
yägut	یاقوت	sapphire, ruby
yahud	یهود	Jews
yahudi	یهودی	Jewish
yahudiyyat	یهودیت	Judaism
yäl	یال	mane
yaldä	یلدا	the longest night of winter
yaqe	یقه	collar
yäqi	یاغی	rebel, outlaw
yaqin	یقین	certain, positive, sure

yaqinan	يقينا	surely, certainly
yaqmä	يغما	plunder, booty
yär	يار	friend, companion
yaräq	يراق	braid, harness
yaraqän	يرقان	jaundice
yäri	ياری	help, aid, assistance
yäru	يارو	a guy, a chap, a fellow
yäs	ياس	jasmine
yašm	يشم	jasper
yätäqän	ياتاقان	bearing of a car
yatim	يتيم	orphan
yävar	ياور	helper, aid
yaväš	يواش	slow, slowly, softly, gentle
yaväš yaväš	يواش يواش	gradually, little by little
yäve	ياوه	nonsense, absurd, vain
yäveguyi	ياوه گويی	talking nonsense, babbling
yax	يخ	ice
yax zade	يخ زده	frozen
yax zadan	يخ زدن	to freeze
yaxčäl	يخچال	fridge, refrigerator
yaxdän	يخدان	icebox
yaxe	يخه	collar
yaxšekan	يخ شكن	ice pick, ice chopper
yäxte	ياخته	cell
yäzdah	يازده	eleven
yäzdahom	يازدهم	eleventh
yazdän	يزدان	god
yegän	يگان	unit (army)
yegäne	يگانه	unique, only one, sole
yek	يک	one, a, an, single
yek bär	يكبار	once, one time
yek daf³e	يک دفعه	suddenly, all at once
yek dar miyän	يک در ميان	every other, alternatively

yek ho	یکهو	suddenly, all of a sudden
yek jänebe	یک جانبه	unilateral
yek naväxt	یکنواخت	monotonous, tedious
yek pärče	یکپارچه	solid, integrated
yek šabe	یکشبه	overnight
yek tarafe	یک طرفه	one way, biased
yekdande	یک دنده	stubborn, persistent
yekdast	یکدست	pure, uniform, unmixed
yekdigar	یکدیگر	each other
yeki	یکی	one, someone, somebody
yekjä	یکجا	altogether, in a lump
yeksän	یکسان	identical, equal, similar
yekšanbe	یکشنبه	Sunday
yeksare	یکسره	one way, straight
yektä	یکتا	single, unique
yeyläq	ییلاق	summer quarter
yeyläqi	ییلاقی	summer residence, villa
yobs	یبس	dry, constipated
yobusat	یبوست	constipation
yod	ید	iodine
yomiyye	یومیه	daily
yomn	یمن	blessing, grace, felicity
yonje	یونجه	alfalfa
yunän	یونان	greece
yunäni	یونانی	greek
yureš	یورش	attack, raid, assault
yuzpalang	یوزپلنگ	panther

Z		
za³f	ضعف	weakness, feebleness
za³ferän	زعفران	saffron
za³if	ضعيف	weak,
zäbete	ضابطه	standard, criterion
zabt	ضبط	recording, confiscation
zabt kardan	ضبط کردن	to record, to confiscate
zadan(zan)	زدن (زن)	to hit, to beat
zado xord	زدوخورد	fight, clash
zäher	ظاهر	appearance, obvious, look
zäher šodan	ظاهرشدن	to appear
zäher säzi	ظاهرسازی	pretending, faking
zäheran	ظاهرا	obviously, apparently
zäheri	ظاهری	superficial, outward
zahr	زهر	poison, venom
zahrdär	زهردار	poisonous
zajr	زجر	torment, torture
zajr kešidan	زجرکشیدن	to suffer
zakät	زکات	alms
žäkat	ژاکت	jacket, pullover
zälem	ظالم	cruel, brutal, ruthless
zälemäne	ظالمانه	unjust, ruthlessly
zalil	ذلیل	weak, abject
zamäd	ضماد	plaster
zamämdär	زمامدار	ruler, governor
zamän	زمان	time, duration, era, tense
zamänat	ضمانت	guaranty, warranty, bail
zämen	ضامن	guarantor, safety bolt,
zamime	ضمیمه	attachment, annex
zamime kardan	ضمیمه کردن	to attach
zamin	زمین	earth, ground, land, floor
zamin xordan	زمین خوردن	to fall

zamin larze	زمین لرزه	earthquake
zamin šenäsi	زمین شناسی	geology
zamine	زمینه	background, field, basis
zamir	ضمیر	pronoun, conscience
zamzame	زمزمه	whispering, murmur
zamzame kardan	زمزمه کردن	to whisper, to murmur
zan	زن	woman, wife
zan gereftan	زن گرفتن	to marry a woman
zanamu	زن عمو	paternal uncle's wife
zanande	زننده	repelling, shocking, obscene
zanäne	زنانه	womanly, female, feminine
zanäšuyi	زناشویی	marriage
zanbäbä	زن بابا	stepmother
zanbaq	زنبق	lily
zanbäz	زن باز	womaniser
zanbil	زنبیل	basket, hamper
zanbur	زنبور	bee, wasp
zandär	زندار	married man
zandäyi	زن دایی	maternal uncle's wife
zang	زنگ	bell, dial tone, rust
zang zadan	زنگ زدن	to ring bell, to call, to rust
zang zade	زنگ زده	rusty
zanjabil	زنجبیل	ginger
zanjalab	زن جلب	cuckold
zanjir	زنجیر	chain, shackle
zann	ظن	suspicion, doubt, mistrust
zänu	زانو	knee
žänviye	ژانویه	January
žäpon	ژاپن	Japan
žäponi	ژاپنی	Japanese
zar	زر	gold
zarabän	ضربان	beating, pulse
zaräfat	ظرافت	delicacy, elegance

zarar	ضرر	loss, harm, damage
zarar kardan	ضرر کردن	to lose
zarb	ضرب	multiplication, rhythm
zarb kardan	ضرب کردن	to multiply
zarbe	ضربه	stroke, hit, impact, beat
zarbe zadan	ضربه زدن	to stroke, to hit
zarbohmasal	ضرب الم ثل	proverb, saying
zard	زرد	yellow
zardälu	زردآلو	apricot
zardčube	زردچوبه	turmeric
zarde	زرده	yolk
zarf	ظرف	container, utensil
žarf	ژرف	deep, profound
zarf šuyi	ظرف شویی	dish washer
zarfiyyat	ظرف یت	capacity, valency
zargar	زرگر	goldsmith
zarib	ضریب	coefficient, index
zarif	ظریف	delicate, fine, elegant, frail
zarih	ضریج	shrine, tomb
zarräfe	زرافه	giraffe
zarrät	ذرات	particles
zarre	ذره	particle
zarrebin	ذره بین	magnifying glass
zartošt	زرتشت	zoroaster
zartošti	زرتشتی	zoroastrian
zarurat	ضرورت	need, necessity, emergency
zaruri	ضروری	necessary, essential
zarvaraq	زرورق	foil
zät	ذات	essence, nature
zäti	ذاتی	intrinsic, innate
zätorriye	ذات الریه	pneumonia
zaväl	زوال	decline, downfall
zavvär	زوار	pilgrims

zaxämat	ضخامت	thickness, coarseness
zaxim	ضخيم	thick, coarse
zaxire	ذخيره	reserve, stock, saving
zaxire kardan	ذخيره کردن	to store, to stock, to save
zaxm	زخم	injury, wound
zaxmi	زخمى	injured, wounded
zaxmi kardan	زخمى کردن	to injure
zäye³ šodan	ضايع شدن	to spoil, to rot, to be wasted
zäye³e	ضايعه	damage, loss, wastage
zebh	ذبح	slaughtering animals
zebh kardan	ذبح کردن	to slaughter animals
zedd	ضد	contrary, against, opposite
zedde yax	ضد يخ	antifreeze
zegil	زگيل	wart
zeh	زه	cord, rim
zehär	زهار	pubis
zehkeši	زهکشى	drainage
zehn	ذهن	mind, memory
zekr	ذکر	mention, recital
zekr kardan	ذکر کردن	to mention, to recite
zel³	ضلع	angle, side
zelände no	زلاند نو	new zealand
zellat	ذلت	lowliness, suffering, misery
zelzele	زلزله	earthquake
zelzelezade	زلزله زده	victim of earthquake
zemestän	زمستان	winter
zemn	ضمن	meantime, while
zemnan	ضمنا	by the way, meanwhile
zemni	ضمنى	implicitly, implied
žen	ژن	gene
zenä	زنا	adultery
zenäkär	زناکار	adulterer
zenäzäde	زنازاده	bustard

zendän	زندان	prison, jail
zendänbän	زندانبان	jailor
zendäni	زندانی	prisoner, inmate, captive
zendäni kardan	زندانی کردن	to imprison
zende	زنده	alive, live, lively
zende šodan	زنده شدن	to become alive, to revive
zende bäd	زنده باد	long live
zendegi	زندگی	life, living
zendegi kardan	زندگی کردن	to live
ženeräl	ژنرال	general
zerä³at	زراعت	agriculture, farming
zerang	زرنگ	clever, smart, cunning
zerangi	زرنگی	cleverness, smartness
zereh	زره	armour, shielding
zerehi	زرهی	armoured
zerehpuš	زره پوش	armoured
zerehšekan	زره شکن	armour-piercing
zerešk	زرشک	barberry
žest	زشت	gesture, manner
zešti	زشتی	ugliness
zeytun	زیتون	olives
zibä	زیبا	beautiful, nice, pretty
zibäyi	زیبایی	beauty, elegance
žimnastik	ژیمناستیک	gymnastics
zin	زین	saddle
zinaf³	ذینفع	beneficiary
zip	زیپ	zipper
zir	زیر	under, beneath, high pitch
zir kardan	زیر کردن	to step over, to run over
zir nevis	زیرنویس	subtitles
zir sigäri	زیرسیگاری	ashtray
zirä	زیرا	because
zirbanä	زیربنا	infrastructure, foundation

zirdaryäyi	زیردریایی	submarine
zirdast	زیردست	inferior, subordinate
zirpirähan	زیر پیراهن	undershirt
zirpuš	زیرپوش	underwear
zirpusti	زیر پوستی	subcutaneous
ziršalväri	زیرشلواری	underpants
zirsigäri	زیرسیگاری	ashtray
zirzamin	زیرزمین	basement, cellar
zirzamini	زیرزمینی	underground
zist	زیست	life, living
zistan	زیستن	to live
zistšenäsi	زیست شناسی	biology
ziyäd	زیاد	many, much, plenty
ziyäd kardan	زیاد کردن	to increase
ziyäderavi	زیاده روی	overindulgence
ziyäfat	ضد یاف ت	party, reception, feast
ziyän	زیان	loss, harm
ziyän didan	زیان دیدن	to lose, to be harmed
ziyänävar	زیان آور	harmful
ziyärat	زیارت ک ردن	pilgrimage
ziyäratgäh	زیارتگاه	shrine
žo³an	ژوئن	June
zob	ذوب	melting, dissolution
zohr	ظهر	noon, mid day
zohre	زهره	venus
zohur	ظهور	appearance, outburst
zoj	زوج	couple, pair, even number
zokäm	ذکام	cold, flue
zoläl	زلال	transparent, clear
zolf	زلف	lock of hair
zolm	ظلم	injustice, cruelty
zolmat	ظ لمت	darkness, gloom
zomorrod	زمرد	emeralds

zoq	ذوق	talent, zeal, enthusiasm
zoqäl	ذغال	charcoal, coal
zoqäl axte	ذغال اخته	dogberry
zoqälsang	ذغال سنگ	coal
zorrat	ذرت	corn
žu³an	ژوئن	June
žu³ye	ژوئیه	July
zud	زود	quick, early, soon
zudbävar	زودباور	naïve, credulous
zulbiä	زولبیا	a type of sweet
zur	زور	power, force, coercion
zur goftan	زور گفتن	to bully, to force
zurgu	زورگو	bully, oppressive
zurxäne	زورخانه	gymnasium
zuzanaqe	ذوزنقه	trapezoid
zuze	زوزه	wailing, yelping
zuze kešidan	زوزه کشیدن	to wail, to yelp

To see other books from the same author, visit
www.yavardehghani.com

Printed in Great Britain
by Amazon.co.uk, Ltd.,
Marston Gate.